BEYOND
PARTICIPATIVE
MANAGEMENT

BEYOND PARTICIPATIVE MANAGEMENT

TOWARD TOTAL EMPLOYEE EMPOWERMENT FOR QUALITY

G. RONALD GILBERT
ARDEL E. NELSON

Quorum Books
New York • Westport, Connecticut • London

Library of Congress Cataloging-in-Publication Data

Gilbert, G. Ronald, 1939–
    Beyond participative management : toward total employee
empowerment for quality / G. Ronald Gilbert and Ardel E. Nelson.
        p.   cm.
    Includes index.
    ISBN 0-89930-612-8
    1. Government productivity—United States.   2. Work groups—United
States.   3. Management—United States—Employee participation.
4. Sacramento Air Logistics Center—Management.   I. Nelson, Ardel
E.   II. Title.
JK468.P75G55   1991
353.001′72—dc20   91-11429

British Library Cataloguing in Publication Data is available.

Library of Congress Catalog Card Number: 91–11429
ISBN: 0-89930-612-8

First published in 1991

Quorum Books, One Madison Avenue, New York, NY 10010
An imprint of Greenwood Publishing Group, Inc.

Printed in the United States of America

The paper used in this book complies with the
Permanent Paper Standard issued by the National
Information Standards Organization (Z39.48–1984).

10   9   8   7   6   5   4   3   2   1

This work is dedicated to the men and women who were formerly in the Directorate of Distribution at McClellan Air Force Base. Their extraordinary willingness to respond to the challenge for quality while under scrutiny by others throughout the nation has, indeed, been heroic. Without them this book could not have been written.

Contents

Illustrations

TABLE

Preface

The authors wish to express their appreciation to a few special people whose assistance was invaluable in completing this project. Tom Gannon and Ernest Haim of Quorum Books provided us excellent editorial guidance and support. Ms. Marie L. Levine and Ms. Dalia Y. Emery of the College of Business Administration at Florida International University willingly gave of themselves to assist the authors to meet their production deadlines and provide administrative assistance in the coordination of the manuscript.

Jan Gilbert and Jean Nelson made incredible sacrifices while we labored over the manuscripts during the past year. Both edited our work and offered invaluable suggestions for improvements.

None of these people is responsible for what is said in this text or any other oversight that may be found by the reader. That responsibility falls directly on the authors. Whatever faults are uncovered here do not in any way reflect on them. However, if one should find a particularly polished piece in the text, most likely it has been more of their doing than ours.

It is the hope of the authors that our work makes clear that the innovation through Project Pacer Share and quality improvements reported in this book were accomplished by American employees, no less government employees. They revitalized what America is all about: experimentation, working together, empowerment, team play, innovation, practicality, and performance excellence. Their work points to a new beginning in America to further the cause for quality, productivity, and mutual respect.

Introduction

Throughout America a revolution is occurring in the way organizations do their business. Organizations are focusing on getting quality to the customer, and they are recognizing that quality first must be from within before it can be provided for others outside the organization. Key to getting that internal quality in the organization is to go beyond permissive "participatory management" to full empowerment of the employees themselves in the decision-making process. Teams within the workplace are being developed, both technically and behaviorally, to take charge of getting quality to the customer. These teams are challenging the role supervisors have been tasked to play in the traditional design of American business and government. Some teams are performing better than ever before without their supervisors—they have become self-governed.

This book is about quality and one organization in the federal government that initiated some major changes to improve quality in the workplace and to the customer. The program is called "Project Pacer Share" (PPS). It was authorized under the Civil Service Reform Act of 1978 and is sponsored by the U.S. Office of Personnel Management (OPM). Although it is still in its demonstration stage, it is rapidly being expanded while its host organization has undergone radical reorganization, leaving the project under new leadership. Opinions about the effectiveness of the project differ, based on who is the evaluator.

RAND, the "objective" third-party evaluator of the effort, is guarded about the project's success. However, RAND indicates that the impact the project has had on employee morale, supervisor relations, and team performance has been significant. RAND indicates the project has not made any significant impact on the bottom line, for example, reduced costs and improved productivity. Yet, it may have made this judgment without reference to the underlying, shifting defense budgetary process and the continuing failure of federal wages to keep pace with the real cost of living—key intervening variables that influence the system in which PPS has been introduced.

The host organization (Air Force Logistics Command's Sacramento Air Logistics Center) was so delighted with it that it opted to substantially expand it based on what they viewed to be hard-core, multimillion-dollar savings. However, recent commandwide reorganizations have put this effort on hold. The OPM, the other sponsoring institution for the project, is more guarded about the project's viability than the Air Force. OPM's position is that the program is not doing what it was supposed to do in terms of fulfilling its obligations as a demonstration project for that office.

The authors are in agreement about the quality model proposed in this book, having worked together for over three years to effect the changes described. Nelson was the primary force behind the development and design of Project Pacer Share, the demonstration project that this book introduces and describes. His perspective is tied to his organization. He experienced the day-to-day struggles, administrative challenges, and resistances to change that took place within his own system and in the Air Force and federal community. He has actually done what many hope to be able to do—he instituted major change in his organization from within. He writes about his experiences when getting things started and on their way to implementation. Few, if any, have demonstrated the genius for actually making radical change from within the system. His words in this work are the words of a "true believer," the person who believes that he has seen evidence that the current organizational paradigm has failed, and he has made a "leap of faith" into the new paradigm for quality—that which PPS is all about.

Gilbert is both an academician and practical scientist. As the primary outside consultant to Project Pacer Share during its first three years of implementation, he introduced a process termed "Tactical Planning and Team Building." It became a primary organizational development intervention in Project Pacer Share, radically expanding Nelson's initial "autonomous team" ideas. It went beyond the introduction of team building as an organizational exercise, to team building as an organizational imperative. In team building, members of the team engage in substantive decision making based on their education, training, and formation in team activities; process focus; and interpersonal communications. Every employee in the organization went through his workshops where the quality approach, team building, tactical planning, customer-oriented leadership, and self-initiated followership for one's customer were introduced.

Because we recognize that our own experiences have biased our perceptions about the program, other employees and union representatives in the host organization also report about various events as they occurred in the project.

Part I, Chapters 1 and 2, is presented by Gilbert, giving his model of where large organizations in America have been and where they need to go in order to make the transformation to the quality approach.

Part II, Chapters 3 through 6, presents the recollections and critical thoughts about the constraints of the Civil Service System and development of Project Pacer Share by Nelson. They deal with his experiences as the change agent within the Air Force. They describe the organizational and interagency realities from his perspective. His description of what happened in the formation of the project is highly subjective and deals with the idiosyncratic aspects of the challenges one may expect when undertaking a massive design in organizational innovation. The accounts by Nelson in Part II are his alone. They recall the trials and tribulations he experienced when attempting to get the program started and the realities that go with it when challenges from within and external to the organization are at play.

Part III, Chapters 7 through 12, describes various processes, tools, and techniques used to help make the transformation to quality in the project. It includes the overall change strategies employed, and includes Gilbert's specific training and development tools to include Tactical Planning and Team Building, Leadership, Followership, and Nelson's Essential Process Management (EPM). Personal accounts of events and applications of the tools and processes introduced in this book by its authors are included in the Appendixes. These accounts have been written by union leaders, managers, and nonmanagers alike.

In Part IV, we discuss the results of the project. We describe the unexpected consequences that have occurred from our points of view.

Demonstration projects like Pacer Share exist in highly charged and changing environments. As open systems, they influence and are influenced by many factors. At the time of this writing, Project Pacer Share's original host organization has been radically changed as a result of Air Force reorganization, Defense spending cuts, and executive choice. The project is under new leadership. Like the U.S. Housing and Urban Development's "Model Cities" demonstration project of the late 1960s, parts of its program have been adopted elsewhere before the demonstration itself has finished.

Whenever possible, we have both contributed to each section of the book. Sometimes this has resulted in a synergistic strength that attains goals beyond the expectation of either of us. It has resulted in a more balanced presentation, even when, as the words in the text will reveal, balance may not always have been achieved. Nelson lived inside the organization everyday while Gilbert worked with the organization more as a third-party, external resource.

In October 1990, it was announced that McClellan Air Force Base (MCAFB) received the "President's Quality Improvement Prototype Award" for that year. The major factor in the granting of that recognition to the Air Force Base was Project Pacer Share. The major factors cited in the award to promote Total Quality Management: the application of Essential Process Management, statistical process control (SPC), quality circles, team building, team facilitation, and other tools to promote organizationwide employee participation in problem solving were originally derived from PPS.

The "President's Quality Improvement Prototype Award" represents a tribute to the over 1,800 men and women in the Directorate of Distribution at McClellan Air Force Base who willingly undertook the challenge for quality. They demonstrated practical wisdom in creating the project components. They willingly went forward to be the first in making such a sweeping attempt at reform for quality in government. Through persistence and trial and error, they found effective ways to implement Total Quality Management (TQM) in the Department of Defense. Without the leadership of labor and management at McClellan Air Force Base and their day-to-day hammering out of collaborative arrangements between the two, the project would never have been tested. They performed both ingeniously and heroically.

During the war to free Kuwait, Operation Desert Storm, McClellan AFB was a large supplier to the Air Force's Middle East theater of operations. The same men and women who had been involved in Project Pacer Share and the quality-focused tools and approaches introduced here were able to demonstrate logistical support of heroic proportion. They were "world record" setters.

The program remains controversial, as it is still in the demonstration phase, and if universally applied across government agencies would radically change the civil service system. The extent of the project's effectiveness is variously defined and debated by RAND, the Air Force, organized labor, individual employees, academicians, and the OPM. However, as the debate about the project's worth continues, many of the project's innovations are being adopted throughout the federal government as well as other organizations in government and business alike.

It is our erstwhile hope that this book will further the knowledge base and application of tools to advance the quality model in America. In doing that, we will have attained our objectives.

PART I

The Quality Imperative

With the excitement of world capitalism and the decline of communism in Europe and Russia, the free world has replaced the centralized social planner with "customers" who influence incremental redirections for quality in every choice they exercise. With the new entrance of the East Bloc of Europe (and possibly Vietnam, North Korea, and other Communist nations) into the world marketplace, the future of the world is being guided more by these consumers than by those in charge of the states in which the consumers live—it is indeed a new world order. The successful organization and nation in the decade of the 1990s will be expert at customer-oriented behavior. It will provide such outstanding work for the customer that it will become the customer's choice for products and services.

The call to provide quality to the customer is not just a call for business. It is as much the challenge of government as it is for the private-sector entrepreneur. The viability of a nation's tourism industry depends as much on the way the immigration department personnel treats the tourist as the way the hotel treats the tourist. It is government that keeps the streets safe and the courts that ensure social justice and reasonableness in conduct prevail. The tenets of good government parallel good business. Just as a business wants to make a good impression when the customer enters the store, so, too, a nation seeking to gain tourism support needs to pay attention to the way the visitor is treated at entry. For too long, both government and business in the United States have taken the customer for granted. It is time to meet the challenge for quality here in America.

One can't run a good customer-oriented enterprise with unsatisfied people working in the enterprise itself. Whether in a small store, factory, hotel, hospital, or large federal bureaucracy, to get quality to the customer, the organization needs to get quality to the people who work there.

Part I introduces the call for quality in America and identifies what organizations need to do to make their transformation to what the authors term "the quality approach." A new paradigm for management is posed. Although it is theoretical, it forms a basis for understanding the rationale for Project Pacer Share.

A Call for Quality Worldwide: The War of the Peacekeepers

A new war has emerged and is worldwide. It is a war that is much more sophisticated than the types that most of us have known in the past. It is not a war based on the availability and use of deadly weapons mixed with the luck of the battlefield itself. The war of which we speak is not ever decided in a single decisive battle like Napoleon's Waterloo and Hitler's D-Day. Rather, this war is going to be won and lost every day through a myriad of skirmishes whereby the winners and losers are decided by the customer.

The war is spreading at an alarming rate. In the eighties, it seemed to be confined to manufacturing—producing products for others in a quality, defect-free, manner. In the decade of the nineties, it has spread throughout industry and government. Quality is the name of the game, everywhere.

Now that much of the Communist East Bloc has joined the West in capitalist competition, the stage has been set for a continuous series of skirmishes among competitors that are driven by one objective—to become the "customer's" choice.

In a market-driven economy, winning is decided by one thing—the ability of the supplier to deliver quality in such a way that the customer will decide to return once again for the product/service received. The customer returns because the service or product received was perceived to be the very best available. In the market-driven economy, one gets to the winner's circle every time a customer is satisfied.

In closed economies and where the market is protected by political barriers, such as when we were deeply entrenched in the East–West cold war or in closed markets like Cuba or North Korea, the customer has little choice. Therefore, the organization does not have to be as sensitive to pleasing the customer as it is to pleasing the political hierarchy under which it exists. However, in a purer market-driven situation, such as we have now, where the customer has the opportunity to procure the very best product or service he or she can find, it is entirely different. In such cases, where the customer has the option to "vote" for the vendor of choice every day with every service or product procured, a totally different approach to doing business is required.

Today, a new approach to leading people, to managing organizations, and to serving the customer is required for the organization to succeed. The decade of the eighties conclusively demonstrated to American-trained managers that the approach they were using to manage their people was becoming outmoded. More collaborative approaches to planning, organizing, leading, and controlling the organization create the type of productive, customer-driven efforts throughout organizations that are essential to gain customer loyalty.

The decade of the eighties demonstrated that the future was not necessarily going to rely on the ways of the past in American business and government. The most highly prized industrial heroes, like those having the "Harvard MBA," were not able to lead their own organizations to long-term success. Chrysler, Ford, and General Motors were not out-competed by other companies because these three automotive giants did not have enough Harvard MBAs. No. They were out-competed because they were not as customer-oriented as were their competitors. They failed to remain in the winner's circle because they relied on traditional ways of management for efficiency, and short-term "maximum" gains of their organization's resources, while letting their customers drift away and discover better products and services elsewhere.

Perhaps the most blatant example of the mind-set of the losing manager in the old way of doing business was the leveraged buyout (LBO) fracas, which represented the "smart" way of doing business in the eighties. The LBO resulted in some (few) people making a great deal of fast dollars. However, very often they did it at the expense of the millions of members of the work force, the loyal and dedicated people who gave their lives for the plant, airline, bank, hospital, or corporate conglomerate. To place the organizations in positions for buyouts, the "profit-guzzling" managers and corporate accountants quit investing in new technologies, equipment, work-force education, and the like. They worked deceptively to show greater profits and healthier bottom lines to their prospective new owners. By doing so, these companies were seriously weakened, whereas companies from other countries were investing in the very things that American organizations needed so that they could compete in the next decade.

This same orientation to selfish, short-term thinking on the part of the most skillfully trained American managers led to the collapse of our financial institutions—to the tune of at least $500 billion. The failure of the savings and loan institutions in America was due to the same thinking that led to the defeat of the American auto industry. The smart leaders of the financial institutions made dollars very quickly; however, over the long term, they failed their customers. A favorite pastime of children in America used to be playing a game called Monopoly.℠ The future business leaders of America learned to engage in very creative finance (even cheat a little) in order to buy out the board and beat the others on the team. Most Americans can recall how they purchased "Board Walk," the utility plant, or the other exciting properties so eagerly. Sometimes we even went to jail, but nobody really stayed there very long. However, nothing in the game ever taught us about the people who might work in, or depend on, the places we bought and traded so casually. The game did not teach us to take into account the effect of our transactions on people. What happened to the tenants who lived in those hotels? How did our new ownership affect the work force in those companies, plants, and hotels? Where was the "customer" in all of this? The game never taught us to look at these issues. Yet, it is these issues that make the difference in the customer-driven economy that currently prevails.

DECLINE IN QUALITY IN THE PAST DECADE

According to former U.S. Trade Commissioner to Japan, Clyde Prestowitz, in 1982, the United States was number one in the world in economy, industry, manufacturing, and military. Within a decade, it has lost that title to Japan, a nation about half our size in population and with about as much land as the state of Montana, but not as rich with natural resources as that state.

David Garvin (1983) reports that American air-conditioning manufacturers yield 63.5 defective parts for every 100 air-conditioning units they produce, whereas Japan had a rate of 0.9 defects for every 100 like units. David Garvin (1988) reveals that Japan, Britain, France, and Italy are experiencing a higher annual growth rate in manufacturing than the United States (1979–1986), and that the United States is spending less than Europe, Asia, and Japan in automation. The Japanese, West Germans, Swedes, and others have demonstrated their superior abilities to build better-quality automotive products. Brazil, Argentina, New Zealand, and others are becoming highly competitive with us in their abilities to produce agricultural products—where we once clearly dominated the global marketplace.

The ramifications of these changes are not just tied to business. They also have tremendous implications for American government as well.

THE NEED FOR REVITALIZATION

Our democracy has become lazy. Elected officials have been permitted to function as though their first task was to get reelected. They gerrymandered their way to their own political support. They created defense contracts to support their own constituents, but not necessarily to support the greater good of the entire community or nation they were officially tasked to serve. They authorized public works to be built that were not needed. They approved vast public expenditures that were wasted. They approved the wholesale distribution of weapons to nations like Iraq, which were later turned against us, and they let our weapons get out to our own streets as well. They cow-towed to special interests and avoided the tougher decisions tied to our long-term national interests. They permitted our schools to decline to the point where now over half of the math and science students in the graduate schools in America are students from foreign countries. Elected officials discussed ways to tax and ways to spend while skirting our cancerous national debt and the disenfranchisement of our black community, where there are more black males between the ages of eighteen to twenty-two in prison than there are in college, and the likelihood of being murdered is higher for a young black male living in the inner city than it was for his cohort in either Vietnam or the recent war to free Kuwait, Operation Desert Storm.

Our nation has accepted a political style of incrementalism and self-survival. Also, we have turned important organizations into huge bureaucracies that have become too rigid, wasteful, and unresponsive to the people they serve. The larger the organization, the less likely the organization is responsive to the people it purports to serve.

Our political leaders were elected by a first-class nation. Our government leaders were appointed to provide first-class services and products for our great nation. But, in fact, we have created many second-class services as a result of our own political laziness, our failure to assume responsibility for the behavior of our elected and appointed officials. We have created a system that rewards those who listen to special interests rather than to the logic that comes naturally when the long-term interests of the customer are taken into account.

Our national debt and the debt of our cities, counties, and states attest to the benefits of the old way of doing business and government in the richest, most prosperous, most gifted nation in the world. It is said the average adult in America has less than $2,000 saved. Such is a statement about our own will to make sacrifices. Today, few Americans think the heritage they will give their grand-children will be as promising as the heritage our grandparents gave us. It is time to make a change in America. We need to engage in another way of doing business.

A CALL FOR CHANGE

This book has been written to introduce the types of changes that can be initiated in the workplace and, by doing so, create better, more quality-driven products and services to the customer. Our nation is dedicated to guaranteeing the individual rights. It has built-in protections to assure such rights are upheld. Yet, we have designed and established means of managing people that impede, rather than facilitate, individual progress and the realization of one's own potential on the job.

ABOUT THIS BOOK

This book is about how to manage organizations for quality and lead the people in them into a total quality approach. It identifies how to make a difference for America through new ways of doing business. It introduces a new paradigm for organizational design that is based on absolute customer-focused and process-centered behavior. It draws upon an actual case in government where the quality approach is being developed and demonstrating itself to lead to better organizations with more productive, happier employees and ''delighted'' customers. It also presents methodologies used to make the transformation to the new way of doing business, ranging from the initiation of desired change from within the organization and the actual tools used to reeducate the members of the organization to perform the ''quality way.''

The name of the project is Project Pacer Share (PPS), a project sponsored by the U.S. Office of Personnel Management and hosted by the U.S. Air Force (USAF) at McClellan Air Force Base (MCAFB), Sacramento, California. It began its fourth year of demonstration in February 1991. It is an authentic attempt to get beyond participative management and create true partnerships for quality by all in the workplace. Fitting, it seems, that it would be underway in a government founded on just such a set of concepts in 1776. The quality approach to management is an extension of the quality approach to managing a first-class nation. You can't have a first-class nation without first-class places to do business.

The authors were personally involved with the Air Force program. Nelson, an Air Force civilian manager, an individual who came up from the ranks in the old system, steered the project from concept to sponsorship, design, development, and initial implemenation of the demonstration. He was the internal institutional change agent. Gilbert, a university professor, organizational behavior specialist, and management consultant, designed and implemented some primary interventions and tools of measurement used by the project to facilitate the shift of the work force, itself, from the old efficiency approach to the quality approach.

SUMMARY

The world of work is changing. Tomorrow's organization will be more pressed to deliver quality to its customers than ever before. The challenge for service quality is particularly pertinent to America, because, with the globalization of capitalism, greater emphasis will be placed on the customer to decide about the merit of the product or service being rendered. With competition being heightened worldwide, organizations can no longer do business as usual.

Chapter 2 addresses the fundamental differences between past organizational behaviors and practices and those that are essential for total quality.

REFERENCES

Garvin, D. (1983). ''Quality On The Line.'' *Harvard Business Review* 61 (September–October): 64–75.

———. (1988). ''The Productivity Paradox.'' *Business Week* (June 6): 100–103.

Past Failures in Doing Business: The Efficiency and the Quality Paradigms

The call for quality in America, and that which is advocated and described in this book, may be illustrated through an example one of the authors (Gilbert) witnessed in industry when working as a consultant with the top management of a Detroit-based automotive and industrial parts manufacturing company—the management of the company was in a situation where it had lost a lot of money and market position due to Japanese and European competition. The company had long been a chief supplier of parts to General Motors, Ford, and Chrysler. However, it had recently lost some major contracts. It had to lay off 28 percent of its work force. Both management and labor were laid off—it hit all levels.

During its strategic planning session, it became clear why this organization had lost its competitive position with its customers. It had failed to be customer-oriented. It shipped too many defective parts, which caused its customers to have warranty problems. The workers did not have a stake in the organization; they did not share the concern for quality that management had learned was essential in order for them to compete. Their involvement in the decisional processes associated in the design, manufacture, marketing, and evaluation of their products was at a minimum—decision making was left to those in the "salaried" or "professional" positions.

When competing with the Japanese, this American company could not demonstrate the long-term stability of its work force, because it had too much turnover. It had too many defective parts per shipment, and it took too long to modify its engineering and production capabilities to meet the changing demands of its customers.

Out of desperation, it sought a joint venture with a Japanese competitor—doing the work in America with American workers, and with shared Japanese ownership and managerial expertise. According to them, the Japanese had "deep pockets," meaning the Japanese had more money to finance innovation than did American businesses. (The Japanese were more long-term-oriented in their business practices, whereas the Americans were more interested in the fast buck without ample resources for long-term investment opportunities.) Their proposal for a joint venture was turned down by the Japanese for two major reasons. The American organization made too much profit at the expense of its American customers, and it did not demonstrate sufficient partnership with its workers— essentially, it could not guarantee a quality product over the long term for the benefit of its customers.

At the Strategic Planning Workshop, the marketing executive (who was under the gun to get contracts, fast!) revealed that the Japanese are so dedicated to assuring only quality parts are shipped to the customer that the parts are inspected four or five times before final shipment, whereas in his manufacturing company, 4 percent of the parts that were sent out were defective. He revealed that the Japanese firm had improved its processes to the point where it was cutting back on its inspections because they were not necessary. They were cutting back while the American firm was increasing the intensity of its own inspections, as its own manufacturing processes resulted in too much variance in the quality of the work manufactured. It was the high degree of variance that required added inspections and rework in order to retain the business the American company already had. The challenge for the Americans was not to increase its market share, but to hold on to the market share it already had.

The new president of the company (turnover was high at that level, too) revealed an interesting story. In his first days on the job, he talked with the workers on the line to learn what he could do to help them produce better-quality products. The workers told him that if they had *less* supervision, they could do their work better. They revealed their supervisors would give them too many conflicting orders and instructions, which most of the time did not make sense.

The president soon came to realize that most of his workers had been doing their jobs for many years. They knew their jobs well. They knew what to do, but were not given the opportunity to contribute to the process of producing quality products as full partners of the firm. They were not asked their opinions about what to do to improve things. They did not identify with the emphasis on corporate profit when they knew such would lead to inferior products—"Who cared about them?" they wondered.

He also learned that most of the workers usually had answers to the problems they identified, but were not asked for them by their management. It was as though the workers were not respected by their management/supervision for having exceptional expertise. Many of those in supervisory positions were threatened by their subordinates if the subordinates had good ideas.

It did not take the new president long to recognize the company had too many people telling the workers what to do. He started his turnaround strategy to get the company back on its feet by first cutting the fat from the management levels. Too many leaders, not enough followers. He soon learned that his instincts about the workers were right. It was followership behavior at every level that was necessary for the company to improve the way it did its work and to become customer-oriented.

Well, the story is still unfolding. There are no guarantees in business, but things have improved a lot. The manufacturing firm has dedicated itself to quality—getting the job done right, the way the customer wants it, doing it on time, and with a dedication to the customer's long-term success.

It revised its thinking about its organizational goals, too. In the old days, before the global competition became a reality, its first and foremost obligation was to make as much profit as possible over the short term for its stock holders. Now its obligation is first to the customer, giving the customer a quality product. Its next goal, in order of priority, is to provide a positive partnership with the entire labor force by sharing the responsibility and benefits that come from ongoing customer-oriented behavior. Each employee is given greater opportunity to reach and fulfill his or her own potential at work. Thirdly, the firm committed itself to giving its shareholders a "fair" return for their investment.

Essentially, this company chose to demonstrate *customer-oriented behavior* that furthers its long-term success. By doing so, it also turned its situation around. It has established itself as a bonafide supplier to its customers, once again. It has received international recognition for the quality of its product and organization by its industry. It has regained a profitable position for itself. However, this time with the customer's success in mind, as well, it wants to do better. There are no guarantees except that if it is to stay in business, the challenge for quality improvement will be never ending. The company will have to seek continued improvements to assure customer quality in all that it does.

Through its renewed dedication to quality for the customer, it has attained more profitability for the long term, provided its stock holders a better investment, improved the prospect of long-term employment for its workers, and contributed its share to an improved quality of life and competitiveness for its country.

Throughout the nation, we are being challenged to perform differently, to perform with the customer's interests in mind. This choice is not merely tied to managerial preference or style. It is not puffery tied to the most recent management fad. Rather, it is essential to our being able to compete in the new global economy that has emerged and will determine the future of America in the decade of the 1990s.

Today, the Japanese produce 75 percent of the world's video cassette recorders, single-lens reflex cameras, and motorcycles. They also produce 50 percent of the world's commercial ships, 40 percent of its televisions, and about 33 percent of its semiconductors and cars (McCallum, 1986).

Japan is developing new markets and new products, focusing on telecommunications, robotics, bioengineering, lasers, and fashions. It has an unwavering commitment to never-ending expansion of product and market development.

GETTING TOP-QUALITY WORKMANSHIP AND COMPETITIVENESS BACK IN AMERICA

Can America still compete? The answer is "YES," but the solution does not rest with chief executive officers (CEOs) like Lee Iacocca, Ray Kroc, or Victor

Kiam, who have been so widely touted and who are paid so well for their efforts. True, these leaders have made excellent contributions and deserve special recognition, but what about the hundreds of thousands of workers, like you and me, who also give to their organizations through excellence in their self-initiated followership to their customers? Who has written about them? The workers are the key to America's future (Reich, 1987). Although we hear of the great heroic deeds of the Victor Kiams, Donald Trumps, Lee Iacocca's, and many others like them, as is more fully discussed in Chapter 10, they represent the old paradigm of management, where great leaders were glorified. In the new paradigm, great leaders would be more like Don Peterson, recently retired CEO of the Ford Motor Company. Although he may be an unknown to the reader, it was because he never put himself on television as did Iacocca and Kiam. Rather, he put the true heroes on the Ford commercials—the Ford people from every level who made up the teams at Ford and were dedicated to the customer. Peterson knew that these workers are the key to the company's future, not just those in the boardroom or in the executive suites.

It is widely known that Japan went through a metamorphosis, from mediocrity in its production capability to excellence in quality during the past 15 years. The big companies there, like Toyota, Canon, and Nissan, are well known to us. But what about their leaders? What are their names? Why don't we know them? Maybe it is because the Japanese are *first* followers for their institutions, highly dedicated to be of service and to bring respect to their organizations and their nation through their own efforts.

The prospect of renewed competition, of establishing organizational quality in America, lies within the collective will of the American people and their ability to demonstrate unflinching quality service to their customers. To do this means we will need to radically shift our way of doing business from short-term efficiency-oriented approaches that focus on quantity and rapid profit to quality products and services to our customers over the long term.

THE QUALITY IMPERATIVE: A NEW APPROACH TO DOING BUSINESS

One vestige within our democratic political systems that still lacks openness, power sharing, and democratic participation in decision making is the structure of organizations in business and government. In our organizations, power sharing is not a guarantee. In them, power is asymmetrically distributed, with those at the top having most, and those at the bottom required to negotiate for minimal means of participation in policy planning, decision making, and profit sharing. Those at the top often have too much say in the destiny of those who are called to do the work.

The very organization that is essential to assuring the continuous implementation of our democracy, the federal government, may well be among the least democratically managed administrative systems in our nation. Being the largest organization in the nation, it is bound by outmoded and dysfunctional political policies and directives, rigid rules, and poor incentive systems. It is ruled through bureaucratic structures and control mechanisms that tend to impede, rather than invite, the full use of the work force's competencies. Jobs are too narrowly defined and performance appraisals may be more of a political tool than a mechanism that functions to reward desired performance. In such systems, morale may be low, and the employees may lose their commitment to customer-oriented excellence.

The actual case example, Project Pacer Share (PPS), used in this book describes one attempt to further democratize organization life in the federal government. It is the broadest, most wide-sweeping effort to create a more flexible, responsive, and participative work environment in the history of the federal government. It seeks to go beyond mere worker and labor participation in areas traditionally protected and controlled by management to broad-scale control sharing with all in the work force to get the job done right for the customer. It seeks to get beyond participative management to authentic ownership in the obligation and approach taken to get quality to the customer by all in the organization.

It is based on W. Edwards Deming's (Deming, 1986; Walton, 1986) principles of quality management, which have been widely applied in Japan and some American organizations (such as the General Motors/Toyota NUMMI plant in Fremont, California; Ford Motor Co.; Florida Power & Light; and within the Department of Defense (DOD) under the title of "Total Quality Management" (TQM)). It is designed to improve the quality of work life, of product, and of customer support, while reducing costs of doing business in government (i.e., productivity is an automatic product that happens because of the quality focus versus intending productivity and having to worry about quality).

The need to create more inviting environments for employees to produce their best on the job has been a challenge to American industry and government for many years. In 1972, the Work in America Institute identified eleven areas that were considered to be the most important in the 1980s. Six of the eleven were directly related to pay and benefits, two dealt with participative management, two were related to alternative work schedules, and the other was related to job stress. According to Walton (1986):

The quality of work life is no longer simply an issue of compensation and benefit programs; more and more it involves the human factors at work. It concerns what people require from their work environment so that their needs as people, not just workers, are met.

The private sector may be ahead of the public sector in most areas in the design and implementation of more participatory modes of managing people. There appears to be a major pay-off to treating the work force as a partner in the management process. Because of the demonstrated long-term benefits of real employee empowerment, some private-sector companies and government organizations are now beginning to undertake the transformation to a more employee-centered, team-oriented, collaborative approach to their way of doing business. They are starting to get involved in more democratic forms of organization because of the benefits that such forms have demonstrated when applied elsewhere.

When we speak of empowerment, we are referring to employee involvement in self-managed work teams and problem-solving groups, and employee accountability for quality performance. These empowering organizations are characterized by having less hierarchical and more flexible work designs; they have cooperative partnerships between their management and the employee union or representative association. Employees share in broader pay and benefit schedules such as gain sharing, or profit sharing, where the work force has a greater voice and responsibility in getting quality to the customer.

The Japanese management phenomenon has given cause for the American managers to get beyond their ''smart decision making'' and management-by-objectives (MBO) techniques, and join with their work force in partnership to attain their shared goals. Through collaborative management, Japan has risen to a position of global dominance in product reliability and quality. It has experienced a transformation from having a reputation of ''junk producer'' to the hallmark of quality products and services. It has internalized the TQM philosophy throughout its industries. The Japanese success story through TQM coupled with America's decline on a global basis has led to organizational ''soul searching'' throughout the United States.

THE BUREAUCRATIC, CLASSIC EFFICIENCY AND THE QUALITY APPROACH

In response to the U.S. Air Force's mission to maintain defense readiness with a primary civilian work force, a radical shift in the way of doing business was proposed at McClellan AFB. It required the action of Congress for it to become a reality. At McClellan AFB, Project Pacer Share, a TQM oriented approach to logistics management, has been initiated.

The emphasis in this TQM approach under way at McClellan AFB is to build on and mobilize the talents and abilities of the entire work force. It assumes the worker can produce more, better, and quicker, more accurately, and economically, and will want to if empowered to do so. It views the worker to be in partnership with management. Not only is the worker viewed to be a full partner in the process, so, too, is labor. The union, itself, is viewed in the quality-driven organization to be an essential player on the team.

The key to TQM is the redistribution of power, responsibility, and accountability from the few at the top of the organizational hierarchy to the entire work force. It pertains to democratic supervision, horizontal and vertical job enrichment, employee incentives to attain organizationwide goals, broader pay and benefits tied to organization performance, training and development, and safe working conditions, as well as the bottom line—getting better quality to the customer, on time, when the customer needs it, and with a product that facilitates the customer's long-term success.

Collaborative leadership is essential in the TQM process. The TQM model represents a radical paradigmatic shift from the normal way of doing business in government and industry. It means the emphasis is placed on everyone, rather than the few heroic, visionary leaders to get up to the standard needed for the organization to create delighted customers. In the quality approach, everyone is expected to behave heroically, to share in the creation of the vision, and to assume responsibility in problem solving to get top quality to the customer.

Figure 2.1 illustrates some differences in assumptions that represent the typical federal system and the new quality-oriented system that PPS has been designed to become.[1]

As is depicted by the classic efficiency model, we Americans have confused a few things about work and what it means. We measure our work performance more by how fast and how many products we can turn out and the speed by which we can make money, produce outputs, or services than the suitability of our contributions for those we serve—the customer. To win the new game, the game to become the customers' choice as a result of the "delight" they receive from our product or service, individuals, organizations, and our nation need to be committed to quality work that is customer-oriented, committed to the customers' long-term success.

This demand may be even more critical in government than it is in business. It is not just the bureaucrats of government; it is the political leadership, as well.

Public elected officials are often seen to be driven more by short-term decisions that facilitate their reelection and their party's gain than what is in the best interest of the United States. This is clearly demonstrated during budget preparation. In 1990, it became clear that for the long-term good of the country, the federal deficit had to be reduced substantially, for it had become an economic cancer. It was constricting America's quality of life both domestically and internationally.

To address the national deficit, Democrats and Republicans alike agreed that added taxes needed to be introduced as well as reduced expenditures in federal services needed to be undertaken to substantively deal with the debt choking this nation. It was the members of Congress up for reelection who chose not to increase taxes and reduce the spending, which both the Senate and President Bush had proposed. Rather, they chose a platform better suited for their own reelection. Those members of Congress who chose the course for their own reelection were as guilty of impeding quality in America as those businesses that build and sell an inferior product, investment, or service to their customer just to make a short-term profit. In either case, America gets ripped off, and we can't continue to operate this way. In business and in government, in profit and politics, America needs to seek the long-term course for quality.

When the quality course is short circuited, such action leads to polluted streams, oceans and beaches, smog and dangerous air quality; degenerating

Figure 2.1
Comparing the Bureaucratic System to the Quality-Oriented Approach

Dimension	Classic Efficiency Model	Quality Model
Organization design	Bureaucratic, functional units	Nonhierarchic, process teams
Locus of attention	Top of pyramid	Everyone at direct point of contact with the external customer or production activity and internally within the teams
Positive role model	Heroic leadership	Self-initiated followership for the customer
Primary control mechanism	Extrinsic rewards and punishments from management	Intrinsic rewards and team sanctions
	Performance appraisal tied to merit pay	Ongoing coaching, role clarification, and organizationwide awards
Star performer	Upward mobile, fast burner	Team player, customer focused team
Blame For poor workmanship	Worker	85-94% system or process, 6-15% assignable causes
Role of leader	Control through management by objectives	Facilitator, trainer, developer
	Legal authority	Inherent authority
	Boss	Partner/team leader
Primary means of team communication	Staff meeting, written instruction	Process improvement activities
Decisional power	Ownership/ management	Entire work force plus labor
	Power by position	Management by fact
Dominant theme	Compliance with rules and efficiency	Personal and team commitment to absolute customer satisfaction
Quality	A destiny: an end product	A journey: a process

forests and agricultural lands; loss of wildlife; substandard education; and increased prejudice and crime. It yields products that may not work properly, products that may need to be returned, replaced, reworked, or discarded. It means waste. It facilitates distrust and alienation and breaks down the precious social interdependency and mutuality between the organization and its customer or supplier that are essential for the quality approach to exist.

The core assumption in the quality approach to doing business is that through partnerships between oneself and one's customer—management and the work force, subassembly to subassembly, organization to organization, supplier to producer, producer to customer, supervisor to worker, and worker to worker— long-term success is enhanced. When one serves his or her customer, he or she also serves his or her country. The greater the dedication to quality service in all that we do, the greater the success of our nation. Each of us *does* make a difference.

As customers, we all value suppliers with a quality orientation toward serving us. This being true, then, naturally, those of us who have a quality orientation will be more successful over the long term. We will be in greater demand than others.

Quality means:

- designing what your customer wants and *needs* (i.e., addressing not only your customer's current wants, but your customer's *future* needs, perhaps even before the customer is aware of them);
- preparing what your customer wants on time, the way the customer wants it;
- assuring your product facilitates your customer's success through your follow-up and support;
- committing yourself to continuous, never-ending improvement of customer support to assure yourself that you will remain the customers' choice in the future.

Quality is the responsibility of management and workers alike. We all share it, but it begins with management's commitment to this definition.

MAKING GOVERNMENT A QUALITY PLACE TO WORK

In America, government is the ultimate preserver of quality. When our streets get too unsafe, it is government that takes charge. When the air we breathe is too polluted, government is the key to turning that situation around. When man, machine, and nature disrupt our lands, our soil, and our great outdoors, government takes the reins and ensures the quality of our lives. It is true that it has been the quality of our national defense organization that enabled our nation to prevail during the cold war—through it our democracy and our economy were able to endure.

Yet, government is plagued with a reputation for mediocrity. The federal government is the largest organization in the country. By size alone, it is destined to be less efficient, inflexible, and less responsive to its customers than organizations of smaller size and with less political direction. Also, depending on the political and economic times and sensitivities, it is the employer of the last resort whose employees are managed by a civil service system that has taken the lead in ensuring employee rights in America, but has stifled the organization's ability to provide quality to the customer.

THE QUALITY APPROACH REPRESENTS A NEW PARADIGM

The quality approach is not simply another cognitive alternative that is being offered to managers and workers; it is a profound shift in understanding about the meaning of work and the rational systems that we employ to support it— our organizational behavior.

We use the term "paradigm" to imply a shared set of beliefs and underlying, subconscious assumptions about a particular phenomenon as it relates to our world (Kuhn, 1962). History is bursting with examples of significant paradigm shifts. Columbus' demonstration that the world was round rather than flat opened up all types of new possibilities in thinking and acting—it changed human behavior. New paradigms give cause for new rational thinking and scientific investigation to support the underlying assumptions of the paradigm itself. In turn, they also encapsulate perspective and deter other explorations that would not fit within their own underlying assumptions.

When the earth was viewed as the center of the universe, philosophers created rationales to support man's role and the roles of the stars and planets and all that fell within them to support that paradigm. However, when it was decided that the earth is not the center of the universe, people like Kepler and Copernicus could be stimulated to investigate things never before imagined.

What the quality approach offers is an orientation to management and organizational behavior not imagined before. It is that profound. The criteria to evaluate it must be drawn from the new paradigm rather than the old. The changing paradigm will place great strain on managers and their employees.

Smith and Peterson (1988) have identified a cognitive process that they term "event meanings." These occur over time as a result of routinized "best-response" patterns when exposed to decision-making situations. Although event meanings create ready activation of the routinized reponse, they tend to discard all other choice solutions. This is done for conceptual and emotional convenience. Collectively, these response patterns form cultures from which prescribed, anticipated social interaction takes place. The bureaucratic system described before is one of these cultures so formed over time. The project discussed in this book attempts to change that culture and create a culture for quality.

We have termed the American approach to doing business to be the classic efficiency-oriented (bureaucratic) paradigm. As a result of global competition and the realization that the customer is going to make or break us, the customer has gained new importance and has forced us to collide with our own working set of assumptions about management and organizational behavior. The quality approach offers a new paradigm for doing business where the customer is the "center" of the organization's world.

Employees and managers who have been socialized into the old efficiency-oriented approach have routinized response patterns to decision making that need to be changed to accommodate the new quality paradigm. They will manifest themselves in how we decide to plan, direct, lead, control, coordinate, reward, select, promote, analyze, and evaluate organizational behavior from the perspective of the impact they have on the customer.

SUMMARY

The quality approach has been contrasted with the working paradigm of the past. The quality way represents a major shift in organizational design and performance. It is not just theory. Right now, the paradigm shift is occurring throughout America.

Part II describes practical problems that co-author Nelson found in the past federal Civil Service System (CSS) that needed changing to enable his organization to perform more effectively within the quality paradigm. It also provides an alternative, more quality driven approach to managing people—a process that is currently in demonstration at McClellan Air Force Base, where he worked. He provides background information about the extrarational events that paved the way to create the alternative that was never before considered in the old paradigm.

The conditions that are described in Chapter 3 are impediments that are not just representative of the federal government. They exist in greater or lesser degree in every large organization that exists where the bureaucratic form of management exists—where the behavior of people is controlled by extensive rules and regulations. The conditions to be described are part of the major reason our nation has taken a new, hard look at the quality approach, and the federal government has sponsored PPS and other efforts to move beyond participative management.

NOTE

1. This dichotomy was detailed in an unpublished paper presented by G. R. Gilbert, C. Krum, and A. E. Nelson. "The Pacer Share Project: A Federal Demonstration Perspective On Pay, Gainsharing, and Quality." Western Social Science Association, Portland, Oregon. April 1990. See also G. R. Gilbert. (1989). "Making Government a 'Quality' Place to Work." *Government Executive* (November): 58.

REFERENCES

Deming, W. E. (1986). *Out of the Crisis*. Cambridge, MA: Massachusetts Institute of Technology, Center for Advanced Engineering Study (MIT/CAES).

Kuhn, T. S. (1962). *The Structure of Scientific Revolutions*. Chicago: University of Chicago Press.

McCallum, J. S. (1986). "The Japanese Industrial Miracle: It is Not hard to Explain." *Business Quarterly* 51 (Summer): 41–47.

Reich, R. B. (1987). "Entrepreneurship Reconsidered: The Team As Hero." *Harvard Business Review* 3 (May–June): 77–83.

Smith, P. B., and Peterson, M. F. (1988). *Leadership, Organization, and Culture: An Event Management Model*. London: Sage.

Walton. M. (1986). *The Deming Management Method*. New York: Dodd, Mead.

PART II

Quality in Government: Failure, Promise, and Project Pacer Share

Co-author Nelson played a major role in constructively confronting unsound governmental practices that impede customer-oriented quality. Unlike most critics of organizational practice, he not only deftly identified unsound practices, but he steered his organization to implement new ways of doing business in government based on the quality imperative.

In case study style, he describes the faults with the present personnel system in the nation's largest employer, the federal government. Then he relives his journey as he and others created an alternative to the old way of doing business, which is founded on the principles of quality management. Finally, he describes Project Pacer Share, a nationally supported demonstration project for improved quality currently underway at McClellan Air Force Base, Sacramento, California. Nelson headed the project's design team and directed the overall project during the first three years of its five-year demonstration effort. The project is sponsored by the U.S. Office of Personnel Management and, though still in its demonstration stage, many aspects of its design and technology are being transferred to other organizations, both public and private.

Brief statements about their own recollections regarding the early conceptualization, design, and start of the project are provided in the Appendixes by two other key employees who worked with Nelson on the project design team. Dan Fuchs describes the difficulties of getting participation from top-level managers in the early design phase. Although there was an extraordinary attempt to get their involvement, many in management were passively cooperating until they learned the project would, indeed, be implemented. Upon implementation, when the project directly began to change their lives, they became deeply involved. Colene Krum, a member of the design team from the start, describes the development of the project from her perspective as a design team member who surveyed organizations in both the private and public sectors before the project components were designed and proposed for implementation.

The Problems with the Existing Civil Service System

There can be no question that the U.S. Civil Service was created to solve major problems and that it has accomplished great things. It has, by and large, achieved the end of the political spoils system, exactly as it was intended to do. Through it, over time, the various Congresses and Administrations were also able to leverage progress for both the federal worker and those served by them. It helped bring to an end hiring and promotion practices based on discrimination (of whatever particular bent—age, sex, race, color, handicap condition—take your pick), political favoritism, graft, and the many other ills that afflict a spoils system.

If all that is true, and it is to some degree, what is the problem? The problem is that the improvements in the U.S. Civil Service System (CSS) were slowly grinding to a halt; not being lost, but just not being further improved. Like so many institutions that preceded it, the CSS was sinking into a morass of its own making, becoming bogged down with excessive bureaucracy, and seemingly infinitely multiplying regulations. The CSS had created its own bureaucratic realities. It had created an overlay of weighty rules, procedures that caused too much restriction on the present and insufficient focus on the future.

The federal personnel system, and all the managers and would-be leaders who were governed by it, was being increasingly focused on "maintenance of the status quo." And that status quo had, despite its many good points, incorporated into itself many management practices and organizational design concepts derived from past theories and practices that were better suited for mechanisticlike, efficiency-oriented systems of an industrial age than the quality-driven organization needed for the next decade and beyond.

Certain aspects of the CSS were being rapidly invalidated by organizations and nations that had begun to adhere to the new quality model. Both in terms of content and theory of humanity, some of the practices in the CSS were antithetical to what America stands for. These policies, practices, and procedures, and the organizational structures they created and demanded, were directly sti-fling the improvement efforts of federal employees and their organizations.

Managers and nonmanagers alike were prevented from affecting needed change, prevented from providing the American public the never-ending im-provement of quality service and support they had every right to expect (and, yes, to demand). Indeed, the "quality" of public service grew to become the butt of many jokes, an example of what quality service "was not."

"Good enough for government service" has become the expression for medio-crity, for example, for products and services that are substandard. One could say that it is an anachronism that today's slogan, "good enough for government ser-vice," has become the equivalent to what "Made in Japan" was in the 1950s.

However, the Japanese, driven by crisis, were responsive to new ideas. They learned how to change their ways of doing business in order to viably compete in a world that demanded better quality. They undertook the journey for never-ending improvement, and today they, not we, are the quality capital of the world.

Over time the public has learned to expect, and accept, less timeliness, re-sponsiveness, courtesy, care, and reliability of and from its government agencies. Today, our government and all public agencies need to undertake that same quality revolution—the revolution undertaken, not only by Japan and many Far East nations, but by the newly emerging "United States of Europe," the Eu-ropean Economic Community.

Given the changed economic order in the world today, a world based on global capitalism, where the United States no longer has the luxury of carrying a huge national debt and bank rolling government inefficiency, it has become clear that the federal government needs to change its own way of doing business. This must start with how it manages its people. It needs to facilitate innovation and commitment for quality. Our federal government is the nation's largest employer. It has the greatest opportunity and obligation to provide quality to the nation. Yet it is employing an outmoded approach to management. Change is needed now. The federal government needs to conduct itself in such a way that every service, every customer contact, every product is of such quality that it meets the ultimate standard of a mighty nation's success—it is good *enough* for gov-ernment. Every freeway should be built as though it were built for the mightiest people on earth—just like the Roman Appian Way. Every employee must be treated with the respect due one who possesses full citizenship. Every employee must be expected to fulfill his or her obligations to the workplace just as the workplace is expected to protect the rights of the employee.

But that is not the way it is now. With the exception of the military at war, an insufficient number expect excellence from government, be they consumers, clients, Congress, supervisors or nonsupervisory employees. It is time for a change.

WHAT WENT WRONG?

What went wrong? Let's examine those elements of the CSS, however well intentioned in their original form, that have become the major issues that the jointly sponsored U.S. Department of Defense's (DOD) and U.S. Office of Personnel Management's (OPM) Project Pacer Share demonstration project addresses and attempts to resolve.

We will examine the Federal Civil Service Classification System, the supervisory grading system, reduction-in-force (RIF) procedures, the dependence of the system on a fixed-salary schedule only and, lastly, but most significantly, the annual employee performance appraisal system.

Position Classification System

In the Federal Civil Service, all positions (i.e., "jobs") are categorized by the following considerations:

(a) Is the job "white collar" or "blue collar"?
(b) What basic "profession" or "trade" is involved in this job?

The answers to these two queries are used to determine the "job series" of any particular position in the federal CSS. Currently, the CSS recognizes over 700 of them.

Then a third question is raised:

(c) Within each series, what levels of knowledge, skill, and ability are called for in "this" job?

The answers derived from this question are used to determine which of fifteen different "Pay Grades" to assign to the job.

Today, the CSS has a classification system that is essentially a matrix measuring $2 \times 15 \times 700+$. But there are some further complications. In the "blue collar" classification system, there is a separate group of pay levels for a type of job called a "work leader," which supplements the supervisory/foreman positions, and serves as a kind of "crew boss," and yet another separate group for supervisory positions.

Shred Codes

Additionally, there is the ability to further break out each of the series, and pay classifications, on individual "position descriptions" by adding duties from some other series, or classification, or pay system, or particular set of skills applicable to "this job." This is done, in the Air Force, for example, through the use of what is called a "shred code" (i.e., a further "shred-out" of the basic computer skills code), and beyond that to another level, by a "subshred."

For example, a specific job might be classified as a "Supply Systems Analyst" and placed in the basic 2003 Job Series (2003 is the number assigned to the jobs called "Supply Systems Analyst," already a subdivision within the basic 2XXX "Supply" area). Then the job might be further broken out as one carrying a shred meaning "a Supply System Analyst who works with automated systems," and then further specified by the specific organizational background, location, or setting of those automated systems.

Classification Specialists

Now it should come as no surprise that to understand the system that divides federal employment into over 20,000–50,000 (there is widespread rumor that no one knows the actual number) possible specific grade, series, and pay plans is not an easy task. Indeed, it is so complex that the expert understanding and application of the system has its own "series," that is, a series/profession whose incumbents have the job of determining what series, grade, and pay plan everybody else is in.

Beyond this, every one of those series has its own official "Classification Guide," a document that may require twenty to thirty pages of guidance, references, cross references, and task descriptions. This 500,000+ pages of documentation, in turn, must be written, proofed, coordinated, printed, and distributed to the hundreds of personnel offices throughout federal agencies around the world, where "Classification Specialists" wait to apply them.

Ripple Effect

But the complexity and cumbersome nature of the CSS does not end there. As technologies change in the workplace, so, too, must jobs change. That requires more staff work for personnel specialists who are needed to update, reproof, recoordinate, reprint and redistribute, and restock and reisssue those "guides." As one of these guides changes, it frequently has a "ripple effect" (some would call it a "domino effect") as it generates further changes across whole groups of series, which can, in turn, come back to impact the series whose change started it all.

Classification Audit

But we are still not done. Massive "classification audits" and surveys are routinely conducted in federal agencies to assure that the guides are being "properly applied to local jobs." These may result in reclassification or "downgrading" (reducing the pay grade) of specific jobs or groups of jobs, which, in turn, launches a regular series of "appeals" through the classification system for "reconsideration" of the audit action. This bureaucratic exercise leads to a tremendous expenditure of resources that could be used more productively in some other way.

High-Grade Control

The structuring of the system into the fifteen pay grades has also resulted in the institution of "high-grade control" systems to restrict and reduce the number of white collar employees in the top three pay categories of the GS/GM pay plans. The GS, or General Schedule, is the white collar pay system, and the GM, or General Manager, identifies white collar supervisors in those same three grades. Both GS and GM have the same top three pay grades/pay ranges: the GS (or GM) 13, 14 and 15.

How Did It Get Like This?

At this point, a person could logically ask, "Why are there all these series, pay plans, and pay grades and their supporting bureaucracies in existence?" Unfortunately, there does not appear to be a logical answer. Like Topsy, "they just grew." As new technologies came into use, sometimes a new "series" was developed for it, and sometimes not. And, no, there was no set of specific rules as to when this happened and when it didn't. Sociopolitical forces played as much in the decision process as the specific technologies, or the mission of the organization. Please note, we do not say this is "wrong," it is simply reality.

There are three inputs to any system: the essential mission, the technology, and the sociopolitical (human). We must acknowledge and account for all three in every system or court disaster. Likewise, as pay accelerated in the nonfederal sector, sometimes due to those new technologies, and sometimes just due to failure to raise federal pay to match the private sector, the response of the federal classification system was to "add a new grade" or to promote to the next higher existing grade. This is known in federal jargon as "grade creep."

Promotions

Now, to "move up" through the system, that is, to reach a higher pay grade, a person has to go through the merit promotion system. This means that to progress from one pay grade to the next (e.g., to be promoted from a GS–3 to a GS–4), every time there is a complex series of screenings and reviews, this 21,000+ matrix is involved to assure that all the rules were followed. Past jobs held in the matrix (each categorized by a series and grade identification to one of the 21,000+ cells of the matrix) do, in truth, relate to and qualify potential candidates for the series and grade of the new position.

If all of this begins to sound just a little Byzantine, keep in mind that we are dealing with the simpler part first. To further complicate matters, many of the series have "time limits." This means either a requirement that a person must have spent a specified length of time in a certain series and at a certain grade level before qualifying for promotion to the next "higher" grade or that there must be a certain time spent in several series at certain grade levels. Coupled to this, not all the series allow or practice promotions the same way. Some go from "grade to grade" (e.g., from a 3 to a 4 to a 5 to a 6 to a 7). Other series have what are called "two grade intervals" (and go from a 5 to a 7 to a 9). Which ones? Well, that depends on how the Classification Guide was written (or revised), and all the rest of the "information" on series and grades.

If even this system, as complex as it is, ended there, perhaps it could be saved. After all, in intent, it was an "honorable system," designed to end the "spoils system."

But it does not end there. Standards are not uniformly applied, and application can vary from department to department within the same agency, or across agencies, or between geographic locations, or even from office to office, as managers struggle to "get their people the best deal."

That variance, in fact, is one of the causes for all those audits noted before. The "classifiers," as it were, now become a police force out to "catch" managers and agencies "gaming the system," empowered not to improve the system, but to enforce the status quo. This results in the continuation of a system so complex that getting it changed is nigh onto impossible and takes enormous amounts of time and effort. But neither technology, nor the private sector, is going to wait for all that to happen. The result is that federal managers see their ability to compete with the private sector swept away. They are unable to recruit and retain the quality of people the American people have a right to expect in jobs of public trust. And each year it gets worse, driven by the series and grade pay limitations lagging years behind the real world.

Pay Adjustments

The current administration's efforts to get "regional pay" for some jobs in the "white collar" pay plan is an attempt to respond to this situation; but, it should be noted, only when the system made it impossible to recruit and retain secretarial and clerical help in Washington, D.C. Unfortunately, all it does is add another element/dimension to the matrix. Rather than simplify, it further complicates. And not just by adding the "Where are we?" question to the pay question. The establishment of geographic rates tremendously complicates the question of geographic moves by some federal workers (those in the lower grades), as has already been experienced in the blue collar pay plans that are already geographically differentiated. The "geographic pay" response must be fairly labeled as "another work-around" versus a cure, a Band-Aid (TM) when radical surgery is called for.

Impact and Promise of Technology on Jobs and the Personnel System

Further complicating the classification issue is the rapid spread of automation and related technologies across the entire work force. This is particularly true in the area of computer skills. Classifiers themselves were largely unprepared for and unskilled in computer technologies and their application (via applications software) in the "microcomputer revolution." They have been totally caught off guard by the need to cope with executives who "keyboard" and former "secretaries" whose use of spreadsheets, graphics programs, and data bases has allowed the replacement of entire rooms full of accountants, mainframe programmers, and computer support personnel, analysts, draftspersons, and various other staff professionals. Indeed, the potential benefits of automation on the classification system itself have been missed.

Technology Transfer

The medical and engineering professions have, for several years, used various programs, either in conventional data base or advanced artificial intelligence (AI)/expert systems to help them. This help has ranged from the analysis of complex data (e.g., the medical systems of a patient) to the ability to "advise" them of the probable best analysis of a medical diagnosis. Likewise in the legal profession, lawyers routinely link to online, nationwide data bases/research programs to assist them in case analysis and research.

Not so the federal classifiers. Turning instead to the hundreds and thousands of pages of printed data, they daily, nationwide, continue their manual processing and research. Though the application of such existing technology could have radically simplified the classification task, and given some consistency to classification decisions, it has not happened. That same "mind-set" that could not recognize that a "secretary" running a spreadsheet was doing a job far more complex and valuable than the old series classification called for (i.e., she's/he's still using a keyboard isn't she/he?) also prevented classifiers from understanding the impact of technology on their own job.

Not, mind you, that we believe that such automation is the correct answer. To automate a process that need not exist may save some money, but it is still 100 percent wrong. By automating a job that shouldn't exist at all, the investment in such automation gives tacit management ratification to the need for that job. Thus, we make it all the more difficult to finally eliminate what we have now spent money to improve.

The waste that could be eliminated by automating the classification process, though substantial, is not the major waste. No, the major waste is not in the salaries of the classifiers. Nor is it even in the wages of the thousands of people involved in the typing, filing, printing, distribution, and maintenance of the classification standards and their related position descriptions (even if costing millions of dollars a year). The major loss is at least an order of magnitude beyond that. It is related to improving a system that shouldn't be there in the first place, as noted before. The major waste is in the loss of the potential contributions of all the people that could have been freed to contribute to the maximum of their capabilities in accomplishing their agencies' mission and cannot do so in the present system. It is the loss of the entire two million plus federal employees' ability to realize their own potential goals through more productive applications of their knowledge and skills on the job. It is in the loss of the freely given contributions that could have come from a motivated, free, empowered work force—a work force now artificially constrained by a system based on control versus commitment, on "scientific management" versus people-centered leadership, on mediocrity versus excellence, on compliance versus improvement.

The great loss is the loss of hope that many human beings employed in government had first dared to expect of their employer; for many, they chose to work for government to serve their nation and to perpetuate the principles of the world's greatest democracy through their own work. However, in their work situations in the federal government, due to a great degree as a result of the constraints placed on them through their work situations as described before, they found themselves contained and severely limited in their own job situations. Over time, many lose hope in what they may do.

Many readers may say, "It can't be that bad." What we have set forward is nothing but simple facts, verifiable by a visit to any federal personnel office. Unfortunately, if anything, it is worse, as we will see.

Supervisory Classification System

The Supervisory Classification System is that portion of the Civil Service that controls the manner in which the pay and "grade" of federal supervisors are determined. Though there are some minor variations, the current supervisory grading criteria for both blue and white collar supervisors, first of all, assigns one of the job series (area of job specialization, as before, for the nonsupervisory positions) of the people being supervised to that job. If, for example, the people in the area being supervised were GS–2003 Supply Systems Analysts, then the supervisor would be a GS (or GM, more on that later)–2003 "Supervisory Supply Systems Analyst." Likewise, the second-level supervisor (and third, and fourth, and succeeding levels of supervision "up the chain of command") would also be assigned a series and job title corresponding to the series of at least some of those supervised. Besides just the name of the series, the requirement for being in and from that profession (be it a pipe fitter or logistician) is also included. It is important for it attests to the person having held one of the immediate preceding jobs in the same "career ladder."

An example may help illustrate this. To become a GS–2003, Supervisory Supply Systems Analyst, at grade 11, you had to be a journeyperson GS–2003–9 (and before the 9, a 2003–7, and before; you get the idea). Likewise, before becoming a second level GS–2003–12 Supervisory Supply Systems Analyst, you had to have been that GS–2003–11 first-level supervisor. And so on, up the management pyramid. The result of this is the "building in," the formal incorporation, of career "stovepiping." You not only "could" stay with a single career field your entire working life, sometimes you were encouraged to do so, because your series both (a) excluded all other series from consideration for promotion in that field, for example, to be promoted to a GS–2032–12 Packaging Specialist, you needed to have been a GS–2032–11; and (b) offered attractive promotions right from entry trainee level up through fairly high-paying management jobs at the 14 and 15 pay levels.

In the case of co-author Nelson, he entered the federal civil service in just such a series when he began his federal career as a GS–2032 Packaging Specialist Trainee, in 1969. He advanced directly up the ladder from GS–2032–7 to GS–2032–9 to GS–2032–11 to GS–2032–12 (first-level supervision at his location; other locations have GS–2032–9 levels of supervision) to GS–2032–13 (second level), totally in one series and in one organization. It was only due to the severe DOD cutbacks after Vietnam that resulted in the elimination of many positions, including his, that he had the opportunity to learn, firsthand, that the world was a bigger place, with further horizons than those encompassed by the packaging management field.

Although career ladders could act for some in this beneficial way, for the majority, these vertical career paths were much shorter, locking people into low-paying jobs with little future (including the lower grades of some supervisory jobs). The 318 Clerical Series "died" at the GS–5 level, with little possibility for advancement. The 322 Secretarial Series, with a handful of exceptions, "died" at the 7 level, and hundreds more "died" at the 9 and 11 levels. As each "career ladder" ended, the "incumbent" had a choice: plan to retire at that level or move to a totally different career field. In most cases (including supervisors), this meant going down in pay/grade, even down to an entry-level trainee position. Such a person had to bet "on-the-come" that he/she would be successful in the training (some aren't and "go back") and recover in future years what they had lost in the one or two years of the training process. But many more, by far the majority, cannot, or will not, take those risks, and we incur the dual societal loss of losing what they might have contributed to a new job and what they, in turn, could have contributed to society (including themselves) by finding and testing new horizons.

The effects of such restrictions are, of course, directly opposed to the quality model. The quality model requires a committed, involved work force, understanding and supporting each other in true team fashion to achieve never-ending improvement in delivered product and service. Rather, we see the federal employee, with each passing year, become more frustrated with the restraints. We see him or her become more unwilling to give his/her all, more angry at the structure and those who manage it (even for managers, who focus that anger at "the next levels up"). With this increasingly adversarial model, management (that "next level up," at whatever level that might be) becomes increasingly frustrated with "them" (read: "anyone below"), with "the unwilling." They increasingly impose, and still impose, more restrictive rules and regulations, forcing at least minimal compliance in performing organizational tasks. And slowly but surely, the system, so honestly conceived, moved into a system of control and compliance versus the required system of commitment and improvement.

Layering

But there is another aspect of the Supervisory Classification System that is also causing great financial loss. In the CSS, the pay/grade of every supervisor/manager is directly related to both the number of people supervised and to the pay that those people receive. And if you are thinking that this promotes inefficiency, you are right. A few examples will make this clear.

Example 1: Supervisor/manager X is a third-level foreman in an aircraft repair shop. She is a WS (i.e., a blue collar Wage Supervisor) –12, a third-level supervisor. She has four WS–11 subordinate second-level supervisors reporting to her. If she determines there is a way to "flatten her organization," and eliminate the need for those subordinates (or, say, all but one WS–11), so that the twelve WS–7 and WS–9 first-level supervisors in the organization report directly to her, saving the government well in excess of $100–150,000 a year, what will the reward be? In the current system, she would be demoted or moved to another job, and her position would be reduced in pay for whoever followed her. How much motivation does this possibility provide supervisor X?

Example 2: Let us suppose that rather than determine how to "flatten" her organization, she decides to increase the number of subordinates at the WS–11 level from four to eight. What is the result in this case? Well, believe it or not, the usual result is to promote supervisor X from a WS–12 to a WS–13. What kind of motivation is found here? Right again, "empire time," "bigger is better," and "the more the merrier."

Example 3: Manager Y is forming a new division. It is to be an important organization, with an important mission, say, for example, the design of a new accounting system to support a 10,000-person organization, with a budget of $300 million for salaries/benefits alone. Manager Y determines that to get the talent he needs, the position will have to be established at a GM–13 pay level (GM means General Manager; supervisory/management positions above the GS–12 are normally placed in this pay plan, created by the 1978 Civil Service Reform Act). No problem! All that has to be done is to use a formula to build a pyramid. One GM–13 equals three (or more) subordinate GS–12s; each 12 equals three (or more) subordinate 11s; each 11 equals three (or more 9s, and some 7s, 6s, 5s, etc.); and so on, to the bottom. Never mind if the actual job requires all those subordinate positions. Never mind if all those people are really needed.

The formula says that's the way you support that GM–13. Move whatever functions and tasks necessary to get that pyramid into place. Create them, if needed; just get them. Move them from some other organizations that have a higher ratio of 12s to 13s than strictly needed (or 12s to 11s, etc.). No matter if you break up a process, or complicate formerly simple chains of communications, or add new layers to organizations, or create unnecessarily complex reporting chains. No matter if some of the "moved-in"/created functions/processes have no relation to the main accounting purpose, or if the technologies, or customers, or output services and/or products have no relationship to each other. No matter if the members of the new organization are so different they can't even communicate with each other, or the new GM–13 doesn't have the foggiest idea about what some of these people do for a living. No matter! That's not the purpose. The purpose, the sole purpose, is to support that pyramid that holds up that GM–13 position. Unreal? Unfortunately, no. Every day across this country, every one of these cases, and sometimes cases that combine the examples, is being played out in the various agencies, offices, and departments that make up the administrative and judicial branches of the federal government. There are some exceptions regarding the specific titles, grades, and rules, as in the diplomatic service, but the approach is the same in all.

Reduction in Force

In the CSS, there are many categories of "appointment" to a job. The principal ones are "temporary," an appointment to a known, time-limited job, usually for a period of one year or less (but that may be extended if the job situation requires it); "career conditional," the normal manner of entry to a federal career (one-year probation followed by two years of more "controlled"—requiring greater justification to terminate—probation); and "career," the type of appointment of a "permanent" federal employee, that is, one who has completed the three-year conditional-probationary appointment.

In actual fact, the career-conditional "probation" is best classified as a fiction; few such "probationary" conditions are ever enforced and, on average, once "in the door," the only time full career status is not reached is when the agency enters a severe budget-cut crisis.

When such budget cuts occur, as now, in the Department of Defense, with the literal disappearance of the threat of the Soviet Bloc, and the reconfiguration of budget priorities within the administration, Defense Department agencies enter the truly Byzantine world of "Reduction In Force" (RIF). With all the grades, series, and types of appointments we examined before, it is, as you might imagine, not exactly an easy task to sort out all the ins, outs, priorities, retention rights, etc., of all the employees impacted by a RIF.

To illustrate this best, we will look at how a "typical" RIF action might take place. For our action, as it is imaginary, we will look at Mythical Air Force Base (MAFB), Los Angeles, California. Mythical AFB is, let us suppose, a base of the Air Force Systems Command Space Systems Division (in charge of the design and acquisition of the nations's space satellite communications system). When the Air Force receives its budget from Congress, there will be a certain portion aimed at the slow down of the acquisition process. This will slow down the buy, let us say, of some systems (including satellites), or the elimination of certain other new acquisitions (including satellites), or the elimination of certain existing systems (including satellites). Added to this, there will be a "general cut," aimed at no specific system, or involving the closure of some bases (which may or may not involve the end of the mission of those organizations stationed at those bases). From all of this, Mythical AFB will receive a certain "quota" of reductions, some to dollars, some to manning levels, perhaps some to facilities (up to base closure), and some to activity levels supporting some of the satellite systems managed by (designed and acquired by) the base.

These "as-yet-not-totally-specific-reductions" (a reduction of 320 civilian positions does not say which jobs) now enter the formal RIF process.

First, management must determine where the specific reductions are to occur, in which satellite programs (or base support/facilities programs) will there be specified cuts (i.e., directed reductions) and to what level.

When such reductions are specified, the personnel office and management next identify the specific job series and grade levels that will be lost, and the number and organizational identity of each.

Next, the people who occupy all such jobs in those organizations are identified and they are "ranked" by:

(a) Veteran's preference (veteran versus nonveteran), and, within the veteran category, disabled veteran versus nondisabled veteran (10-, 20-, or 30-point disability, depending on the nature of the disability).

(b) Within each of these four categories, incumbents are ranked by seniority (first as career-conditional versus career, and then by the number of years seniority within which of those two categories the employee falls in).

(c) The score of the last appraisal, and special consideration/awards that may be given extra retention points.

This 10-part ranking (series, grade, vet/nonvet, three-way disability, seniority, appraisal, "special" points) gives us our "first-round" identity of people who will be affected by the RIF. But hold on, we have only just begun. You see, each of these "first-round" RIF candidates has a job history. And that job history has to be compared with the job history of every other person at the installation, in each of the categories (of the 10 noted) to see if the first-round candidate has "bumping rights" (i.e., a higher ranking in the 10-way matrix than someone else in the RIF population). This is done first among any other incumbents in the same series and at the same pay grade. This includes other "qualifying" series, where the job qualifications of the incumbent's series have a cross qualification, or in a series in which the incumbent had previously worked (at the same or higher grade). If so, then that person becomes the RIF candidate and the whole process starts again for that "second-round" choice.

If this first "screen" doesn't identify a "second rounder," then management can wave "series" requirements and the second-round "bumpee" may be in any series. If that doesn't find a second-round bumpee, then we begin the screen, in like manner, at the next lower grade down and do it all again. And then to the next grade, and the next, and . . . you get the idea. And each time a bumpee is identified, we do it all over, from the top, for that person.

The result is that the apparently straightforward reduction of 320 positions can result in upwards of several thousand people being displaced. All will be changing jobs. All will have to learn new skills. And the actual 320 that are separated will be totally unknown for weeks, except that we know that in 90+ percent of the cases, they will not be the occupants of the jobs being eliminated and initially identified. Which means, of course, that the positions actually eliminated will come from the bottom, the lower grades, where the people who have the least seniority are usually found. That will mean the reductions will be at the lower salary ranges, not where originally planned. That, in turn, will require new reductions to reach the original set dollar reductions, *and we will do it all over again*. This new round will involve even more of the work force than the first time through. Before we are finished, we will have disrupted an amazing percentage of the work force in "bumps," moves, transfers, and, ultimately for some, actual separation, and all the training needed to bring all those newly moved people up to speed. Thus, we have not only the costs of all the calculations, paperwork, and counseling involved in the actual moves, but the very significant morale factors involved in the initial uncertainties, the fear of not knowing from one day to the next whether "I'll get bumped or not, and if I do, what's next." Added to this is the anger of having worked for years, in many cases, to leave a certain career field or job and then suddenly finding oneself back in it. Or we must cope with the fear of entering a new (or old) job field with totally new technological requirements and not knowing if "I can cope with that or not."

Small wonder that for years many professional personnel specialists and line managers have claimed that the long-term costs of any RIF far exceed any short-term savings. But, then, that is the exact conflict, isn't it? The conflict of the long-term thinking of the quality model versus the short-term thinking of the efficiency model is exactly the issue we address in this work.

A clearer focus of those differences is found in the attitude that embodies the RIF action. Here we find the view that the quick fix of firing people is *the only way to go*. It directly runs counter to the long-term payoffs that come from the work force when management opts for their reeducation, protection, and dedicated out-placement services instead of the RIF. These longer-term-oriented options are expressions of loyalty to those who have been loyal to their organizations.

Recently, while undergoing the threat of a RIF and employee displacement, a federal manager said, after having to remove several key supervisors from their jobs, "It is only business," as though there was nothing personal in the decision; yet, the decisions he had to make were obviously painful for him. He was being a good functionary of a corrupt system. He had no other choices as long as he was to stay in the system.

Quality organizations demonstrate their dedication to human values over mere dollar signs. They don't just seek more; they seek quality for the long term.

RIFs create tidal waves of fear. Mention the word "RIF" in any federal agency and watch fear raise its ugly head.

Dependence on Fixed Salary

One of the normatives of the Industrial Revolution model (and, perhaps, even before) has been the fixed salary. This is often expressed with the aphorism, "a fair day's pay for a fair day's work." In the CSS, this translated into the "pay grade" system described at the beginning of this chapter. The intent was good, we are sure, and probably ran something like "to assure that equal pay for equal tasks is paid to employees." However, it totally ignores the basic principle of intrinsic self-motivation that derives from ownership of the enterprise, and may well run counter to the basic American ethic of distributive justice.

First, let's look at intrinsic self-motivation. Assume you are a member of a work force of twenty-seven government workers, all receiving that "fair wage." You notice that there are six of you at the same salary grade, say, GS–9. You will all get the same wage regardless of what you do, how hard you work, or how much smarter you work. Why should you work any harder? Or why should you take any action to correct a situation where one or two are consistently late to work? Without your compensation being directly tied to the success of the organization, but only to "being there," it's "no skin off your nose"; so you do nothing. As a matter of fact, if most people follow the dysfunctional behavior, they will get "on the case" of the "good worker" and try to bring down his/her behavior to the group norm, all because there is no financial reward/penalty for doing anything else. Oh we know the old saw, "money doesn't motivate!" Well, we're sorry; it is clearly a motivator of people who work. Maybe the relationship between money and motivation is not linear (every added dollar is not directly correlated with added motivation). However, the unfair distribution of money paid out on the job will clearly trigger motivation; often, the dysfunctional, destructive, type—just wait until your salary is cut by your management while others' salaries are untouched and remain the same, and feel yourself get motivated! Is money a "best" motivator? No, it is not. However, when it fails to demonstrate respect as an incentive, it can readily turn into a destroyer of organizational quality.

When pay plans in organizations tend to separate people in such a way that removes some from full participation in the organizational decision-making process, such a system will seriously inhibit human potential and organizational collaboration for the customer. Such is the case in the CSS.

Second, let's look at the ethics that may be involved. Is it ethical for an organization to contract with you and your fellow workers for one job, and then, because you all pool your energies, talents, and efforts "above and beyond the call" of that original contract and the organization does better, you do not share in the rewards as a group? Also, is it ethical for an organization to limit the recognition of all members of a group of employees who demonstrate excellence in their work by only permitting a given quota (say, 10 percent) of the employees to be recognized for work done by the entire group? Is it any wonder that some employees have learned that, in their system, they will not be rewarded for the work that they do? Indeed, they have come to believe that pay and work are not connected. Some have learned that one's politics in the organization is the greater corollary with their pay. Such assumptions about organizational life in the CSS raise doubts about the ethical conduct of the institution itself by its employees.

The Annual Appraisal System

Although all of this is harmful, we have saved the worst for last. By far and away the worst part of the CSS (or most any personnel system) is the practice of annual appraisals, merit ratings, and associated merit pay, and appraisal-based promotion systems.

We know that this flies in the face of much conventional wisdom. Yet, we hope that before we are done, you will understand both the truly statistical insanity of any annual rating system and the destructive influence it has on people. We will demonstrate the psychological impossibility of implementing the team structure, essential to the quality model, in any environment using an annual rating system based on individual performance alone.

Finally, we will demonstrate the philosophical contradictions inherent between any such rating/merit system and the basic American philosophy of the dignity and worth of the human person. We will begin by exposing the straightforward statistical (mathematical) falseness of any annual rating system (Deming, 1988; Scholtes, 1988). That proof is based on both the nature of the natural distribution curve and the work of Dr. Walter Shewhart, of Bell Labs, in the 1920s. Dr. Shewhart developed the now famous theory of control charts, used by organizations worldwide in the development and application of Statistical Process Control (SPC). What control chart theory indicates is that for a process in control, all performance variance was due to the system itself as opposed to any "special cause." What this simply means is that no matter how far "below average" a person's performance was, if that system, by statistical calculation, was in control, then the variance of that individual was due to faults within the system rather than a result of the individual's actions. Further, no matter how high "above average" the performance was, if that system, by statistical calculation, was in control, then that variance is caused by the system, not the individual. We now end up punishing or rewarding the person for his or her below-average or above-average performance, which is not the fault of the individual, but rather the "fault" (whether good or bad) of the system. Isn't it true that whenever we fail to attain our work objectives, we can find cause for our failings in the same aspect of the system that has failed or helped us? Yet, performance appraisal focuses cause for our exceptional performance on ourselves.

Beyond the intuitive feelings of being treated unfairly in a performance-appraisal cycle, given what Shewhart had identified as the cause for exceptional job performance (the system, not the employee), the work force would now have statistical evidence/proof they ''worked for crazy people'' and that they could not trust the system if it ties reward and punishment to the review of individual job performance.

Setting the statistical issues aside does not resolve the problem. Psychologically, the entire appraisal system is inappropriate to the quality approach to performance. First, as a simple application of the ''Pygmalion'' effect (or self-fulfilling prophecy) demonstrates, the giving of any lower appraisal programs the receiver for lower levels of output, that is, we get what we expect.

But there is a more insidious psychological effect of appraisals; it makes collaboration impossible. Annual ratings as Deming maintains make sustained collaboration, without which teamwork can only be partial, *impossible*. Not difficult. Impossible.

Although some degree of cooperation is possible where high internal competition exists in a group, true sustained commitment to a common good in which all members of the team give freely of their talents for the good of the group over a sustained period of time is not possible. In situations where the management of a group focuses on individual performance rather than team performance, the group may realize only temporary bursts of enthusiasm or a partial participation, hedged in protective psychological mechanisms.

So statistically and psychologically, the annual appraisal cannot be sustained. But more far reaching than that are the philosophical implications of such a system. There is an inconsistency in a system that purports belief in the individual and that treats the growth experiences of education and training as expenses verses investments; and rates, sorts, and grades them as though they were inanimate parts of a machine system rather than vital resources having unique roles to play. There is a problem in any system that blames individuals for that which they do not control. And the annual appraisal/merit system rating does exactly that.

A CALL FOR CHANGE

The next chapter describes the development of PPS from concept to design to implementation. As a case study, it describes the workings of an internal change agent, and the events, opportunities, challenges, and pure luck that made it possible to gain support both within and outside the organization for the project. Clearly, change in the system is needed if the federal system is to facilitate greater quality from its employees and managers.

SUMMARY

Clearly, if half of what preceded is true, the personnel system in the federal government is in need of revision if quality is the objective. If one were in business for himself, he would not permit such practices to exist in his own company.

Recognizing the need for continued improvement, the Civil Service Reform Act of 1978 authorizes innovative approaches to improve the way the federal government manages its people. Through it, federal employees like Nelson, the men and women in the Directorate of Distribution (DS) and the American Federation of Government Employees (AFGE) were encouraged to offer an alternative approach to personnel management, more facilitative of the quality approach described in Chapter 2.

In the next chapter, an alternative approach, PPS, is described. It was approved for implementation by the very agency that it was created to change, the U.S. Office of Personnel Management (OPM).

REFERENCES

Deming, W. E. (1988). *Out of the Crisis*. Cambridge, MA: Massachusetts Institute of Technology, Center for Advanced Engineering Study (MIT/CAES).

Scholtes, P. (1988). Unpublished article for Joiner and Associates, Madison, Wisconsin.

4

Creating an Alternative System: A Shaky Beginning

The year is 1980. The location is McClellan Air Force Base (MCAFB), Sacramento, California, in the Directorate of Distribution (DS) of the Sacramento Air Logistics Center (ALC). The organization has a working population of over 2,100 people. Its mission is the physical distribution of the receipt, storage, issue, and worldwide transportation of billions of dollars of material in storage at MCAFB. Employees of the organization are under the U.S. CSS with all its incumbent difficulties, as described in Chapter 3. Co-author Nelson returns from the Air Force Institute of Technology. He subsequently initiates the Quality Circle (QC) Program at the Sacramento ALC. That program, modeled after Japanese management approaches, grows slowly but surely. With it grows the knowledge that the work force, if properly trained and encouraged, is capable of exactly what the QC founders in Japan claimed: unlimited improvement. By 1982, the QC Program within DS has grown to the point where it is the largest single geographical location QC Program within the Department of Defense (DOD).

IDEAS FROM INNOVATORS ELSEWHERE

Also in 1982, the Sacramento Air Logistics Center, in cooperation with the San Francisco Regional Office of Personnel Management (OPM) cosponsored a conference on Productivity and the Quality of Work Life in the federal sector. A representative of DOD, Karen Alderman, makes a presentation on the benefits of productivity gain sharing. During lunch, she and Nelson discuss the feasibility of extending the productivity gain-sharing efforts to the QC process at MCAFB. Also on the program at that conference are speakers from the Navy Research and Development effort at China Lake, California. They make a presentation on the Civil Service Reform Project, the first in the nation, under way at the Weapons Research and Development Test Center at China Lake, California.

Part of their presentation deals with the nature and the process of establishing a Civil Service Demonstration Project. Further discussions at the conference between Nelson, Alderman, the China Lake Demonstration Project personnel, and representatives of the San Francisco Region of OPM explore the feasibility of establishing a Civil Service Demonstration Project at MCAFB. All these discussions raised hope that the CSS could be changed and, by so doing, help improve performance among the federal work force.

Nelson is convinced that, as voiced by Donald Devine, Director of OPM, "The problem [in government production] is not the people, the problem is the system," that is, that government employees, both managers and nonmanagers, are just as productive, creative, and enthusiastic as anyone else in any other organization. But they are hampered in their efforts to improve their jobs and their processes by the nature of the bureaucratic system in which they work.

INTRODUCING THE IDEAS BACK HOME

Encouraged by those conversations, back home in DS, Nelson approaches his Deputy Director, the senior civilian in his organization, Gerald Tompkins, to discuss the possibility of establishing DS as a site for a U.S. Civil Service Demonstration Project. He is encouraged to continue his exploration of the possibilities. Meetings with representatives from the Directorates of Personnel (DP) and Maintenance (MA) at MCAFB revealed the fact that they also are interested in exploring the possibilities of a demonstration project as they, too, have been excited by the China Lake presentation. A temporary working group to explore the possibilities is then established at the Sacramento ALC between DS, MA, and DP. Over the course of the initial months of this discussion, it is quickly revealed that the interests of DS go far beyond "pay banding," which was the new approach presented by China Lake. Based on Nelson's experience with the QC process, he already is proposing an end to the areas of job series, grade levels, supervisory classifications, and the documented difficulties with the RIF procedure for the reasons noted in Chapter 3.

As it becomes clear that DS is interested in much more than simple pay banding, the MA and DP lose interest and decide to drop out of the project. Nelson, again encouraged by Tompkins, contacts Claude Fahrina, the Deputy Director of the Directorate of Material Management at MCAFB. Mr. Fahrina is, at that time, the only top-level Senior Executive Service ranked executive at MCAFB. He and Nelson discuss the basic concepts of a project that would serve as a model for the U.S. Government. They consider an alternative employment model without series, without grade, with new management/supervisory grading criteria that eliminate all references to number and grade of people employed and without the threat of RIF on permanent employees. Mr. Fahrina encourages Nelson to continue his development of the concept and together he and Tompkins arrange for Nelson to discuss further possibilities with the Commander of the ALC, Major General Dewey K. K. Lowe. General Lowe and Fahrina both encourage Nelson to go to Santa Monica to talk to RAND and Project Air Force, which is the portion of RAND dedicated to providing managerial advice and guidance to the U.S. Air Force. This meeting takes place in early 1983.

Checking with the RAND Corporation

The first meeting with Project Air Force reveals that there is not much that branch of RAND can do to help, because by internal company regulations and corporate charter, they are restricted to advise on projects that involve only the U.S. Air Force, and, by definition, a U.S. Civil Service Demonstration Project involves impacts far exceeding those that would be contained within the Air Force. Contact through Project Air Force, however, is made with James Hocek, then Director of Manpower Mobilization and Readiness for the RAND Corporation. Dr. Hocek's area is not restricted to projects involving the Air Force only. Intrigued by the proposal and the possibilities of it, Hocek commits RAND to an initial support, at least in concept, of project development and says he will do what he can to enlist the support of the RAND Board of Directors, realizing that initial funding of the project itself is at least several months away. Note: This began a relationship with RAND Corporation that continued until mid-1991, with RAND serving as a third-party project evaluator, that is, serving as the neutral evaluator on behalf of OPM with the obligation to report success and/or failure of the demonstration project, Project Pacer Share (PPS), that eventually was created and is currently underway at MCAFB. This relationship is now ending as OPM wants to change evaluators and conclude RAND's role with PPS.

The Start of a Decision Team

Encouraged by these results, Nelson proposes the establishment of a "Tom Peters-type Skunk Works," that is, a small dedicated group of people whose total function will be to explore the feasibility of the project design. Such is approved and it is headed by Nelson.

It also is at this point that one of the most critical decisions in the project is made. Based on his research, Nelson advises Tompkins that no such design is possible or desirable without the full collaboration and partnership of organized labor. A meeting is convened with the three unions that represent the total work force of DS. A general discussion of the research on the project to this point— its initial proposals to broaden skills and move to a generalist concept that is team-based, without grades, with a new manner of grading managers and supervisors, and with a new manner of protecting permanent employees—is presented to the three unions. Based on the sheer number of employees represented by the American Federation of Government Employees (AFGE), it is suggested that the three unions might be able to come to a position where AFGE would be selected as the prime representative of organized labor to represent the interest of all unions in the project. DS proposes the appointment of a full-time repre-

Figure 4.1
Organization Chart for the Directorate of Distribution in the Early Phase of Project Pacer Share

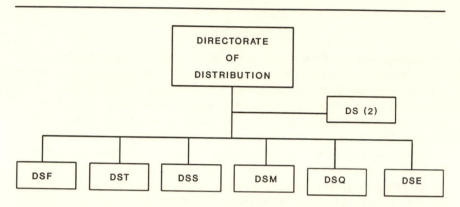

sentative of organized labor to serve as a government-salaried member of the design staff whose sole job would be to represent the voice of organized labor in the development of the project design itself. It is felt that the demonstration of a partnership between labor and management would begin the shift that is necessary to help make the CSS a model for all employment in the United States. All three unions agree with both the necessity of the changes proposed and with the proposal to have the AFGE represent the interest of all organized labor. At this time and continuing to the present, the AFGE represents close to 90 percent of the nonmanagerial employees within DS. The second largest union representing the petroleum workers comprises another 7 to 8 percent and the engineers' union represents about 1 to 2 percent of the overall DS work force.

Organized Labor Joins the Design

With the agreement of organized labor, the beginning of this historical project takes another major step forward, and the Pacer Share Project Office is officially formed and designated with the symbols SM-ALC/DS (2). The entire design staff consists of one representative of organized labor; two DS project analysts, Dan Fuchs and Colene Krum, who still remain as the key project office design analysts; one management assistant; and Nelson, serving in a part-time position, because his full-time job remained in the normal management chain of command.

Figure 4.1 depicts the DS organization departmentalized by division. When the design team [DS (2)] was created, DS consisted of five main divisions. After the project implementation, DSE was added as the training division (see Chapter 7) and DSQ was eliminated, whose function was quality assurance. The people from DSQ were transferred to more direct production-oriented roles.

TESTING THE WATERS WITH OPM

In early 1983, Nelson meets with the San Francisco office of OPM. They discuss some preliminary details of the project the design staff wish to undertake. They agree it is time Sacramento made contact with the Washington OPM and in particular the Research and Design staff that has oversight responsibility for all demonstration projects. [At this time, there is still only one OPM-sponsored demonstration project, the original one conducted by the Navy both at the China Lake location and at Naval Ocean Systems Command (NOSC), Point Loma, California.] Nelson, the project manager, together with project analyst Krum, proceeded to Washington, D.C., for the initial meetings with OPM. Those meetings were conducted in a most positive manner.

Kathy Cunningham was at that time the manager of the Research and Development test office overseeing the demonstration projects for OPM. She was excited by the concepts proposed by Nelson and Krum and responded with most positive support and guidance in how to prepare the ''concept proposal'' to OPM.

Back in Sacramento, the design staff proceeded to develop the concept of the proposal, put it into rough-draft format, and prepared to ''brief-it-up'' the chain of command through the U.S. Air Force.

W. EDWARDS DEMING PROVIDES THE GUIDING PHILOSOPHY

It was also at this time, late 1983 and early 1984, that Nelson began to have the first contacts with the philosophy and teachings of Deming. Deming's approach to managing for quality would become the basis for the overall project approach. Deming demonstrated the total invalidity of the annual appraisal system. Up until this point, there had been no intent to modify and/or change in any serious manner the annual appraisal system. Nelson then held initial discussions with both labor and management on the problems that might be inherent in the appraisal system. All parties agreed, however, that in the initial presentation of the design concept, the appraisal system would be left somewhat intact. The project office then prepared and delivered the initial concept briefings to the ALC Commander, Major General Lowe, in late February 1984. They received his approval to proceed to Headquarters Air Force Logistics Command. In early April, Nelson briefed the Air Force Logistics Command staff, directed at that time by General Earl T. O'Laughlin, on the basic concepts of the project, and received an enthusiastic endorsement from General O'Laughlin, who on the spot approved the concept. He sent it on to Headquarters Air Force with an enthusiastic endorsement letter. The concept paper that was prepared along the guidelines given to the project office by OPM itself received rapid review and approval, and the project office proceeded immediately from concept preparation to project design.

AN END TO PERFORMANCE APPRAISALS

Starting in 1984 and for over the next three years, all the senior management members of DS attended the now famous four-day Deming seminars conducted by Deming. This led to the realization that the project would also need to include the total elimination of performance appraisals. The DS design team and the DS management agreed that performance appraisals were more harmful to the quality approach than they were helpful (see Chapter 3 for further explanation).

PPS TAKES SHAPE

In lieu of performance appraisal and its classic efficiency-oriented approach, PPS would adopt as its central philosophy the Deming 14 Points. PPS now contained its total major design elements:

(a) the elimination of job series;

(b) the elimination of pay grades as established in the CSS;

(c) the change in the manner of determining the pay and grade of managerial and supervisory employees;

(d) the total elimination of annual appraisals;

(e) the establishment of gain sharing; and

(f) the establishment of a new method of hiring employees, called the Demonstration On Call (DOC) employee, to protect the permanent employees from ever facing RIF again.

Pushing the Concept Forward

After defining the elements that comprise PPS, a proposal was prepared to be sent up the bureaucratic channels in the Air Force and on to OPM. Following the sending of the proposal from the AFLC Commander to Air Force Headquarters, there was somewhat of a pause prior to the Air Force's endorsing it and transmitting it to OPM for final approval. This was due to the revolutionary character of the personnel system being proposed in PPS along with less than enthusiastic support from the Headquarters AFLC Office of Personnel.

Fortunately, at this same time, Sacramento ALC attained a new civilian base personnel officer, Betty Maddox. Ms. Maddox was unique among those at the higher levels of civilian personnel management in that she immediately embraced and endorsed the underlying concepts behind PPS. She requested that Nelson accompany her to a meeting of Air Force Logistics Command personnel officers to be held in Phoenix, Arizona, shortly after concept approval by General O'Laughlin took place in the fall of 1984. Nelson briefed the concepts of PPS at that conference to a less than enthusiastic reception by the other base personnel officers and the representatives from Headquarters Air Force Civilian Personnel.

At one point, the then senior civilian in charge of civilian personnel for the Air Force actually asked Ms. Maddox if she wanted him to put an end to this project. Ms. Maddox not only said, "No," but said she enthusiastically supported it. It was in large part due to Ms. Maddox's continuing and enthusiastic support over the next several years that much of the project's progress was able to take place.

Support Weakens Back Home

Back at the Sacramento ALC, the management champion of the project, Mr. Tompkins, retired. (Tompkins was the buffer and protector of Nelson, the internal change agent.) One of the observations of Deming comes into play here; that is, that one of the deadly diseases of American management is mobility of management. By this, Deming means that top management moves so frequently from position to position, from organization to organization, that the manager is frequently not in place long enough to understand either the nature of the business that they are charged with managing, the inner workings of the system over which they have charge, nor the impact, good or bad, of the decisions that they make. This is not to say that many of these individuals are not excellent people with exceptional gifts and having great talent. It is to say that they frequently have a very short time to make their mark in the system that still has the corruption of annual appraisals and ratings and dysfunctional competition within teams. Individuals (fast trackers) must make their mark quickly and frequently do so at the expense of the organization. They demonstrate they are invaluable to their organizations, get promoted as a result, and then rapidly move on to some other organization only to repeat that same process of actions.

The new replacement for Mr. Tompkins was indeed a gifted and talented person, a person who had climbed from the bottom ranks of an organization to the top, but had never managed within DS before. Not understanding the reasons for the project's development, there was little common ground for understanding what PPS was supposed to do. In addition, that person had risen up in a system that was the classic model that promoted and rewarded those who were tough "heroiclike" managers. As might be expected in such a situation, openness, freedom of information, equality, the ability to push decisions down, and not to force top-level involvement in every decision, even every important decision, were simply concepts not in the manager's lexicon. It began a period of difficulty; had the project not had the already existing approval of the ALC Commander, the four-star Commander at AFLC Headquarters, and Ms. Maddox, the lack of support from the new leader at DS might have proven fatal to the project itself.

However, by this time, the U.S. Air Force had decided to proceed to gradually send the proposed project design to OPM. Little known to anyone at that time, except the project staff, because of the earlier mentioned support of Kathy Cunningham from OPM's office in charge of demonstration projects, an interchange of draft copies of the proposed project concept had already taken place. This resulted in the actual wording and actual typing of the concept paper with the direct help of the OPM office to which it was to be sent. The Air Force then sent the concept paper across to OPM. The content of the Air Force cover letter was less than enthusiastic and it was anticipated it would be several weeks, perhaps months, before OPM could respond. To the dismay of many in the chain of command, within a week OPM had said, "Yes, let's go for it," and the concept was officially established as approved and it moved from a proposed concept to a "design phase" of the Civil Service Demonstration Project.

PPS Gets Added Support from Personnel Specialists

Ms. Maddox, after the concept paper had OPM approval for project design, established a team of personnel experts to assist the DS team in the actual development of changes to the law and CSS policies that would be required to bring Pacer Share to full flowering. The team included Bill Waggoner, who was from the world of labor relations; Ben Ragsac, who was from the world of personnel staffing; and Jack Givens, who was specifically brought out of AFLC headquarters, where he had served as Chief of Classification, to head up the team. Though there were others assigned at various times to the project office, it was due to the support of these three and their insights to the project that much of the final design was able to be developed.

The Stilling of "Circles"

Opposition within DS to much of what the project stood for was beginning to grow. Most resistance to the project came from managers raised in the old school of noncollaboration and top–down decision making. This was probably most visible in what happened to the QC process within DS. By this time, 1986, Nelson had been promoted and was now the senior civilian over an organization of some 580 people in DS. Through the circles, his organization had achieved a substantial reduction in required personnel and yet was producing at higher levels of quality than before. His organization received the only "outstanding" rating given by the AFLC Inspector General to similar organizations, commandwide. Still, overall, QCs were not doing well DS-wide—especially in one other division of DS. Management opposition to circle meetings (e.g., to accept the right of people to examine work processes and make suggestions for change) was growing.

Under Tompkins there had been a QC steering group that was the only authority allowed to disapprove a Quality Circle suggestion, and they had done so only twice in the history of the circle movement from 1980 through 1984. That steering group seldom met now. As a result, circles lost their forum in which to present many of their ideas and concepts. In addition, there was a "new" matter of opposition that began to appear.

As Nelson saw it, "the problem with circles is that they were too successful." Management tended to cooperate with the circles, but it would not fully get behind and collaborate with them. The circles would make a suggestion for change, and then nothing happened. Well, it didn't take long before the frustration level of circles began to grow and numbers began to decline. From the high of 103 active circles at the retirement of Tompkins, the circles went steadily downward. By 1986, and the time of the next new change in directorate management, active circles had dropped over 50 percent to only forty-two active circles.

OPM Shifts Ground

Changes in management at OPM, Washington, D.C., slowed down the project. Cunningham's position had changed. She had been very supportive of the project and had overridden much of the opposition that had begun to appear within OPM. The office that Cunningham had occupied experienced a series of temporary appointments. During that time period of revolving leadership, the project office received little active guidance from OPM. They all awaited the appointment of a permanent leader to replace Cunningham so they could press on.

During this time, some conflict that broke out between the DS PPS design teams and OPM. Partially, this was due to DS having taken a rather unique stance, not taken in any of the demonstration projects before, in that they took a "holistic" approach to the reform of the CSS. Rather than attempting to address one of the "symptoms," as the other demonstration projects such as China Lake and its focus on pay banding had, Pacer Share addressed much of the CSS, excepting only those elements regarding Equal Employment Opportunity (EEO), retirement, and veterans' benefits. PPS offered a multiple-intervention approach that complicated the measurement of the effects of the interventions themselves. There was difficulty in reaching adequate understanding on the part of all concerned as to what should be measured, what would be included in the design, and what results could be attributed to the multiple interventions underway given various research designs that might be used.

These difficulties were somewhat repeated with the RAND Corporation. As PPS began to grow, and the RAND measurement staff began to assemble, there was some difficulty in communicating the nature of PPS as an integrated system, the results of which could not be attributed to any one given intervention, that is, that all, interdependent and interactive, played a tightly linked role to produce a synergistic whole.

Through it all, the project continued to grow and thrive as the design went forward for approval review. The personnel team working with the DS(2) group led the way in the identification of specific laws to be waived, specific wording that needed to be placed into the personnel regulations, and specific changes in procedures that would be required on the personnel side of the house. The DS PPS design team proceeded with identification of the changes necessary in the proposed joint labor–management consortium (partnership) that would develop the detailed operating procedures and instructions DS would operate in the eventual PPS. (The personal commentaries of project analysts Colene Krum and Dan

Fuchs on this are in the Appendixes). To this point, however, resistance remained strong at OPM, at least in some of the offices outside of the demonstration project office, and among many key managers within the DS staff. Many good people, loyal to the old efficiency-oriented paradigm, simply "could not see" the facts; the new quality paradigm was coming. Quality was "blowin' in the wind."

SUMMARY

The development of the formal nationally sponsored program to demonstrate an alternative way of managing people in the federal CSS was more evolutionary than rationally planned, starting from scratch. Many "extra" rational events and circumstances combined to get the idea from concept to a formal project design that was supported by OPM, the U.S. Air Force, and Congress. The next chapter introduces the program components of Project Pacer Share (PPS), a project designed to help government move further along toward the quality model.

5

The Design of Project Pacer Share for TQM

As described in Chapter 4, initial support for the project was often murky. However, actual design of the details of Project Pacer Share was accomplished by a team consisting of three representatives from DS: led by the project design officer, Nelson; Jack Givens of the Directorate of Personnel; and James Cortese representing the Comptroller's office. The design effort itself was to span the better part of three years (1984–1987).

The overall coordination of the effort by the DS design team was not an easy task. There were differences among the design team members themselves regarding the philosophy, content, and scope of the project. In large part, these differences were due to the administration (at that time, the administration of President Ronald Reagan), emphasizing the pay-for-performance (merit pay) aspects of the CSS. This emphasis was antithetical to the concepts of TQM as based on the teachings of Deming on whose philosophy PPS was to be based.

This necessity to eliminate the performance appraisals became clearer as the team examined not only the pure statistical invalidity of the performance appraisals, but the far more serious psychological and philosophical impacts of the annual rating, grading, and sorting of human beings. Probably the greatest impact that would be totally contrary to the TQM implementation was the negative effect performance appraisals had on the formation of teams. It negatively affected team play on the Quality Circles, because there was observed an almost annual waxing and waning of enthusiasm in the circles following performance-appraisal reviews.

The battle to eliminate the performance appraisals was not easily won. Nelson was the strongest advocate for its elimination. He prepared a position paper and educational briefings to enable others to understand the need to eliminate performance appraisals from the system (Nelson, 1987). He relied on other major businesses that had eliminated appraisals and merit rating systems while improving quality to build his case (see Pearce, Stevenson, and Perry, 1985). After much debate, the elimination of performance appraisals had become an integral part of PPS.

The elimination of the appraisal added a significant amount to the project design. In the past, it had been an instrument in the selection of individuals eligible for promotion. Now it was gone, and an entire new promotion system had to be developed. And another barrier to team play had been removed.

CONSOLIDATION OF PAY GRADES: PAY BANDING

The promotion system was radically simplified by the design team's completion of the consolidation of pay grades. The definition and delineation of the various types of work into fifteen grades and ten steps for the white collar, and five steps for the blue collar (see Chapter 3), of the various jobs in the CSS had been judged to be a relic of a past technology. The design team completed the effort to consolidate these grades into the pay scales and comparable grades shown in Table 5.1.

Pay banding, going from a promotion system that involved fifteen grades to one that involved four, eliminated a vast number of promotion actions and radically simplified the entire process. This allowed the development of an adequate promotion system based on actual competencies and an interview process that would be a collaborative labor–management effort. The elimination of the traditional pay grade series into the four pay bands also met with a lot of resistance. The establishment of grade series within the CSS dates back a long way and carries a long history founded in trade unionism.

In Total Quality Management (TQM) the Team is the Hero

Total Quality Management (TQM) is nothing more nor nothing less than focus on the customer. We begin with a focus on the external customer. The purpose of an organization is to serve a customer. Without such a focus, TQM, good management, and continued company existence are not only impossible, but may be viewed as antithetical to the continued improvement of society itself. Given that focus on the customer, we must ask what is the level of focus. The answer is 100 percent.

The goal of TQM, indeed of any company that has succeeded in the past, whether it knew the initials TQM or not, has been and must be customer "delight." Please note that we do not say customer satisfaction. Those organizations, those companies, and those corporations that focus on customer satisfaction will indeed have satisfied customers who will go elsewhere when someone else can satisfy them more. TQM is focused on building customer loyalty through providing a product and/or service of never-ending increasing quality. They're focused very much on the external customer, on their wants and needs.

That means that the TQM company and/or organization, be it in the private sector or government, is focused on not only the current wants of the customers,

Table 5.1
Relation of Pay Bands to CSS Grades

PROPOSED PPS PAY BANDS   OLD CSS PAY GRADES

White Collar Pay Bands	GS Grades
I	1
	2
	3
	4
II	5
	6
	7
	8
III	9
	10
	11
	12
IV	13
	14

Supervisory Pay Bands	GS/GM Grades
I	5
	6
	7
	8
II	9
	10
	11
	12
III	13
	14
IV	15

Blue Collar Pay Bands	WG Grades
	1
I	2
	3
	4
II	5
	6
	7
	8
III	9
	10
	11
	12
IV	13
	14

but the future needs of the customers. When future needs actually materialize and turn into a want, the TQM company and/or government organization is already there, standing by to delight its customers with what they now want but did not anticipate in the past. This concept of TQM is critical to understanding the rest of the development. Because if we are focused on the external customer's delight, that delight can only be accomplished by an internal work force, at any level, that is self-motivated to never-ending improvement. That customer delight cannot be accomplished by an organization that is focused on control, on mandatory compliance with a management-driven set of standards, product rules, work rules, personnel rules, internal audit rules, and the like. It can only be accomplished by a company/organization whose management realizes that its obligation is to build an environment in which the members of the work force can grow, can continually improve its own capabilities in providing to the next person in line, that is, the internal customer, what is necessary to build the product or service that will delight the external customer.

Now that sounds so simple, and yet that is so difficult. Many companies claim dedication to the service of the external customer in product and/or service and yet treat the internal customer, the ''employee,'' ''the worker'' as if they were dirt. And then they wonder why these downtrodden members of the organization, abused, appraised, ranked, rated, sorted, and mistrained, do not achieve the goals of customer satisfaction. Clearly, unhappy, angry people are not highly focusing their attention toward customer delight in any organization.

Now we come to another of the more difficult propositions of Pacer Share, and indeed any TQM effort. It is the job of those in management to understand that the external customers belong not to them but to the nonmanager. Furthermore, those nonmanagers that produce that product and/or service are the customers of management; they are the people that management is supposed to serve. Note: One of the better series of references and books on this subject is that based on the philosophy and practices of Ian Carlzon of Scandinavian Airline Systems (SAS). Carlzon (1987) is documented and taught in this country by Karl Albrecht (Albrecht and Zemke, 1985; Albrecht, 1989).

In order for the design to adequately focus on service of the external customer and the internal customer, we can draw a direct correlation between the changes made in Pacer Share and customer service as we have set it forward thus far.

First, in order to service the customer, one cannot be tied down by artificial restrictions of what one is capable of whether in depth or in breadth, that is, the organization must incorporate within itself, in its personnel system, the principles of both vertical and horizontal job enrichment and teamwork. Long preached but seldom realized, the PPS does in fact accomplish this through the elimination of both series, that is, career paths, and grades that designate specific pay levels for specific levels of performance within a given career area. The series/grade combination prescribes what one can do within a narrowly defined career path, grade, and pay level. They also limit employee development and actual employee performance as they inhibit cross training, teamwork, and mutual coverage among members of the team.

END OF GRADE CREEP

The development of a customer-driven team is, of course, also related to a change of focus by management. The grading system of the individual federal supervisor is another problem. We can hardly build a sense of customer delight and teamwork when the focus of the managers is on building the size of their organization in order to get themselves promoted. Therefore, we can see the direct link to the next Pacer Share intervention, which is elimination of the number and grade and pay of subordinates as having any relationship to the pay and pay level of the individual manager, to dispel grade creep as described in Chapter 3. This allowed the manager to accept suggestions proposed by the work-force teams that would streamline and eliminate waste from the system and decrease the number and pay of people in the organization.

DEMONSTRATION ON CALL (DOC)

One of the key elements of management theory in the past has been the need to protect the technological core of the work force. In the more common language of perhaps the nonmanager, we might say that loyalty starts at the top. This translates into the simple statement that those who have been in the company longest deserve more loyalty than newcomers. Many organizations in America have realized this in their no-layoff policy. Others, still failing to realize this, randomly cut, chop, and release without any understanding of the underlying principle involved. PPS represented the first attempt to recognize this on a serious manner in the U.S. Civil Service by establishment of the Demonstration On Call employee (DOC). The idea was relatively simple. It was to protect the career employee from ever having to face the probability or the possibility of a RIF. This mechanism made it possible to place all new hires into a "buffer zone." That buffer zone would be used for any required release of employees, any reductions in force, any problems with dollars while the permanent work force, though perhaps having to be retrained, and/or reeducated into new areas, and new competencies, would never be threatened with reduction in pay status, reduction in grade, or being forced out the gate.

PRODUCTIVITY GAIN SHARING

The last change, Productivity Gain Sharing (PGS) did not require permission from the OPM. PGS is a program whereby organizationwide savings are shared by both the organization itself and the work force. It is like a profit-sharing effort; however, productivity gain is the unit of analysis rather than profit.

Gain sharing is not an award. It is not a reward. It is simple recognition of the equity of the situation in which, when an organization does well, then those who are members of the organization should do well, also. And that should be equal, across the board, with no distinction as to rank, grade, and/or particular role, which is beyond the capability of the individual member to determine in any case.

The PGS change was one that the design team struggled over greatly. There are as many ways to approach the philosophy behind PGS as there are companies that have attempted an implementation. Percentages that go to the work force and percentages that go to the organization vary widely; what is used as the basis for the calculation varies widely. The design team ultimately decided on following an industrial-engineering model, largely due to the influence and re-spect for the Deputy Director of Distribution during the majority of the design phase of the project, Gerald Tompkins, who was an industrial engineer. Though this approach was to later prove fallacious, the initial gain-sharing effort was therefore based on industrial-engineering standards, earned hours, computation of overhead hours, standby time, method–time–motion (M-T-M) studies, and all the other elements of an industrial-engineering standard. And that is in fact the gain-sharing formulation that was presented in both the initial and the final Pacer Share designs.

As discussed in Chapter 5, it did not work. This resulted in the redesign of the gain-sharing effort based on line-item cost. Now we have presented all of the elements of the project itself, the *end of series,* the *end of grades,* the *end of the performance appraisal,* the *change of manner* in which a *supervisor/ manager's pay in grade* is set, and *Productivity Gain Sharing.*

SUMMARY

As the knowledge and the realization of TQM and its underlying philosophy spread across the design teams, the final design rapidly began to take shape. The delay, as noted before, was not due so much to the production of the design as it was necessary to sell it within the Washington, D.C., arena. This is not to say that it was easy to sell within the Sacramento, California, arena. For as Machiavelli has pointed out in his classic works, you will not find support for the change to a new idea from those who benefit from the continuation of the old. Therefore, it should have been forecast with more accuracy that those who benefited most from the existence of the current system would not be foremost in their support and endorsement of the new PPS system.

The design of PPS took a great deal of time because no one was willing to commit the resources required to prepare for it until the project was actually approved for implementation. Then "shock therapy" took place.

One is reminded very much of the television commercial some years ago for a particular brand of battery. The commercial opened with a young boy coming into a kitchen with his mother and saying, "Mom, the Martians have invaded, can I go fight the war to defend the earth?" Mother, replied, "Of course, son." Whereupon son grabs his ray gun, powered by the brand name of battery and one is shown scenes of the son's face smiling and firing his ray gun with flashes of light around him. The commercial continues with the son running back into the kitchen and saying, "Mom, mom, we're winning." And mother abstractly turning from the stove only partially, paying no attention, saying, "That's good, son, you just keep it up." The son goes back, flashes of light, and again the son reappears at the kitchen door saying, "Mom, mom we won." Mother says, "That's nice, son, congratulations." Son says, "Mom, we beat the Martians, can I bring one home to dinner?" Mother says yes and the son enters the kitchen with a nine-foot-tall insect and mother faints. This commercial depicts how Pacer Share was introduced. Although there was participation by many in its development, it was not authentic involvement. Thus, when the project was eventually authorized for implementation, many were in shock.

The significance of the paradigm shift involved in Pacer Share literally blinded those in the old paradigm to the possibility of it ever being implemented. Therefore, though there was some acceptance and some lip service about it, and some resistance, of course, few believed permission would be granted for the test to actually begin. Therefore, when the design was completed and comments were gathered, much of the work required to actually implement Pacer Share was yet to be accomplished. The various specific operating instructions (that crossed the "t's" and dotted the "i's") on all of the internal measures, practices, and techniques had not been done at the implementation phase and were only gradually coming to be understood.

TQM, and Pacer Share as a personnel management system designed to help the implementation of TQM, is a major paradigm shift. Therefore, the title of the chapter may perhaps be misleading. Pacer Share represents a beginning of a recognition that TQM perhaps might be a better way to go. Pacer Share helped introduce this concept to the federal personnel sector just as Don Peterson introduced quality at Ford, David Luther at Corning, and others in various industries across the country began and supported the change. No one has effected it, no one has completed it; the successful total implementation of quality as a focus in our governmental and private organizations still remains years in the future. But Pacer Share, and private-sector projects like it, has in fact made a beginning.

REFERENCES

Albrecht, K. (1989). *At America's Service*. San Diego: University Associates.
Albrecht, K., and Zemke, R. (1985). *Service America!* New York: Dow-Jones Irwin.
Carlzon, J. (1987). *Moments of Truth*. New York: Ballinger.

Nelson, A. E. (1987). *Performance Appraisals, Fact or Fancy*. Sacramento, CA: Nelson and Nelson.
Pearce, J. L., Stevenson, W. E., and Perry, J. L. (1985). ''Managerial Performance Based on Organizational Performance: A Time Series Analysis of the Effects of Merit Pay.'' *Academy of Management Journal* 28(2) (June): 261–278.

Mobilizing Support for the New Way of Doing Business: A Peek Behind the Scenes

Now that the idea for Project Pacer Share had been clarified and defined in operational terms for TQM—pay banding, gain sharing, elimination of performance appraisal, change in supervisory grade criteria, expanded use of a nonpermanent work force (DOC employees)—it was time to move on to the next stage, which we associate with institutional change. It was time to build sufficient support for the project to overcome the vested interests of resistance that are always certain to occur. The project design team had done its work thus far. However, to move the project from concept to reality, broad-based support from every level and every political entity would need to be mustered to overtake the fear that such a radical reform would create among those who were in position of control and served as functionaries in the present system that Pacer Share was designed to change.

To get the support needed to bring about change within the system, the project design team realized very early that it had to go beyond the chain of command, even ignore it at times, to muster sufficient support from outside the system so the system would redirect itself toward the quality approach. Otherwise, those in control of the system would prevail with their attitudes of "If it ain't broke, don't fix it." The design team realized early on that the system's "customers" at headquarters and Congress would be much more effective in getting management's attention than those within the system who were assigned to the project design team. Thus, external political support was viewed to be key to the future life of the project.

ORGANIZED LABOR BECOMES A PARTNER/ADVOCATE

The most obvious source of support needed by the project design team was the political support engendered through the partnership being welded with organized labor. In the public sector, this link is *essential*. By law, most federal employees are forbidden access to the lobbying channels necessary to gain the support of the legislative bodies that have substantial influence over the executive functions of government. Legislators with their budgetary power can convince administrative agencies like the U.S. Air Force and the OPM to test a new concept.

It is risky business to go around one's chain of command in any organization, but this is what was essential for project survival. Nelson and his project design team knew the potential benefits of the project experimentation and recognized the need to take risks to keep it alive.

In 1985–1987, one of the most important links was that formed between the project and the national office of the American Federation of Government Employees (AFGE) in Washington, D.C. The partnership between the project and the local union soon expanded to the national level. The union provided the project political liaison with congressional representatives, who themselves were open to the core concepts of TQM that the project embraced. These congressional representatives were not on just one side of the political aisle. No, they came from both Republican and Democratic sides.

POLITICAL SUPPORT

Early political support for the project was found. Senator Ted Stevens from Alaska and Representative Pat Schroeder from Colorado endorsed the project's purposes early on. The key members of their staffs, as much as the elected representatives themselves, carried the understanding of the project forward and helped the project office achieve its goal of being permitted to conduct the test. One cannot underestimate the important role staff members of public elected officials do play. Without their help, PPS would not have been approved. First and foremost among the political alliances that were formed, and the one that would be most critical to the project's initiation, was that formed with Congressman Vic Fazio, the Congressman in whose district McClellan Air Force Base lies. Many times Congressman Fazio's assistance played the deciding role in leveraging approval for project continuation.

Support by one member led to interest and eventual support by others. Each new congressional advocate led to the opening of new doors to others. By 1987, the project design team had mustered sound external support from Congress. But it needed further support from within the Department of Defense and the U.S. Air Force. This came more by chance and opportunity than it did by design.

In the mid–1980s, one of the Quality Circle facilitators hired by Nelson had a link on the outside of the Air Force to Lieutenant General Anthony L. Palumbo, then commander of the California National Guard. General Palumbo, in turn, had close links to the Reagan administration, dating from the days when President Reagan had been Governor of the State of California. Using this chance contact, Nelson met with General Palumbo and outlined the general thesis of the project and the desired change. Nelson also described some examples of opposition to the project that were beginning to appear at the administration level, most notably from new leaders and bureaucrats in the Office of Personnel Management. General Palumbo offered to intervene with the contacts he had within the Reagan administration, beginning at the Secretary of Defense level, and with the Attorney General, to see what he could do "to help the project succeed."

POLITICAL HELP

The contact with General Palumbo opened the door for Nelson to make "at-will" contacts within the Department of the Air Force to help the administration provide assistance in overcoming some major hurdles, when needed. Of course, great discretion had to be exercised in the activation of this particular channel. Only rarely did the contact point ever become exercised. The contact, Dennis Kenelly, was a political appointee in the Department who was serving in the Mobility and Reserve Affairs Office. On numerous occasions, however, Nelson did have lengthy conversations with Kenelly, provided him status reports and briefings on Nelson's not infrequent visits to Washington to brief the project to the official channels, and ask for any assistance he deemed necessary. One of the first such contacts with Kenelly resulted in the issuance of a letter of support from then Secretary of Defense "Cap" Weinberger. One would need to be a member of the Department of Defense, and a member of the services, or far down in the civilian structure to realize the impact that such a letter has. In the letter, Weinberger stated, "I fully support this project [PPS] and request that you inform the personnel involved in developing it of my appreciation for a job well done" (Weinberger, 1985). The very existence of the letter as an endorsement resulted in a surge of morale and renewed hope among the project advocates in management, labor, and the project design team.

CHANGING OF THE GUARD: NEW SUPPORT FROM THE TOP

The next significant event within the project was a change in military and civilian leadership within the DS. Although Deming cites "the mobility of management" to be one aspect of the fourteen deadly diseases to quality in American management, the change in leadership gave a breath of fresh air and new support for the project design team.

At first, the new civilian deputy, Carl McRorie, appeared not to be much more open than his predecessor toward the basic principles of the project. However, he soon became a willing collaborator, seeking to learn about the quality approach and identify how he could lend his support to get the project approved. Within nine months of his tenure in DS, PPS officially began its five-year demonstration effort. McRorie inherited PPS along with several other major change activities destined to take place in the DS about the same time. Thus, PPS was not the only high-priority program on his agenda. This placed added emphasis on the design team to educate him regarding the project in terms of its content and politics.

Almost one year later, Colonel David Naehring was transferred from Headquarters AFLC, where he had served as Chief of Supply. He had a background in distribution and he generally supported the concepts behind Pacer Share. He and McRorie (Deputy Director) now were supportive of the project, as they continued to direct the overall DS efforts—including PPS.

LABOR HELPS ENCOURAGE BUREAUCRATIC COOPERATION

In 1987, the staff of the project together with Deputy Director McRorie, and a representative from the civilian personnel office at Sacramento, visited the Washington, D.C., Office of Personnel Management to discuss apparent holdups in the consideration of the project design that seemed to be coming from the OPM itself. The meeting was convened to iron things out. Relationship and trust between the two agency representatives had declined since the early phase of the project's creation. A brief presentation of basic concepts was given by the project team. During the course of discussion, the OPM posed an objection to the Air Force on a project element. John Mulholland, the National Vice President of the AFGE came to the defense of the Air Force.

Later, when the OPM objected to a statement made by the union, it was the Air Force, represented at the meeting by Mr. Earl Aler from the Headquarters of the Air Force Civilian Personnel Office, who came to the defense of the union. This collaborative partnership between labor and management demonstrated the project had its act together—it had formed an alliance with its constituents. OPM held its ground in that meeting and sustained its objections. Following the meeting, John Mulholland from AFGE contacted his AFGE congressional liaison and set up a series of briefings the following day for McRorie and Nelson, Air Force Headquarters staff, and the union, with key congressional staffers on Capital Hill. This series of meetings, facilitated by the AFGE, led to bipartisan support for all of the project concepts and the resolution that the project could indeed expect support from both sides of the aisle on PPS.

Within two weeks, a letter from some twelve congressional delegates, Senate and House, had been sent to OPM asking why the project was being held up. The importance of mobilizing this congressional support was later confirmed by Senator Ted Stevens of Alaska, who stated the project "wouldn't have happened without extreme pressure" from Congress. Lesson learned: Union leaders are potentially powerful allies when attempting to cut through the system.

POLITICAL APPOINTEE PUTS ON THE PRESSURE

Within a matter of two months, a follow-up meeting to discuss the project's design, final approval, and publication of that design in the *Federal Register* had been arranged at the Sacramento Air Logistics Center. Personnel from the OPM Headquarters in Washington attended that meeting. Shortly after the meeting began, it was clear that the OPM still had strong objections to implementing the test project, had no intentions of allowing the publication of the test design documents in the *Federal Register,* nor allowing the initiation of the test project. At this point, Nelson absented himself from the meeting and placed a call to his political contact within the Secretary of the Air Force's office. That discussion "laid it on the line" as to exactly what was happening, who was present at the meeting, what their objections were, and what the nature of the problem was in Nelson's opinion. Within one hour, a call was placed from Washington, D.C., to the OPM executive who was heading the conference. He left the room, took the call, and returned with the announcement that the project would be approved as designed and implemented on schedule. Lesson learned: Political appointees are potential allies in overcoming bureaucratic delays.

LABOR ASSERTS ITS INDEPENDENCE AND LEADERSHIP

One year following the implementation of the project, labor was asked to assess the project's progress. Local President of the AFGE, John Salas, together with the DS chief steward, Dave Wheeler, issued a union first-year report that lambasted management from front to back. It cited major problems that were not being accounted for by management, the reasons for the problems, and, in essence, ratified the claim of Deming that "the problem is management."

The reaction by management was predictable and swift. It was based on strong denial and anger. Such denial was, perhaps, the beginning of the classic steps of accepting a paradigm shift or a major change as posed by Kubler-Ross (1969). Management asserted that only some of the union's claims might be partially true, but, overall, the union's position was inaccurate. At a management meeting to brief the Air Logistics Center commanding general, Major General Lee V. Greer, on the nature of the union charges, management suggested the union had overblown the situation, its charges were invalid, not well documented, and involved only a few minor incidents. Greer was not persuaded. Perhaps the union charges were right. He directed the project management to go back to the organization and find out what was really happening on the floor.

Based on this charter from Greer, a management team was formed to look in depth at the union report. A team of senior managers from Distribution, Personnel, and the Comptroller were formed to accomplish this task. The team was facilitated by Nelson. The team validated thirteen of the sixteen claims, admitted that two of the sixteen were more true than false, and had serious difficulties with only one of the union contentions. Management reevaluated its stance, admitted its failing, and began to weld a true partnership with labor and with the work force that was the only way possible to make the project a success. This, then, gave way to a partnership between labor and management that has proved in countless ways to be one of the project's major assets. Lesson learned: True partnerships are possible when all parties have the right to say "no."

MOBILIZATION OF INSTITUTIONAL SUPPORT WITHIN THE DIRECTORATE

The principal vehicle for the mobilization of institutional support for the idea was no more nor no less than classic marketing design. The principles of marketing, the principles of quality management as reflected in marketing, came into play here as the principal driver; that is, find the customer, find what you do for the customer, and cooperate to do it better. Here we are dealing with the internal customers, that is, the members of the organization who provide the ultimate support to the external customer.

Early on, the project design group had come to the conclusion of the need for an internal marketing plan. That need was recognized in 1984 officially by the project team in the preliminary design concept following concept approval by General O'Laughlin. Beginning at that time, the design team began to search for the vehicle by which they could effect (1) awareness, (2) inspiration, and (3) intrinsic commitment by the work force at large to the concepts behind and underlying the project. In 1985, design analyst Colene Krum attended a course at OPM's Western Executive Seminar Center at Denver, Colorado. In that course, she attended a session conducted by co-author Gilbert. She notified Nelson of Gilbert's potential value to the project and pointed out that Gilbert, as part of a contract he held with OPM, would be conducting a one-week session for the Air Force on the subject of program management, communications, and evaluation at McClellan Air Force Base.

As a result, Nelson subsequently arranged to be sent to that course. Impressed with the content of the course, he arranged for a meeting to be held with members of the DS organization involved in planning PPS and Gilbert. Nelson presented the basic concepts that underlie the design of the project and noted its inherent dependency on the development of a viable team-building educational process. He asked Gilbert to propose an approach to team building that would foster the values and goals of PPS. Gilbert met with and discussed the concepts with Carl McRorie and other key members of his staff. They liked the concepts presented and were eager to engage themselves in a process that was much like the PPS effort soon to be launched—something offering much opportunity, but with a lot of risk, for they had never been involved in anything like what they were about to undergo in their careers. Gilbert designed his program specifically for the DS senior leadership team, consisting of thirty-seven members.

The initial Tactical Planning and Team Building session was held. It helped identify areas where the leadership might need to especially focus its efforts as a group. As a team, the group was very businesslike, but not very alert to the feelings of the people who work for them. The team focused on highly participative approaches to problem identification and problem solving while building trust, communications, and a greater sense of teamwork and collaboration. As a result of that first session, over 100 process problems were identified with sound, constructive strategies to fix them proposed and implementation plans put in place through *team consensus*. In terms of the project, the rest is history. That same intervention was extended to every team in the DS. (See Chapters 8 and 9 for more detail.) It excited the will of the work force for TQM and PPS. It demonstrated what can be done through team play for TQM while developing individual and group communications and problem-solving skills when in leadership and followership roles. It became a key tool in the mobilization of institutional support for PPS and TQM within the Directorate of Distribution. (See Chapters 10 and 11.)

Team building cannot be effective within an organization unless it is modeled and practiced at the top of the organization. Deputy Director McRorie agreed with that contention. He also became an immediate advocate for team building, the building of consensus, the passing of inspiration, the building of a vision. Therefore, team building began within the Distribution population at the very top of the organization with Colonel David Naehring, Mr. Carl McRorie, the senior managers of the Directorate, the division chiefs, and key branch chiefs within the organization. It was through this process, which lasted well over three and one-half years, that the Directorate of Distribution began to come to self-mobilization of institutional support for the concepts that underlie the project.

Another key means of mobilizing institutional support for concepts that underlie the project, and part of the marketing plan for the project developed by the Project Office, was the specific assignment of communication of the key project design concepts to the work force by labor–management teams. In this process, key areas of the project were assigned to teams of managers for further development of details. In so far as possible, labor was assigned to as many of those teams as was practical (the sheer number of the teams and the few available stewards from the union side available to be appointed to those teams limited the participation of organized labor in some areas). Even so, internal support began to be developed. Once again, playing a key role in the development and mobilization of that internal support was organized labor. The national AFGE office sent in a key briefer to present the concepts of the project, to have regular meetings with members of the represented work force, to explain key areas of project change, and to voice support for those changes.

Almost with the beginnings of the first briefings, the appearance of resistance took place. And resistance, here again, as Deming has so clearly pointed out in his works, was not from the general rank and file of the work force but from management. Resistance came from those with a vested interest in the maintenance of the status quo. And this should have been forecast; this was exactly the area of resistance predicted by Machiavelli in his classic work, *The Prince*.

In DS, those in middle and upper management were most suspicious and concerned about PPS—later it would be demonstrated that their suspicions were partially right, for they would be affected by the project more than any other group. They were going to be most significantly affected by the new collaborative management model. It was only as the project came closer and closer, with the publication of the actual design itself in the *Federal Register* (set forward in the next chapter) that management began to take seriously its need to prepare for the future, to prepare the detailed operating instructions that it would need to implement, and to even understand the degree of change that would be needed. It was, in a manner of speaking, the approach of the inevitable that began to leverage the actions required to enable the change to take place.

OPM, in its annual first-year report, would soundly condemn the lack of preparation on the part of the DS management structure for total implementation. This, of course, expressed a misunderstanding of the nature of any paradigm shift in that those within the existing paradigm can never prepare adequately for the new paradigm until the new paradigm actually is in effect. To use an analogy, "How does the vacuum-tube industry prepare for the transition to transistors?" Clearly, this is not an easy task when the alternative is not comprehensible.

In DS, slowly but surely, they became aware of the reality of the oncoming implementation of Pacer Share and what it would mean. Such awareness could not be developed via a briefing, memo, newsletter, pamphlet, or meeting. It repeatedly took all of these means of communications. It required one basic understanding. Overcoming resistances that would take place from all aspects of the organization as a result of change would be tied to one basic approach: the project management team would have to dedicate itself to *inform, inform, and inform* throughout the project life. Furthermore, information alone would not be sufficient to educate the work force about the project. It took experience to fully demonstrate that the project would not harm the people, and that it would make things better. Nothing takes the place of successful experience when change is introduced. That is what the tactical planning and team-building activity provided the work force.

SUMMARY

This chapter has attempted to describe some of the behind-the-scenes activities and events that helped develop PPS policy and political support. They have been recalled by Nelson, the major force behind the project's development. Without the support gained through the union and political contacts in Congress, the Department of Defense, and OPM, the application for PPS would most likely still be on the shelf, collecting dust, and soon to be reduced to microfilm for more efficient storage in the "inactive" files of several organizations.

REFERENCES

Kubler-Ross, E. (1969). *On Death and Dying*. New York: Macmillan.
Weinberger, C. (1985). Memorandum for Secretary of the Air Force Regarding New Demonstration Project, October 21.

PART III

Major Intervention Tools and Techniques for TQM

The tools and techniques of Project Pacer Share are introduced. Each has played a major role in helping to make the transformation to the quality approach discussed in Chapter 2. All tools were viewed to be essential ingredients enabling the members of the work force to improve the quality of their work. The strategy, approach, and constellation of tools and techniques employed in the program to help facilitate the transformation of the organization to a quality-oriented approach are provided in Chapter 7. It introduces the DS quality "college" that has been developed for all managers to enable them to learn to think quality rather than mere efficiency. Frank Mason, the chief negotiator for management, discusses how the organization and the union forged a partnership that has been a model for others around the country.

Chapters 8 through 12 provide overviews of the major interventions employed in the project to help make the transformation to quality. Combined they form a constellation of approaches that are essential to make and sustain a cultural change for quality. They comprise sociopolitical and technological tools to redirect leaders and followers through teams to make continuous improvements on the job through TQM-type analyses.

Separate pieces are presented in the Appendix by men and women who worked in the Directorate of Distribution, the organization under demonstration. They describe the applicability of the tools in the workplace, commenting about their own special learnings that have taken place.

The knowledge gained from the project came from the imaginative problem-solving efforts of over 1,800 employees involved in the project's design and implementation. They present their experiences as problem solvers working in teams, applying the tools and techniques of TQM in their own work situations. These employees have had their entire careers affected by the project. They sought to make things better, while they were confronted with the requirement to change. They represent the type of heroic behavior that is needed throughout the American work force.

Managing Change: General Approach, Philosophy, and Tools Employed

This chapter introduces some of the approaches used in the project to jump-start the system toward the quality approach. Relying a great deal on Deming, it presents an overview of the philosophical underpinnings that were encouraged throughout the effort. It discusses how new knowledge was gathered and transferred throughout the system. It describes the eventual development of the organization's own "college" for technology transfer and management development. It presents major structures, tasks, and technologies that were used as part of the overall constellation of project elements to steer the organization from the classic efficiency approach toward the new paradigm, having the customer's needs as the center of concern.

Perhaps the most encouraging aspect of the PPS experience has been an affirmation about collective corporate wisdom. When people pull together and work toward a common goal and there is the opportunity for all to participate, quality decisions can be expected.

APPROACH

Internal Visionaries with Flexible Implementation Plans

Like the design of PPS, where change was initiated from within the organization, the implementation of the project was guided by internal practitioner/managers. The leaders within DS were visionaries as attested to the very fact that they anticipated the TQM movement before it was a credible term in American management. They were flexible in terms of exercising their options when considering how to implement their project.

They were more likely to experiment with new approaches on a day-to-day basis than they were to be dogmatically tied to any one particular approach. The only area where they seemed to be fixed in their approach was in their firm belief in TQM itself. They were committed to make it happen, but very flexible in their consideration of the tools to use to make it come to fruition. They made adjustments to the approach as they proceeded. For them, project startup was a time for flexibility rather than rigid rule making and compliance.

Management of Innovation—External Versus Internal Control

When making such a widespread planned change activity, where both the Air Force and the OPM were committing extraordinary resources and effort to test the program elements of PPS, one would expect the organization would have relied on "expert" outside assistance. But that is not the way it happened. The project was managed entirely by the members within DS. It relied on the collective wisdom of its own people to find its way. With the exception of Gilbert's training and development efforts, the majority of the training-and-development effort came from within the organization, using the talents of the people in DS.

No employee in the organization was a recognized "expert" in planned change or organizational development. About a dozen of the over 1,800 employees had advanced degrees from academe. McRorie, the deputy director and manager of the implementation effort, was the most highly educated person in the organization, having a Doctorate in Jurisprudence (JD) as well as two masters degrees in management-related fields. For the most part, the managers and workers that had primary responsibility for the implementation of the project in DS received their education from practical experience. They were experts at making things work.

The lack of internal "expertise" in behavioral science and organizational development (OD) among the DS implementation team was a contention of the OPM oversight group. It expressed its preference for the project to be managed by an outside OD expert. This was very much resisted by DS. The people of DS "owned" the project, and they did not want it to be managed by an outsider who did not understand the entire system in which PPS was created and would be expected to thrive. Furthermore, the DS leadership felt that PPS was one of many major systems for which McRorie was responsible. He was responsible to manage many other initiatives within the Directorate. PPS would need to be an integral part of overall DS operations. As director of the effort, McRorie would be able to keep the project in proper perspective rather than have it become an end in and of itself and conflict (suboptimize) with the overall integration of all subsystems within the larger DS system. Further, it was believed that to be exportable, it must be able to be implemented by internal resources and that, additionally, excepting Deming, there was no outside expert.

This early difference between OPM and the project has never been fully resolved. There is no way to know if an "outside expert" would have done a better job. From the perspective of the operating organization, it made most sense to run the project from within. From the external, OPM demonstration perspective, it made the most sense to have a person who was an expert at planned change implementation in TQM to manage it. However, in terms of the quality model, the OPM and the Air Force entrusted the demonstration to the people closest to the process—the internal management team in DS. As a result, the Air Force now has a very talented and experienced group of individuals in DS who have attained expert knowledge from the experience and are teaching others elsewhere how to begin.

Program Political Realities at Startup

Project startup occurred without sufficient building of ownership among the host organization's management team, middle and first-line supervisors, employees, organized labor, or the cosponsoring organization, OPM. Windows of opportunity are not left open long when attempting internal innovation. The real-life agency, interagency, and Congressional and labor politics, as explained in Chapter 5, required moving forward with implementation faster than would be the textbook recommendation. That is the reality of organizational life—especially in government. At the time of authorization for implementation, had the work force and labor union members in DS actually had a secret ballot vote, there is more than a 50–50 chance that the program would not have been approved. This is exactly as Deming would predict, that is, "How could they know?"

Planned Change Approaches at Startup

Ideally, according to many, the philosophical approach used in the design and startup of a project like PPS would be a normative reeducative type like that described by Chin and Benne (1969). Its strategy involves the creation of a systemwide process whereby the people to be affected by the desired change are involved in the discovery of the need for change and become committed advocates for it—constituents of the desired change itself. Their commitment is created through their own active participation in reeducative processes introduced by the change agent. The change strategy is targeted toward normative orientations of individuals, whereby their values, attitudes, and relationships change from the old to the new. As such normative changes occur, the members of the system change the system itself. Such an approach is highly desirable but takes time.

At the design phase of the project, a normative reeducation strategy was not practical (see the comments by Fuchs in the Appendix). The manner in which PPS was conceived and its political nature impeded full and fair participation by the work force in the project design prior to its authorization. Participation in the project design was more by representation of various groups within DS, labor, and the Air Force than by direct participation by the employees themselves throughout the work force.

At the time of the project's start, the planned change approach employed by management was more along the lines of the power coercive model discussed by Chin and Benne (1969) than it was normative reeducative. The power coercive approach is more authoritarian than democratic in its beginning. It relies on the compliance of those with less influence and power to affect plans, directions, and policies created by those with more power and influence. Yet it has been demonstrated to be a viable planned change approach. It was used to integrate previously racially segregated troops in World War II, for there was not time to engage the soldiers in the "discovery" of the need for it through their participation in problem-solving sessions. Integration of the troops was just morally essential and, in the long term, was in the best interest of the nation. As the soldiers of different races came to work together, they gained increased respect for one another, and they learned to personally support the policy post hoc.

While normative reeducative tactics were used in the project from the start to the present, the project did have to rely on the power coercive approach to initiate the change. This was how PPS basically was introduced to the work force.

Even though there were public hearings and releases about the project via public notices, the overall design of the project still came as a surprise to many DS employees. Once it was officially approved, the employees were "told" by management (without equivalent support and participation from organized labor) that the project was coming, and then more informed briefings were given them about the changes that were authorized. Such briefings then gave the employees more opportunity to air their concerns and participate more broadly in discussions regarding the tactics to be used in implementation.

Like many other major systems changes, initiating/energizing the quality model may require warlike involvement by the change agents themselves. In making the transformation to TQM from the old efficiency approach, change agents at the top may need to be more forceful than even they may anticipate to overtake the resistance that will occur by those who have internalized the other approach. Without McRorie's forceful support for the project, and the previously noted political actions by the union and Nelson, organizationwide changes would not have occurred. Bad habits are hard to break and it may take traumatic influences to generate the momentum for change, especially if there is an urgency of time.

PHILOSOPHY OF SYSTEMS CHANGE

The organization as a system was viewed as having several highly interdependent subsystems. They include *people, knowledge, structure, tasks,* and *technology.* See Figure 7.1. Changes in any one of these subsystems would affect the entire system as well as each of the other subsystems to some extent. Programs were put in place in PPS to affect these subsystems in a manner that would enable the system to move more toward the quality approach.

The major interventions employed to influence each of these subsystem elements are discussed in what follows. Two major efforts, Tactical Planning and Team Building (TPTB) and Essential Process Management (EPM) are discussed more fully in later chapters.

Figure 7.1
Five-Pronged Approach to Managing the Transformation to Quality

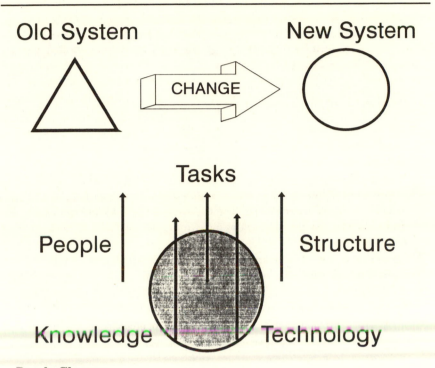

People Changes

Start at the Top

The first focus was on management, for without management's support, the change from the old system to the new is not possible. The expectation that quality is possible requires "vision." The vision of the future founded in quality, with quality permeating every element of the organization, must become the guiding goal.

To accomplish this vision was not easy, but it was accomplished over long months through the persistent efforts of the design team and senior labor and organization management. The vision focused on what government work ought to be. It placed a new emphasis on an old joke about substandard work: " . . . good enough for government." That expectation about government work had become instilled in government itself. Government had become too lackadaisical about the quality of its products and services. At DS, the statement was turned around: " . . . even good enough for government!" implying the very highest of quality, anywhere.

The vision became a new rallying point for them in which they could articulate their belief that there should be nothing better than the quality of the work that government provides. Also, those in PPS would do their very best to assure that the materials and supplies that would be needed by their customers, who defend democracy throughout the world, would be the very best. They rallied around this proposition. As a guiding imperative, the senior managers of DS wrote their own version of Deming's (1986) Fourteen Management Principles, personalizing them for their own organizational setting. The revised Fourteen Principles that applied to PPS are as follows:

1. Create and maintain constancy of purpose. All members of DS, at all levels, must commit themselves to increasing productivity through higher quality of both goods and services, improved relations with all members of DS and their representative organizations, and reduced costs of operation in order to improve our ability to provide customer service.

2. We fully subscribe to and adopt the new philosophy that embraces economic stability and improved performance and refuses to allow commonly accepted levels of delays, mistakes, defective materials, and defective workmanship. Labor and management must accept the role of leadership in this effort, both internally and with external suppliers.

3. We will cease dependence on mass inspection as a way to achieve quality. We will require, instead, statistical evidence of built-in quality.

4. We will work to end the process of awarding contracts and business on the basis of price tag, assuring that quality is a necessary consideration.

5. All members of DS will dedicate themselves to look for problems. We shall constantly improve every process and system in distribution, and work to increase quality and productivity, reduce variation, and thus reduce costs.

6. Distribution shall institute and maintain a strong training program for all members.

7. We shall develop supervisors to become more capable of helping people, improving methods, materials, machines, systems, and processes so as to help all members and the organization to do a better job.

8. Distribution management shall create an atmosphere where all members are encouraged to talk openly about their jobs, make suggestions, question procedures, and participate in the improvement process without being concerned that their careers or jobs are endangered or that they will lose favor with supervision and management. Opportunities for such participation must exist both in the normal day-to-day interfaces and staff meetings between managers, between managers and nonmanagers, and in the special, participative forums of the DS quality circles, task forces, and process action teams.

9. Management will dedicate itself to removing barriers between divisions, branches, and all DS organizations, at any level. All members will work together to become a single team so as to foresee and prevent problems that may be encountered in doing and improving the way we do our mission.

10. Distribution will eliminate numerical slogans and targets, asking for increased productivity unless the methods to attain that increase are also provided. Methods should include guidance related to process analysis and quality.

11. Distribution will eliminate numerical quotas or quantity measurements, unless the essential quality and process/system guidance required are also provided.

12. The Directorate dedicates itself to removing any and all barriers that inhibit all members the right to pride of workmanship. This will be accomplished through the establishment of quality as the most critical internal measure, and the prevention of the entry of poor-quality input into DS.

13. Distribution will institute and continue to support both a vigorous internal program of education and the self-improvement of all its members through off-the-job education and development efforts.

14. Distribution management will work everywhere and always to effect the changes called for by these principles of management.

This is not to say that the mere phrasing of the vision and fourteen points resulted in the desired changes. (It will be years before their meaning is totally absorbed into action.) However, with the articulation of total quality as their overarching goal and the basic philosophy of Deming as their guide, the members of management teams had something to guide them in their journey to quality. Statements like "Even good enough for government" may seem rather simple, mere puffery. However, when they are the result of sincere confrontational dialogue by the people of the senior management team regarding what they would like to become and how they should get there, they represent intense commitment, pride, and purpose.

Team Work for Quality

Given the previous vision, all members of the organization were involved in a program termed "Tactical Planning and Team Building" (see Chapters 8 and 9). It was a program uniquely designed and fine-tuned over time by an external consultant and his firm. In that program, they learned about the quality model presented in Chapter 2 and reminded of the opportunity that was theirs to attain the PPS vision, described before. They learned about customer-oriented leadership behavior and followership (see Chapters 10 and 11) through personal choice rather than compliance. They learned to work together as members of the same team and to identify ways to work better with their customers within the organization. And supervisors learned to behave in a manner that would facilitate quality performance through their employees. They learned to treat their employees as though the employees themselves were also their "customers."

They learned to function more effectively in both their functional (supervisor/subordinate-type) teams and process (interdependent teams consisting of members from several functional teams working on the same work process) teams.

Knowledge

Deming has stated that quality depends on profound knowledge. Such knowledge consists of four parts: appreciation for a system, statistical theory, theory of knowledge, and psychology. Each of these was systematically addressed in the project.

Knowledge of Systems

Systems thinking is essential to TQM and never-ending improvement. Understanding phenomena as systems, being able to get beyond the obvious to appreciate the interaction and interdependency of all things, and being able to detect flow processes that unify the entire organization and by which added value is provided the customer represent a core element in what Deming terms "profound knowledge." Without such knowledge, there can be no hope of a "systematic" approach to process improvement. (See Yourdon, 1975; Yourdon and Constantine 1976; DeMarco, 1978; and Keller, 1987 for more detailed discussions of systems thinking and analysis as they pertain to quality.)

As PPS employees (managers and nonmanagers alike) began to appreciate the organizational interdependencies across DS, it became easier for them to break down the barriers between departments and work groups. They saw they were all part of the same system, all working together to serve the customer. It also became easier for them to accept proposals of change in the overall system. They were enabled to see the increasing tendencies of the teams themselves to focus on their customers and eliminate processes that did not contribute added value The principal tools used to accomplish this were essential process management, essential process analysis, and process flow diagrams (see Chapter 12).

Knowledge of Statistics

When we speak of statistics in TQM, we do not speak of it as it is taught in colleges. What we are looking for here is some understanding of variation, including the ability to detect when variation is due to a special cause outside the system itself. Such variation is expected to be among people, outputs, services, and products. The statistical knowledge needed is about that variation. Specifically, one needs to know the cause of the variance and information about a probable course of action to capture the good variance and to eliminate the variance that has a negative effect on the customer.

In training the work force in statistics, the DS employees were given a fundamental introduction to the techniques of Statistical Process Control (SPC), including the basic tools of data collection, data stratification, types of charts—histograms, Pareto analysis, run charts, control charts—and techniques of process capability analysis. But even as powerful a tool as SPC is, at most, its application will result in 3 to 5 percent of the available improvements that can be obtained overall when TQM is practiced. Generally, far greater gains can be affected through an adequate application of systems knowledge, systems modeling, and group-to-group problem solving through Tactical Planning and Team Building.

Theory of Knowlege

Deming offers a series of characteristics about knowledge. They include the following:

1. Planning requires prediction.

2. A statement that does not provide prediction of future events and explanation of past events conveys no knowledge.

3. There is no knowledge or theory without prediction and explanation of the past.

4. No observation is of value unless it is based on a theory or related to a theory.

5. Interpretation of data must be predictive; the prediction will depend on the knowledge of the subject matter, and, further, it is only when a process is in statistical control that statistical theory can help management predict.

6. Experience must also be grounded, for usefulness, in a theory that will allow that experience to be used for explanation and prediction.

7. An example, an experience, teaches us nothing unless helped with a predictive and explanatory theory of knowledge.

8. We must develop operational definitions between customers and suppliers (internal and external), and those operational definitions can then be used as the basis for clearer communication (effectively accomplished in the project through the use of Essential Process Analysis). (See Chapter 12.)

9. The value of any data is directly related to the manner in which the data were gathered and measured.

10. We must be aware that all empirical observations are somewhat jaded/filtered through the paradigm of the person who is taking the observation/making the measurement (Deming letter, 1990).

These characteristics served as guides for the organization as they moved forward with their problem-solving efforts. They were used to create and use information for decision making.

Knowledge of Psychology

It is through the knowledge of psychology that we come to understand interactions between people. In the project, Jungian psychology (based on Carl Jung) and other existential psychologists were considered guides.

The Myers–Briggs temperament typology (see Jung, 1923; Bates and Keirsey, 1978; Myers, 1980; McCauley, 1981; and Kroeger and Thuesen, 1988) was used to allow all members of the work force to begin their study of the elements of individual and group psychology. All members of the directorate work force, prior to going to team-building sessions, were given the extended Myers–Briggs temperament inventory questionnaire, the results were tabulated and interpreted by Gilbert, and returned to the people during the team-building session. In the session, he then introduced each employee to the Myers–Briggs types, their own temperament preferences, and those of other people with whom they worked. Emphasis was placed on how the temperament types of other people complemented and supplemented others' individual strengths and weaknesses, and how, by combining their efforts, they could more effectively help each other help the customer.

The emphasis was to sensitize the participants to the unique differences, strengths, and causes for interdependencies among one another. It did not place much emphasis on "type casting" participants in rigidly defined categories, as is often the case in Myers–Briggs temperament interpretation. Rather, it focused on the uniqueness and worth of each individual and affirmed the positive nature, ability, and potential in each person directly in the presence of the person's peers.

Nelson, in the Essential Process Analysis classes, also given across the work force (see Chapter 12), continued to use the Myers–Briggs types by indicating how certain psychological types could best contribute to the various phases of process/systems analysis, design, test, and implementation on the work floor. The emphasis was not to confine or limit people by their type, but to enlarge their potential as problem solvers and members of the team.

Examples of other uses of psychological knowledge include the use of the existential school view that sees basic motivation as derived from the intrinsic belief in one's own and others' goodness (essential for TQM). In PPS, the emphasis was on individual strengths and potentials rather than on weaknesses and limitations. Although this basic assumption may appear obvious, early on in the project, many of the individuals attending PPS-related meetings and other organizational functions did not reflect agreement with it. Many employees were "expert" at pointing out negative characteristics of others—especially focusing on management. It was essential to reeducate and redirect employee relations toward a more positive and self-affirming foundation before true participation and teamwork for quality could be expected.

Another psychological approach employed in the project was the adaptation of the model of psychological change, as proposed by Kubler-Ross (1969). She suggests all people go through the five emotional phases when being affected by significant change: Denial; Anger; Bargaining; Depression; and, finally, Acceptance (DABDA). DABDA was used to help explain reactions to the changes within PPS.

Of course, the psychological learning process continues within Pacer Share, as do all the other educational efforts mentioned. Each is central to the TQM process. TQM begins with education, continues with education, and is education, never-ending education in all the phases of profound (relevant) knowledge. It was through the combined usage, therefore, of all of these elements of profound knowledge that TQM as a thought process was introduced to the managerial work force. And as all things have variance, so did the effectiveness of this approach.

Some managers understood immediately and became enthused and continued to be enthusiastic supporters of the changes required by TQM. Others to this day still resist all of the elements of profound knowledge, all the elements of change and, we would suppose, will be arguing about the merits of the changes effected through Pacer Share until the day they die. That is life, neither good nor bad, just a matter of the paradigm with which one is identified.

STRUCTURE

The structure of the organization needed change to accommodate new processes that would need to be developed to provide improved quality to the customer. Organizations designed to promote the old efficiency-oriented system are inappropriate structures for the quality approach.

Work Units

Members of work units started directly interfacing with their peers in other work teams in which they interacted as suppliers or customers in the flow or work process. This started almost immediately upon the introduction of the Tactical Planning and Team Building process into PPS and was reinforced and improved as a result of the Essential Process Management (EPM) programs and every other major effort undertaken by management to reeducate the work force for quality. McRorie and the rest of the DS senior managers also encouraged more lateral communications from unit to unit than the traditional, scalar, chain-of-command approach that is standard in most classic bureaucratic systems (see Fayol, 1949, for more details on this bureaucratic behavior). To illustrate the point, when first attending a team meeting with other work units, one group of technical engineers stated, ''We would like to help DSF [another division] but if we did, we would make our bosses mad at us.'' When vital communications among employees are blocked by the organizational structure, the structure must change.

Flattening and Self-Governed Work Teams

By the end of the third year of PPS implementation, the number of supervisors had been significantly reduced from 207 in 1988 to 136 in 1990 and the organization was ''flattened'' through voluntary measures to reduce the number of levels in the hierarchy. Teams were given the authority to recommend whether or not to fill the vacancy when a supervisor would move or terminate. Many groups elected to manage themselves rather than have their supervisor's position remain and be filled by another person. Self-governed work groups began to sprout throughout the system by the start of the third year of implementation. Teams of employees began to make bottom-line decisions as though they were shareholders in their own company.

It is interesting to note that when teams begin to become empowered, it is often management that has the most doubt about the teams' abilities. As one manager said to his team when they requested time to work on a very important quality process issue, ''Okay, you can take time for it, but don't 'milk' it.'' The idea of employees ''milking'' the organization is alien to those who operate in the quality paradigm, but, indeed, operant among both managers and employees who are enmeshed in the classic approach.

Reorganization

As a result of the change in approach to quality, where those closest to the process are responsible for doing the job right the first time, and for process improvement, one entire division within the DS organization, DSQ, the division charged with administration of the old, inspection-based quality program, was eliminated, with much of its function being reassigned to those on the floor actually doing the work. Concurrently, another division was created, DSE; although substantially smaller in head count than DSQ, it was charged with the mission to create effective on-the-job training for all employees so they could perform their jobs. (See Flaggert's comments in his article in the Appendix.)

Labor–Management Relations

One of the most difficult attitudes to change among managers was tied to the concept of the union. It seems management viewed labor as the enemy. Likewise, labor viewed management as the enemy. Over time, as these people came to know each other and their natures (that is, the senior managers and labor officials), this attitude began to change within PPS.

It has not changed completely yet, nor as much as it needs to. However, the change in attitude between labor and management in PPS has been a significant revolution. So significant, in fact, that on numerous occasions, PPS labor relations has been highlighted at national conferences and workshops. (See reports prepared by Frank Mason, Chief Management Negotiator for DS; John Salas, President of AFGE Local Union 1857; and Dave Wheeler, Chief Union Steward that are included in the Appendix to gain greater insight regarding the evolution of the labor–management partnership that emerged in DS through PPS.)

It is presumed that this change alone as a result of PPS will be a matter of significant interest to organizations nationwide, as they move toward the quality model. The same elements of DABDA, the same elements of the intrinsic belief in goodness/badness, and the same elements of personality as revealed in the Myers–Briggs personality types are all equally valid when applied to senior labor leadership and senior management. The gradual understanding of the psychological differences and strengths between people in these roles has contributed significantly to their abilities to deal with each other, to sit down and collaborate versus negotiate, to share a common vision.

TASKS

Introduction of TQM at any level in any organization results in a significant change to the entire philosophy of the structuring of individual jobs. Contrary to the normative American view, still largely based on the philosophy of Scientific Management, which argues for narrowly defined jobs and rigidly controlled levels of authority, TQM asks for exactly the opposite. In brief, it could be stated that TQM embodies the dual job-enrichment philosophies of vertical job enrichment and horizontal job loading. In PPS this, of course, was formally recognized in the consolidation of series (horizontal job enrichment) and in the elimination of the narrowly defined individual pay grades for the wider pay bands (vertical job enrichment).

This means that TQM rejects the narrowly defined job and along with it the concept of job specialization. The objective of TQM is the development of the multiskilled generalist. Not that every person will know every skill, but as each is incorporated into a team, the team will incorporate sufficient skills so that the team covers the entire range of job duties in a particular process. This, of course, is a challenge to the entire concept of the individual, narrowly defined profession and trade union. Neither the white collar nor blue collar worker escapes the challenge of seeing the path to a more empowered, more fully developed individual expected to exercise more discretion on the job than the restricted, tied down employee of the past, whose every act was detailed via a job instruction written by white collar professionals.

This radical job enlargement on the part of TQM has a significant impact on the entire training and education process within any organization. Entirely new training paths must be developed. Entirely new educational opportunities must be opened to both managerial and nonmanagerial members of the organization. Prior limits to training and education that restricted company- and organization-supported offerings to "job-related" training and education can no longer be accepted. As the quality approach develops, the need for continuous training will increase in order to meet the customer's needs. This vaults the training and education function in any organization far up the scale of importance and should be viewed to be a major organizational function.

We recognize that this may cause shudders to occur within the organizational structure of personnel departments, accounting departments, and system management departments across the entire spectrum of American organizations. To this point, due largely to the suppression of the need for broad skills and empowered educated individuals, the training function, even when it became somewhat sizable, had always been relegated to a relatively insignificant staff position far down the organizational ladder. No longer can this be allowed. In the quality approach, training is a function of job process, not a function of job series or pay grade.

If the path of TQM is followed, it must be recognized by the organization and its leaders that they are building an environment in which people can grow and be prepared for the future. It is precisely in the enhanced empowerment that comes through having a fully educated membership in the organization, it is precisely in empowering individuals to decide on their own and as teams what education and training is necessary for their growth, that organizations will find the path to never-ending improvement. In other words, if we were to formulate an equation, that equation would look like that in Figure 7.2.

Figure 7.2
The Quality Formula

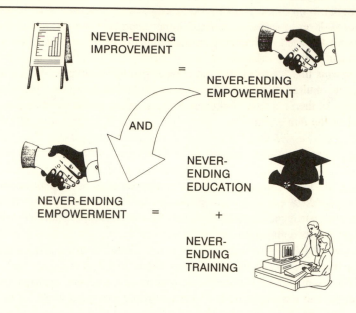

Part and parcel of the new education and training effort is the ability and right of the individual members of the organization to largely select the education and training that may be required for them to develop as individually empowered members of the organization. The staff function of education and training then becomes the supplier to these internal customers in obtaining the support needed for them to continue their never-ending development.

Many people will argue, we suppose, that allowing such empowerment to pass to the hands of the people will result in their taking frivolous courses, unnecessary courses, courses unable to be related to the financial "bottom line." Of course, such a view represents exactly the lack of trust that TQM must do away with. Such a view is based on a belief that people are not good, that people will "take advantage of the system," that people will "rip you off." Nothing is further from the truth when all on the team have ownership in the ultimate outcome and are partners. And through this empowerment of the people to assist in the planning and development of their own educational and training paths, TQM requires the demonstration of loyalty to the people on the part of the organization so that later the organization can have a right to claim loyalty from its members.

This responsibility was recognized early on in PPS. Even before its inception, the function of training was staffed with a member from Headquarters of the

AFLC with a professional background in the training and employee-development field, Jim Flaggert. The training function itself was elevated to formal division status, equal to any other staff or line management position. That training and educational-development organization, under Flaggert's leadership, implemented a document known as a Job Proficiency Guide (JPG), which provides a means to document both the training and the competencies gained by members of the work force as they crossed over traditional professional/series boundaries and became the multiskilled work force that the future required. Jim Flaggert's description of the JPG as a competency based management development tool is included in the Appendix.

TECHNOLOGY

Changing to the new approach required major reeducation with regard to TQM technology. PPS was not introduced to DS through full employee, labor, and management participation (see Chapter 5). Management and workers alike needed to be reeducated to the new way of working together and the new technologies that go with TQM. This reeducation was not considered to be a one-time thing, but an ongoing, never-ending effort.

The DS organization considered the challenge ahead and realized it needed to undertake a systemwide effort to transform the organization to the new technology. The biggest obstacle in the way to making the transformation was old habits that served to support behavior that would support the old system rather than the new. So the organization decided to go off to college. They created their own college within DS and enrolled all managers and supervisors in it.

The DS College: An Androgynous Educational Approach to TQM

One of the tools utilized to change the attitudes and the knowledge of management was the six-year-long internal management education plan within DS. It was designed to provide a common footing and a common knowledge base, a common language, and a common point of reference for all managers in the organization. The process was based on the Malcolm Knowles (1973) androgynous model of education. It assumed that managers, as adults, learned best from themselves, that is, in a dynamic group environment organized in teams versus sitting in a lecture hall being taught by a pedagogue at the front of the room.

To effect this model took a considerable amount of time and education in itself. Textbooks that deal with the subject matter of TQM and its related disciplines as expounded in the theory of profound knowledge were identified and used as sources for a common sharing.

That common sharing was effected by dividing the managerial work force into sixteen teams. Each team was assigned then to attend a one-day class per month with four teams going each day. Thus, in a process of four days, all managers in the work force would receive and discuss the same information.

Material relevant to the particular month's course was distributed to the teams a month prior to the scheduled seminar day. In that month, the teams met, discussed the material scheduled for the seminar, and then each team was assigned the task of teaching one-quarter of the day's material to the other three teams. Thus, learning teams came together, looked at the overall subject matter under review, and then focused on the quarter of the material for which they were responsible (comparing it to their own organizational and work experiences), fleshing out the theory that was in the various textbooks that were assigned, and developing an experientially based teaching outline and materials using real life DS examples.

Some of the subjects included in the college curriculum included:

Introduction to the Quality Model

Customer Identification and Needs Assessment

Leadership and Managership

Communications and Coaching Without Performance Appraisals

Team Building

Labor Relations in a TQM Environment

Introduction to Essential Process Management

Strategic Planning for Quality

Introduction to Business Math, Algebra, and Statistics

Budgeting and Financial Management

Industrial Engineering

Public Relations/EPM Process Promotion

Production Scheduling

The Canon Production System

Advanced Algebra for Managers

Basic Spreadsheet Usage

Instructor Training

Just-In-Time Training

Value Engineering

Product/Process Design

The course schedules were developed, primary instructors from within DS were recruited, and the college began its educational efforts at the beginning of the third year of the project's life.

The androgynous model was not adopted without some controversy. During the initial three or four sessions, a supervisor bitterly complained that he could not be absent from his work group that long because his people "needed" him. After completion of the first year of the study, however, that same supervisor noted that he had learned that his job was to develop the abilities of the members of his team. The material and discussions of the course had enabled him to empower the members of his team. By doing so, the whole team worked better, and he no longer felt he had to be there with them to tell them what to do. This, in turn, freed him to apply other tools he was learning in the course related to planning, interrelationships with other groups and other managers in other areas, and customer relations.

With the planned expansion of Pacer Share into other areas of the ALC and possibly into the Defense Logistics Agency (DLA) it will be of some interest to note whether the planned six-year education process continues and is expanded to cover new managers coming into the system. If one were to ask the managers who have gone through the system about their preference, they would vote for PPS and the quality approach. However, if one were to ask those who are coming into it about their preference, they would probably vote "no," just as it was before the beginning of the process within the DS itself.

SUMMARY

We have addressed the essential areas of change that were required for the introduction of TQM in any organization, with some references to how it was specifically accomplished within PPS, a Civil Service Demonstration Project. In the next five chapters, we begin to examine the concepts of what is necessary to build on this knowledge and mobilize the capabilities and talents of the people in the organization at all levels in order to "enter the new game."

REFERENCES

Bates, M., and Keirsey, D. W. (1978). *Please Understand Me*. Del Mar, CA: Prometheus Nemesis.

Chin, R., and Benne, K. D. (1969). "General Strategies for Effecting Changes in Human Systems." In *The Planning of Change,* 2d ed., Bennis, W., Benne, K. D., and Chin, R., Eds. New York: Holt, Rinehart and Winston.

DeMarco, T. (1978). *Structured Analysis and System Specification*. New York: Yourdon Press.

Deming, W. E. (1986). *Out of the Crisis*. Cambridge, MA: Massachusetts Institute of Technology, Center for Advanced Engineering Study (MIT/CAES).

Deming, W. E. (1990). Handout to conference leaders on profound knowledge. April 4.

Fayol, H. (1949). *General and Industrial Administration*. New York: Pitman.

Jung, C. G. (1923). *Psychological Types*. New York: Harcourt & Brace.

Keller, R. (1987). *Expert System Technology: Development and Application*. New York: Yourdon Press.

Knowles, M. S. (1973). *The Modern Practice of Adult Education*. New York: Association Press.

Kroeger, O., and Thueson, J. M. (1988). *Type Talk*. New York: Delacorte Press.

Kubler-Ross, E. (1969). *On Death and Dying*. New York: Macmillan.

McCauley, M. H. (1981). *Jung's Theory of Psychological Types and the Myers–Briggs Type Indicator*. Gainesville, FL: Center for Application of Psychological Type.

Myers, I. B. (1980). *Gifts Differing*. Palo Alto: Consulting Psychologists Press.

Shingo, S. (1989). *Zero Quality Control*. Cambridge, MA: Productivity Press.

Yourdon, E. (1975). *Techniques of Program Structure and Design*. Englewood Cliffs, NJ: Prentice Hall.

Yourdon, E., and Constantine, L. (1976). *Structured Design*. New York: Yourdon Press.

———. (1990). Unpublished paper on the elements of profound knowledge.

8

Tactical Planning and Team Building

Team Building is an essential part of the overall commitment to continued improvement at all levels within DS. Teams will be utilized in each work area and all employees have the right, obligation, and responsibility to be an active participant.

—Labor Management Council, Directorate of Distribution, McClellan Air Force Base, July 2, 1990

A primary organizational development intervention applied in making the transformation to the quality approach in PPS was "Tactical Planning and Team Building" (TPTB), a process developed and introduced to PPS by co-author Gilbert, an outside consultant for MEDi. He had developed it following over fifteen years experience as an organizational consultant and university professor.

Unlike most organizations that seek to have one-time TPTB workshops, PPS undertook it for the long term and made it a systemwide opportunity effort. Essentially, TPTB consists of ten sequential stages that when followed and managed with unconditional commitment by management, combine to create more effective team performance.

UNDERLYING ASSUMPTIONS

The TPTB process is value-based. It assumes the following:

1. Heroic behavior in the quality organization is found in teamwork. The team is where customer-oriented behavior begins.
2. All employees have valuable information about organizational impediments that are in their way (or are about to be in their way) to doing better-quality work.

3. All employees have sound recommendations about how to solve the problems that stand in their way to doing quality work for their customers.

4. The classic, efficiency-oriented approach to management seldom truly asks for their ideas.

5. The problems they recognize and that are truly in their way to doing quality work do not usually get fixed by those at the upper echelons of the organization without direct input and consultation by those closest to the problems.

6. The people actually at the operating levels of the organization, those actually doing the work, need to be given a larger role in the decisions affecting them.

7. The work team offers everyone an opportunity to excel and gain added respect as individuals, as well as respect for the contributions others provide.

8. Everyone at work deserves respect and no one gets too much of it. People work better when they feel respected.

9. Everyone deserves the opportunity to reach and fulfill his or her own potential, goals, and full use of his or her talents on the job.

10. The causes for lower performance are primarily a result of the system in which people work rather than the people themselves.

11. If the problems in the system can be identified and fixed by the people doing the work, the performance of people will increase, and the problems in the processes on which they work will decrease.

12. Leaders, nonleaders, fellow group members, members of other groups, and people external to the organization—everyone—have the right to be treated as though they were valued "customers" by those with whom they come in contact.

13. To make the transformation from the classic, efficiency-oriented approach to the quality approach will not take place quickly. It will take time to learn the rules, values, norms, and cultural mores of the new way of doing business in the quality approach. It starts with the team and teamwork.

14. Changing organizational behavior is not a one-time thing. It is never a permanent fix. Rather, it is a never-ending process of conditioning.

15. Every employee, every member of the organization, has gifts that, when truly invited, can add value to the system.

16. Teams work best when they know that their performance matters to others and will improve their work as a result of constructive, performance-based feedback from the customer or supplier and from their own self-assessments.

17. Employee work teams, themselves, are capable of greater self-direction and self-control than how they are generally treated.

18. A team works best when the members have the opportunity to share common goals and objectives, and to generate and receive timely feedback about the team's performance.

19. Bureaucratic organizations are more likely to limit rather than expand the potential that employees have to offer. They interfere with the work team members having direct contact with their customers and suppliers.

20. The key to the quality approach is based on the development of smart team play

rather than expert leadership or top–down, control-driven management rules and procedures that tend to constrict the work people do. Quality starts when the team members themselves, are in direct contact with their customers and suppliers and with one another.

The TPTB process operationalized these values and demonstrated that when these tenets are actually behaved, the organization will function more effectively, and people will feel better about themselves and their jobs.

Although these values and assumptions were not originally voiced by all in the PPS leadership, they were foundational to the PPS design. One of the most critical steps taken by McRorie, assigned to be the principal line manager of the PPS organization prior to the project's implementation, was to internalize the philosophy of PPS as his own and to help in the explication of these values.

These values and assumptions served to justify the application of the TPTB process throughout the project. Nothing ever occurred to dispel them. They were reinforced with each TPTB session held until the TPTB sessions were no longer necessary, as the employees themselves took control of the TPTB process in their everyday work. The process eventually became internalized within the system.

The Stages of TPTB

1. *Preprogram Activities.* This included identification of groups to be selected for the program, completion of assessment instruments, needs assessments, facility planning, procurement of equipment, materials preparation, agreement of the program plan and schedule and the like.

2. *Setting the Climate for Excellence.* This included the establishment of the workshop objectives, introductions, and creation of the expectation that the time spent in the program would lead to improvements.

3. *Recognition of One Another's Gifts.* This included the use of the Myers–Briggs Temperament Indicator (MBTI) as a means of creating a supportive environment and to reinforce the belief that each person on the team has gifts and has value.

4. *Introduction to Customer-Oriented Behavior: Self-Initiated Followership and Customer-Oriented Leadership.* This included a review of the classic efficiency- and quality-oriented approaches to management; an overview of the essential characteristics of leadership and followership in the quality-oriented approach; and identification of one's customers in the work setting.

5. *Team-Performance Assessment and Validation of the Need for Improved Teamwork.* This included the assessment, feedback, and validation of overall team performance and the need for improvement.

6. *Identification of Interdependencies and Needs From Between Customers and Suppliers.* This included work group breakouts by key roles in the work process that are highly interdependent as suppliers-customers. It also included breakouts based on supervisor and nonsupervisor interdependencies.

7. *Clarification of Customer Needs*. This included the sharing of needs from customer to supplier; individual and team feedback; and problem clarification.

8. *Designing New Ways to Be Customer-Responsive*. This included creative problem solving and customer-responsive tactical planning.

9. *Contracting for Change*. This included preparation of formal agreements to improve services to one another in the group.

10. *Follow-On Team Coordination*. This included organizing organic teams; handing the ball off to the in-house team-building consultants; putting together the follow-up plan; facilitating opportunities for employees to take control; buffering and linking communications to facilitate team play and continuous performance improvement; training teams to use the Essential Process Management (EPM) problem-solving methodologies presented in Chapter 12, and recording results.

Given these ten steps as key stages of TPTB, we now review some of the actual events that took place during implementation.

Starting at the Top

Prior to the completion of the design phase of PPS, the top-management team of DS elected to attend a team-building program. The top team consisted of the office of the director and deputy director of the Directorate, directors of five divisions, and their branch chiefs. The program was "introductory" in that the top-management team had never been engaged in a retreat-type team-building effort before. There was a lot of resistance to attending the two-day program. The military colonel in charge of the Directorate did not attend nor did the division head of the largest division in the organization.

In spite of assurances by the facilitator (Gilbert), Deputy Director McRorie, Nelson, and the others on the design team, it was very difficult to dispel the fear among some of the soon-to-be participants that the program was going to be some kind of "feely-touchy," nonpractical, childlike activity, if not a complete waste of time.

Preprogram interviews were held by the facilitator and many of the participants to identify needs, set workshop objectives, and prepare for the program. The basic objectives for the program were as follows:

1. To work better together as a team.

2. To gain increased understanding and appreciation of one another.

3. To improve communication among all members of the team.

4. To identify needs each unit in the organization has of one another, as though each was the other's customer.

5. To specify over fifty ways the entire organization can function more effectively as a team in support of its mission to process receipts and issues for its organizational customers.

Figure 8.1
Typical Hierarchical Structure of the DS Team

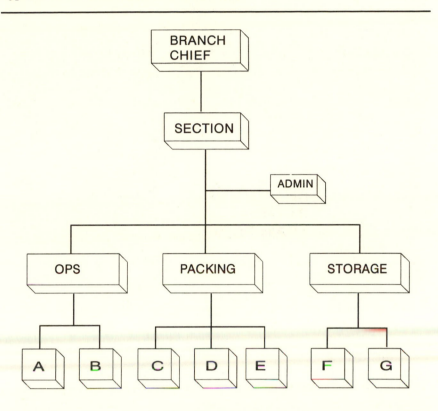

Essentially, the process enabled the participants to "suspend" the organizational hierarchy and learn to behave as though each member of their team and the units that comprised the entire leadership team in PPS were one another's customers. Figure 8.1 reveals the team according to the organization chart. Figure 8.2 reveals the team interacting as one another's customers.

Following the First Session

That initial TPTB effort resulted in over 125 substantive (as opposed to mere attitudinal) ways the team could work more effectively together. More importantly, it demonstrated an alternative approach to the classic staff meeting to working together in creative problem solving. As a result of that initial effort, the expectations of the group were raised regarding the opportunities that the PPS program might offer. Also, it created higher expectations among the top-leadership team regarding the potential of teamwork and empowerment. Everyone in attendance played an important part in the identification and search be-

Figure 8.2
Typical Structure of the DS Team by Process

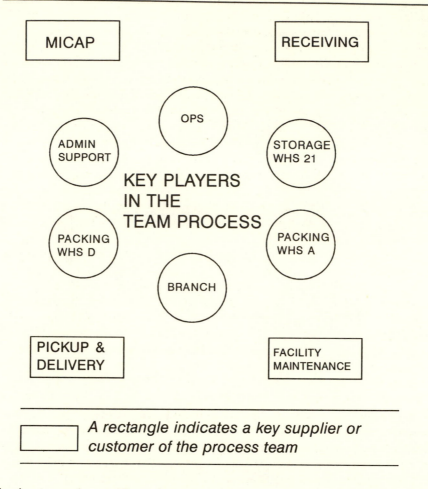

MICAP

RECEIVING

OPS

ADMIN
SUPPORT

STORAGE
WHS 21

KEY PLAYERS
IN THE
TEAM PROCESS

PACKING
WHS D

PACKING
WHS A

BRANCH

PICKUP &
DELIVERY

FACILITY
MAINTENANCE

A rectangle indicates a key supplier or customer of the process team

havior to resolve problems that were raised. The leader of the organization, McRorie, demonstrated his willingness to sit before the entire group and listen to its needs. For many, it was the first time they had ever been in an organizational situation where the communication process not only invited the leadership to listen to its people, but *insisted* on it.

Because leaders do not run their day-to-day meetings that way, it seemed to be antithetical to the right way of doing business. However, as a result of McRorie's willingness to treat his own people with the same type of respect that he would treat any other valued customer, the people began to speak up and identify the real needs they had to do their jobs the right way for their customers. As a result, the process forced the unspoken, informal communications that usually take place after the staff meetings, in the hallways, bathrooms, bowling alleys, pubs, and the like, to be openly discussed. The process opened up communication between the team members to include the surfacing of information that lives in the subterranean levels of the organization, where it is channeled through whispers and winks rather than by open exchange and discussion of differing viewpoints by all on the team.

It is strange that the efficiency-oriented system in which most organizations exist places extraordinary emphasis on displacing power from its natural order to something that is hierarchical. It forces an asymmetrical distribution of power, where the leader has most of the cards when determining what the others are to do. The organization fortifies the leader's power with policies, procedures, and rules that truly separate leaders from those in their groups when it comes to deciding what it is that is to be done. Then, in such organizations, employees are asked what needs fixing by the leaders, and the employees don't share all that they know. Why should they? Where such imbalances of power exist, fear exists as well. People don't share what they know when they feel fear. They also don't engage in spontaneous, free-wheeling, creative problem solving under such conditions.

It seems appropriate that in the classic, efficiency-oriented system, it is the informal system that is a sign of health for it provides outlets for pent-up, suppressed emotion among members of the team. There "confidential" suggestion systems are in place to tap the hidden ideas that employees have, but do not feel they can express openly and receive a fair hearing from their supervisors or work teams. Such suggestion systems make it possible for employees to rise above their work groups, where their talents are seemingly hidden or suppressed.

Contrarily, in the quality-oriented system, the informal system is a sign of pathology—the stronger it is, the less effective the quality-driven system, for it is a sign that the information that needs to be processed by the team is being withheld. Thus, the informal system is brought out into the open without retribution, for it contains extraordinary energy and creative potential and it is fueled by repressive management and team practices that need fixing. In the quality-oriented system, there is no need for the "confidential" employee suggestion box, for ideas are openly expressed without fear of retribution.

Following that initial experience, the TPTB process was expanded to other groups of leaders in the system. Leaders in each division were introduced to the process. Early on, there was open hostility expressed about the team-building effort by leaders in DS. Many did not want to go through it with their own teams. The fear of losing control of their people by involving them more in the problem-solving process was a major obstacle for many to overcome.

Some viewed the process as a threat to their authority and power. They viewed the process whereby they would be forced to listen to their people as a challenge to their integrity as leaders—as though they had done something wrong by being good soldiers in the only system they ever knew. They had always been led to believe that they were the top players on the team in the old system. Now they were being given the message that they were a major part of the problem. Team building and the initiation of employee empowerment was somewhat offensive to them. They knew that many of the employees were inadequate performers and the new attention and respect the employees were getting were not deserved. Indeed, from the perspective of the old system, the team-building process and employee empowerment were inappropriate. But in the quality-oriented approach, team building was the "breakfast of champions" whose contributions were about to implode.

For many supervisors, they had been successful in the old system and now they were being encouraged to behave differently. They had fought hard to earn power and status and to abide by the rules of the old system. Now they were being requested to give up much of what they had attained—status, authority, power, prestige, and personal upward mobility. Much like the good soldiers of any regime about to end, the DS supervisors were informed that the system they had dutifully served was too corrupt to support any longer. They were about to have to learn new rules and play the game very differently, and that was not appealing to most of those in power positions, whether military or civilian.

The supervisors came into their first TPTB session as though they were going into the doctor's office for their first flu shot. Little did they know that some would be subsequently subjected to the process many times before the new way of doing business would take. McRorie, the organizational leader, with the support and exceptional collaborative assistance from the PPS office within DS insisted that the process continue until everyone had the opportunity to experience the invitation to participate more fully in the decision-making process in DS. At times, McRorie and Nelson and the rest of the DS (2) office were not merely unpopular, they were the target of threats and severe ridicule by members of the organization from all ranks. Although team building is more openly advocated in the TQM lexicon today, it was on the frontier then in PPS. Although it was designed specifically for DS, the team-building approach taken in PPS was unique. It was a risky thing to undertake, but each time the process was introduced, it yielded positive results. It demonstrated behaviorally what TQM was about. It made TQM more than palatable; it made it desirable.

New ways of doing business were being identified through consensual decision making and participation. And, although resistance might have been high at the start of the programs, most programs ended with renewed commitment to both personal and organizational excellence by those participants involved.

As the process continued, as more and more people became involved, the people within DS began to treat others as though they were their customers.

As more leaders in the organization began to gain exposure to the TPTB process, there began to emerge a greater appreciation of the wisdom of the group by some in the organization. With each TPTB program, employees and their supervisors were able to identify better ways of working together and to serve their customers.

In the Appendix, Carl McRorie, Deputy Director of DS, and the manager of PPS, offers his perceptions about the TPTB process. Without his personal risk taking and sponsorship of that effort, it would not have been introduced into the AFLC system. He worked closely with Gilbert, the external third-party TPTB consultant; Nelson, the head of the PPS design team; and the managers, supervisors, team leaders, and team consultants in DS to assure this process would be a major building block for quality improvement.

ORGANIZATIONWIDE IMPLEMENTATION STRATEGY

The initial TPTB programs were presented to the top-management teams. All executives, managers, and supervisors were taken through the process to introduce them to it, to explain how it fits into the quality approach and other interventions underway in the system, and to gain experience necessary so they could be more effective when building teams with the members of their own units.

After the initial training for those in managerial/supervisory positions, TPTB training was provided to each supervisor and his or her team working in common processes within each division. It took over two and one-half years to reeducate the PPS host organization through the TPTB process.

Phase I: Resistance

At first, the team-building effort seemed like it was happening in a void. During the first year of implementation, the teams in training focused much of their attention on nonspecific interpersonal issues among the members of the teams themselves rather than on substantive problems associated with getting quality from their suppliers and to their customers. The participants voiced their "opinions" about what was wrong with management in general, their supervisors (who were there in attendance), and both the old and new system in which they were working.

Accounts from one of the very first attempts at team building with a group of warehouse workers might reveal the open hostility, insensitivity, and inhospitable working relations between team members and their supervisors.

My Supervisor Is Crazy

At the start of one session, the team members were asked to reveal their expectations about the value the two-day TPTB program would have for them. An employee said she didn't expect anything to be of value because of her supervisor. It seems the employee had just completed a psychology course at the local community college. She had studied mental disorders and now knew that her supervisor was a "paranoid schizophrenic." As such, nothing would change, because the supervisor, so labeled, would require long-term treatment, and the project was only going to last for five years—not enough time to help the supervisor overcome her "illness."

As the supervisor was sitting about five seats from this employee, it was especially eventful. However, what makes the employee's comments worth noting is that the employee did not reveal any regret that she had said such a thing in front of others about her own leader. Furthermore, the statement never became "famous" in the organization as it was not so far removed from how people working on the "floor" were treated and how, in some units in the organization, they spoke to one another.

(Over time, it became clear the supervisor had a well-integrated, intact personality. Her behavior was very normal. The subordinate's comments were merely hurtful remarks that were not uncommon between members of her team.)

We Are Not Going to Hurt You, Boss

At another TPTB workshop with another group, a supervisor was asked to come up to the front of the room and listen to the needs his employees had of him—the support they needed to do the job in very specific terms. The supervisor left the room to take a break. After a break was called for all, the supervisor was encouraged to return to the room. He remained in the back of the room, in the corner. He did not come forward to listen to the members on his team who were asked to communicate their needs to their supervisor. The supervisor was noticeably scared to the point that his perspiration had made its mark throughout most of his T-shirt. Finally, one of the members of his team called out to him, "Come on down. We're not going to hurt you," in a very soft and caring manner. After hearing that, he wandered to the front of the room to hear about their needs. Throughout the entire time, though, in spite of the efforts of the members of his team, he felt very uncomfortable. When leaders fear their people and do not listen to their needs, they do not qualify to lead in the quality approach to managing people.

Welcome to the Hatfields and the McCoys

At the start of another session, the manager of the division introduced Gilbert, the team building workshop facilitator, to the group. The participants, representing a variety of units in the organization, were very quiet, not out of shyness as much as out of hostility and distrust. Many made it known that they did not want to be there and that nothing good was going to come out of the effort. The attitudes alone were negative enough to keep any team from winning.

After the manager introduced the facilitator and was about to depart for the day, he whispered to Gilbert, "Good Luck! You are about to meet the Hatfields and the McCoys!"

Well, needless to say, that was the start of big-time confrontation, especially between two groups of people that were clearly divided and openly hostile toward one another. Their dysfunctional behavior had been known to management for years, yet nothing was found that management could do to turn it around.

As each group began to identify what was needed of the other so each could do its job better, it became clear that the problem was not in the people, but in the design of the work of the two groups. When one group did what it was supposed to do, it caused more work for the other. Furthermore, it also caused the other to look bad and, on occasion, be criticized or reprimanded. As the two groups came to understand their counterparts' roles, it became clear to them that the problem was not the people, it was the job design.

As a result, the two groups elected to propose a new design to management, where the two groups would form one unit and work out their process problems together, before releasing their work from their units. That solution had been proposed to them by management in the past, but never accepted. As the solution was proposed by the teams themselves, using third-party facilitation to do so, the problem was managed.

Phase II: Team Building Takes Hold in the Organization

Early in the program, especially during the first year, many supervisors and nonsupervisors alike feared the opportunity the TPTB process would offer them. However, after one or two positive experiences themselves, and seeing the progress that others were making as a result of their own participation in the TPTB process when assuming that customer-oriented behavior that the process encouraged and modeled for them, they began to look forward to the time when their team would go to team building.

The addition of the follow-up team-building component (see Chapter 9) made a major difference in getting results from the team building itself. Nelson observed the outside facilitator role (Gilbert) was essential to the follow-up, in-house, team-building consultants, for he could be a coach to them when they felt blocked by the system. At times, he directly intervened on their behalf to communicate their needs to the top when those in the formal chain of command were impeding their efforts.

Also, the follow-up consultants were absolutely essential to the outside facilitator.[1] They were partners. They believed in the program and were expert at getting people on the floor to participate. They went from early motivators of the teams, to the teams' organizers, to the teams' trainers. Today, they have created a new role for themselves in the TPTB effort.

Through the TPTB process, their teams learned to behave in a more collaborative way; they usually work better with one another and their leadership. Even more notable, they began to be more customer-responsive—they took pride in figuring out new and better ways to serve their customers.

Increasing the Organizationwide Support

When TPTB was first introduced in the organization, only a few were for the program and the rest were passive or resistant participants. Trying to get things started was much like a few persons in stadium bleachers starting to stamp their feet to get a cheer going or to build new momentum and enthusiasm for their side of the contest. The feet of these instigators are hitting the bleachers, yet the bleachers fail to move or make any unifying statement; they are insufficient to create a rally on their own. Yet, if the few initiators continue, if they enthusiastically insist in their efforts, others will soon join in. Then others, then entire sections in the bleachers become involved. Soon, the bleachers are moving, shaking, rolling, and even when the few who originally initiated the stamping effort have stopped, the bleachers continue to move. It is as though the bleachers have an energy of their own and are now moving the people. That is what happened in DS through the TPTB process. As the process was continued, and the ownership and support for treating one another like valued customers continued, the process took off on its own—it created its own life support system.

EXAMPLES OF EXCELLENCE IN TEAM PERFORMANCE

The Shuttle Program in Pick Up and Delivery

Following their attendance in a TPTB effort, members of the pick up delivery unit sought to improve the way they were doing business for their customers in receiving, storage, and other drop-off points. They initiated a shuttle program where a driver would shuttle material through the process rather than drop it off and return to pick it up. They also created a method to expedite the handling of material so that at each drop-off point, the material would not have to be unpacked, inspected, and packed again prior to its being released to another drop-off point. As a result of the shuttle program and their commitment to improved team play for their customers, they reduced costs in excess of $350,000 in their first year by the shuttle program alone.

Joe Prater, a driver and dispatcher in pick up and delivery, attended his first team building session in November 1988. He became "hooked" on the process because of the immediate results he and his team were able to see. Joe later became a consultant to other teams and a keynote speaker and workshop leader on team building. His account the impact of team building on his group is included in the Appendix.

Camper Tops for Their Pickup Trucks

Truckers delivering small materials in pickup trucks had asked for camper shells to be purchased so that they could better protect the materials they transported from point to point. This request had been made in the past, but management had concluded it was too expensive to implement. Certain material was transported in open-bed pickup trucks. But when it rained in Sacramento and the material had to be moved in the pickup trucks, the material would get wet and damaged during shipment.

The truckers felt embarrassed for not being able to protect the material when delivering it to their customers. Also, the truckers would often get blamed for doing poor work, when it was not their fault that the material was damaged due to inadequate protection when the material was in transit in the pickup trucks.

As a result of team building, the truckers tried once more to convince their management to hear their case. They used the EPM tools of problem analysis and statistical process control described in this book (Chapter 12) to prepare their case. Also, having attended team building and now recognizing that their subordinates were their "customers," the truckers' supervisors were more willing to listen to the truckers' needs.

The truckers presented their case for camper tops to their management, and the tops were approved for purchase. In a few months, the truckers were able to accomplish what they had fought for and been denied by their management for several years. Now the truckers have more pride in their work, and their customers are getting a better product, with fewer complaints, damage reports to write, and rework.

Donna Wolfe, a driver in the pickup and delivery unit, headed a team problem-solving effort to improve the quality of the handling and transportation of equipment in pickup trucks. Her account of her team effort is included in the Appendix. Today, Donna is a team-building consultant in Project Pacer Share and an instructor in TQM methodologies.

Off-Base Deliveries

The truckers had been excluded from off-base deliveries, because management did not think they could control the truckers off the base. It was thought that the truckers could not be trusted off the base when working on their own time without close supervision. Thus, the organization relied on contractors from the private sector to handle off-base deliveries.

The truckers' team conducted a study and presented it to their management. They found they could deliver material to others off base for 50 percent less cost than the contractors and it would take them only one-fourth the time to get the material to the customer. Management listened to the truckers' report, read their analyses, and decided to let the truckers do work off base. They were given the opportunity to transport material to off-base locations such as Travis AFB, Sharpe Army Depot, and Tracy DLA. Up until that time, all off-base shipping was handled by commercial carriers.

Data were kept on the per-mile cost of the in-house work off base. In the first seven months of implementation, the in-house carriers realized a cost savings of over $43,500 when compared to the costs that would have been incurred through commercial carriers to do the same work. Then came "Desert Shield."

During the Desert Shield build up in late 1990, the team was asked to assist along with the commercial carriers to get ninety-one loads of high-priority material to Oakland, California, for shipment to Saudi Arabia. The team was informed that the material had to be shipped within a two-week time frame. The team delivered the material four days ahead of schedule while saving the government $100,857. The government paid $2,700 for each commercial load, and the cost per load by the DS truckers was $109.

During Iraq's invasion of Kuwait, when the United States and other nations of the world were in crises to send troops and supplies to Saudi Arabia and elsewhere in the Persian Gulf, those truckers were transporting material and supplies off base to other military locations to be sent overseas. They were doing the job faster, with less cost, than their private-sector counterparts. It was their idea, their contribution to provide quality for their customer. They did it better than ever before.

Inspecting Electrostatic Discharged Components

Workers on the receiving line in the warehouse were delayed each time they processed an electrostatic discharged (ESD) component. For when they came upon one, they would have to take the component to another work station especially made to ground them from electrostatic discharges that would possibly destroy the sensitive electronic component. This check was necessary, time consuming, and costly. After team building, some members on the line decided to study the problem to see if there was a better method to process ESDs, one that was less time consuming and disruptive. They "invented" a breadboard-type tray that they could pull out from under the places where they worked. It would give them the protection and necessary grounding on the spot to inspect the ESD without having to travel some 100 to 200 yards to the normal inspection table that had always been used for such purposes. After the ESD item is checked, the breadboard could be placed back under the workstation table, and the workers could return to their normal processing activities. This resulted in a significant improvement in work processing.

Phase III: Beyond Participative Management

It took over two years for the organization to internalize TPTB to be part of the normal, as opposed to the exceptional, way of doing business. The teams gained skills in problem solving through the appropriate applications of EPM, EPA, SPC (described in Chapter 12), and TPTB. They learned to work with their supervisors, and their supervisors learned to work with them. They also learned to work better together as colleagues.

Self-Managed Work Teams

As the teams began to strengthen and become an integral part of the management process, they began to make some extraordinary requests. When a member of the team left the group as a result of transfer, retirement, or resignation, it began to analyze the situation from the standpoint of whether or not that person needed to be replaced or if the team itself could pick up the slack.

Rather than replacing a supervisor at his or her turnover, the team itself analyzed the situation and made a recommendation to management whether or not the team could work on its own without replacing the supervisor. Self-managed work teams began to occur.

In PPS, the teams had incentives to do the work and join with management in taking responsibility to do the work right. They had been given respect. They had been given opportunity to shape their own destiny. They had financial incentive through gain sharing to get the work out faster, on schedule, and without flaw. Most important, though, they had renewed pride and self respect from being the very best they could be for their customer and with their supervisors/partners.

PPS gave rise to new forms of team play. The account given in the Appendix, which was written by Sharon Carvalho, an employee in DS, describes an example of the self-managed work team in action in PPS.

Every intervention used in PPS added value to making the transformation to the quality model. The TPTB process had major impact among the entire work force. Every employee participated in the program. Each received the same intervention. Each learned about team building from the same external consultant. Through it, each employee learned to think in terms of self-initiated followership, customer-oriented leadership, and problem solving based on the needs of the customer. As a result, many employees learned to think of themselves as though they were in business for themselves while working in DS and for government.

The teams demonstrated their ability to a once doubting management, as well. They demonstrated their ability and willingness to work responsibly when given the opportunity and treated as partners. At the time of this writing, the DS has a standing policy that no decision made by a team can be overruled by a manager with the exception of Col. Naehring, the military director in charge of the entire DS operation. He has yet to have cause to overrule one decision made by a team regarding the best way to do the job. Today, there are literally hundreds of teams in place in DS, with members and teams working together to deliver better quality to the customer.

SUMMARY

Overall, in three years, every employee (over 1,400) within the Directorate of Distribution was engaged in the TPTB process with an outside facilitator. Through this process, each employee was given the opportunity to speak up and be listened to by his or her peers, supervisor, and others at higher levels on the management team.

At the same time, every employee, every supervisor, every member of the team, including union representatives and their union officers, were given training in customer-oriented behavior, the quality approach, and self-initiated followership. In the TPTB program, each participant was given training in identifying their customers, searching for and listening to the needs of their customers, application of problem solving to improve their products and services for their customers, and contracting with both their suppliers and customers for improved performance. Supervisors were "forced" to listen to their people, to treat their own subordinates as though they were their customers. Every employee, including those in higher levels in the chain of command were trained in self-initiated followership for customers—even their supervisors were customers whose needs were to be respected.

Each session concluded with an "action plan" consisting of new ways each group would behave in order to support its customers' needs more effectively. These action plans would serve to facilitate continued team development upon reentry to the organization.

This chapter described the TPTB process that was designed specifically for PPS by an outside consultant and then refined in practice to include an internally driven follow-on component. The overall program started slowly and gained momentum over time. It proved not to be a quick fix, but a longer-term developmental process. It created new avenues for communication and problem solving within the DS. It provided new opportunities for the tools of TQM to be used. It resulted in literally thousands of improvements in the way the organization processed its resources. It gave cause for hope among those who had all but lost it in the old system, which PPS was designed to change.

NOTE

1. The team-building follow-on consultants were the reason the TPTB process became internalized throughout the DS. Their contributions to quality have been of heroic proportion and merit special recognition. Their names are Dalene Clausen, Karen Harper, Anita Kordela, Nancy McDonald, Vicki Nelson, Sandi Pang, Janice Peterson, Joe Prater, Princess Putney, Jim Rollin, Lee Tefertiller, and Donna Wolfe.

9

The Team-Building Follow-On Effort

BACKGROUND

As described in the previous chapter, every employee in PPS was trained in Tactical Planning and Team Building (TPTB). During the first year of TPTB, it became clear that many of the commitments to improved customer service that were made in the TPTB sessions were not kept. These commitments were made between workers, their units, supervisors and employees, and management and the work force. Every time a commitment was made and was not kept, another reason for distrust, rather than trust, was created. Each failure in commitment became another blow to the type of continuous quality improvement that was so desperately sought by those in charge of PPS. Every failed promise tended to further tether the organization to the classic efficiency-oriented approach to management rather that help move the system toward the quality approach.

As the team-building effort progressed, people began to report high satisfaction with the TPTB effort. However, once their teams went back to their jobs, many became dissatisfied because the promises made in the initial TPTB session were not always carried out. Supervisors didn't insist on keeping the process going at their staff meetings. Teams failed to meet for continued problem solving. The commitments they made to one another fell through the cracks and were not attended to. It became clear that stronger, more effective follow-on activities needed to be created within the system.

THE EMERGENCE OF NEW LEADERSHIP FROM THE OPERATING LEVELS OF THE ORGANIZATION

One of the outstanding outcomes of the TPTB process was the emergence of new leadership from the floor or the operating levels of the organization. During and following the TPTB programs, employees and supervisors were given the opportunity to demonstrate excellence in customer-oriented behavior and team play. Some excelled. Some whose potential had never been brought to the surface, some unknown to management, and some even possibly blocked by their own supervision to demonstrate their abilities were given a chance at team play. Some took to it like ducks take to water.

Although many teams had reported failure to continue to meet and keep the commitments they had made to their customers during the TPTB program, others had performed remarkably well. A closer look at those teams that had performed well revealed that they generally had the same characteristic: a "grass roots" informal leader had emerged and kept the process going. These individuals had become "true believers" in that they were unflinching in not ever wanting to go back to the old way of doing business and were clear advocates of the quality model. They had a natural ability to demonstrate self-initiated followership (Chapter 11) that was introduced to them in the TPTB program. They also were seen as legitimate leaders by their peers rather than as legal leaders—staff to management but not credible from the perspective of those at the actual operating levels of DS. That is, they were leaders for their peers based on the inherent respect that they had gained from their peers rather than because they were "supervisors." As explained in Chapter 3, most supervisors in the present system were selected because of their suitability for leadership in the classic efficiency system that relied on features of the CSS that had been corrupted over time. The quality approach required teams that would have leadership having popular support from the teams themselves.

Team Building Follow-On Component

An added component to the TPTB effort was designed: the team-building follow-on.[1] The team follow-on activity would require that each team trained in TPTB would select a "team leader" who would serve as the member responsible to convene the teams on an ongoing basis. Each team would have a "code of conduct" that describes how the members of the team are to conduct themselves when working together in team problem-solving activities.

Staff would be needed to coordinate the teams. They would be responsible to work with the external TPTB facilitator prior to the each program, provide a "kick off" at the TPTB start, wherein an actual positive outcome from a previous TPTB effort was presented, to work with the teams as they put together their action plans, and to assure the teams continued to meet with their supervisors and team leaders after the initial program. One of their first obligations after taking the handoff from the outside facilitator was to help each functional work unit select a "team leader" who would lead the team in its discussions and customer-driven team problem-solving efforts.

EMERGENCE OF NEW ROLES

In-House Team-Building Consultants

As part of the TPTB process and an extension of it, the outside consultant and Deputy Director McRorie sketched together a new role in the organization—in-house team-building consultants. These people would belong to each division within DS. In general, they were to be selected because of their proven ability to work well with other people at the process level. They would have also demonstrated inherent leadership with the people with whom they work, as opposed to having been the most senior, most eligible, most affordable, or been the most favored by their supervisors. It was essential that the bureaucratic practice of having supervisors offer the biggest "turkeys" they have to such facilitation roles be checked, as the program couldn't fly with turkeys at such a critical time or for such a vital cause. For the PPS to work, quality had to be number one, and the selection of these key people was extremely important. See Figure 9.1.

The in-house team-building consultant role was designed to facilitate the on-going team-building process within the organization. Each was assigned specific groups; his or her task was to assure the teams met, developed the codes of conduct, carried out the action agendas as promised, tracked all accomplishments, and further trained the teams in the application and use of appropriate TQM tools.[1] These in-house team-building consultants coordinated efforts with one another, Deputy McRorie, the PPS project team, and the TPTB facilitator and management consultant (Gilbert). Each in-house consultant also organized presentations and visitation tours for outsiders from both industry and government who were interested in learning about the organizationwide efforts that were taking place in PPS.

Lee Tefertiller, a member of the pickup and delivery unit in DS, attended his first team-building session in November 1987. He took a lead role in continuing the process within his own unit. The methodology he and his team developed was extended throughout DS. His account of the role of the team-building consultant is presented in the Appendix. Today, Lee provides consultation to others in both government and the private sector in team-building follow-on procedures.

Team Leaders

Team leaders were selected by the members of the team itself. In general, the team leader was not the unit supervisor. In actuality, often the team leader would turn out to be the informal leader of the team, as opposed to the unit supervisor, who was the legal leader. By bringing the two together, it helped bridge differences between the supervisors and their people. In their roles as team leaders,

Figure 9.1
Organization Chart for the Directorate of Distribution with the Role of In-House Team-Building Consultants

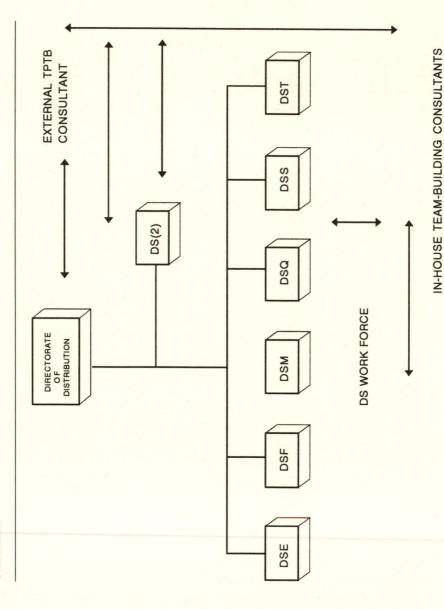

they had the obligation and authority to request guidance from their supervisors, team-building consultants, or others whom they deemed to be resources in the organization, including representation from the union. They were charged with the responsibility to assure team meetings were held on a regular basis.

The team leaders would assure that the team set goals, took minutes, and relied on research and other data-collection methods to help with their problem-solving activities and decision-making processes. David Thompson attended team building with his work unit. He was subsequently chosen to be a team leader by members of his own work unit and offers his account of the emerging role of the team leader in the Appendix.

Recorders

Every team had a designated recorder to keep accurate minutes of all meetings, provide copies of the minutes to all team members and in-house team-building consultants on a timely manner, and to assist the team leader, as necessary. Although the role of the recorder is traditionally viewed to be less important or subservient to the team, it was highly prized by some, for it gave them the opportunity to demonstrate their followership to the team.

Unit Supervisors

The unit supervisors would be responsible to assure that their teams would meet on a regular basis after the TPTB experience. They would work with the team leaders and the in-house team-building consultants to assure that the commitments made in the TPTB session would be kept and the open communications process started in the TPTB activity would continue. They were obligated to allow official time for the team leader to attend any and all team leader meetings scheduled in the directorate. They were instructed to ensure the implementation of all approved process changes that were initiated by the teams themselves and to keep their own leaders informed regarding team recommendations and process changes in work that would have significant impact on the organization and its customers.

Connie Fullmer, a supervisor in the warehouse, has been actively involved in team development training in DS. She has learned and applied the new way of leading and working with others based on the quality approach introduced in this book. In the Appendix, she reports about the role of the supervisor at the workplace where employee empowerment through team decision making has occurred.

Team Members

All members of the teams were expected to participate in the team meetings and team activities. They were expected to abide by the decisions of the team. They were obliged to keep the team leaders, team recorders, in-house team-building consultants and their supervisors accountable to them and the team-building process. As members of the teams, they were to assist in preparing briefing packages and management analyses of key processes under their scrutiny. They were called on to educate and train their suppliers as well as listen to their customers and to one another. They were expected to be in charge of customer quality.

Authority of Each Team

Each team was required to select a team leader. The team had the right to select the team's supervisor or any other team member as the team leader. Whether or not the supervisor was selected the team leader, he or she was responsible to participate in the team process. One division insisted that the supervisor be selected as the team leader, and the rest of the organization encouraged someone other than the supervisor to be selected. By selecting someone other than the supervisor for this role, the team itself is less dependent on the supervisor to do quality work. At first, not every leader is ready to go beyond "participative management" to full empowerment of their people as the selection of a non-supervisor as team leader implies. This points to an important lesson in team development. Start where your client feels most comfortable, build trust, and press on—but not so fast that your behavior justifies the client's fear of the process.

When the work load would dictate postponement of the team meetings, the leader would be obligated to reschedule the meeting as soon as possible, and be responsible to notify all team members, the in-house team-building consultants, and scheduled guests of such changes.

One "resistant" supervisor once refused to permit a team to meet, indicating the work load was too heavy and the organization could not afford to have the team take an hour from work. The team leader and the in-house team-building consultants took the issue to top management. The issue was whether or not management had enough confidence in its teams to let the team decide whether or not its meeting would keep it from getting the work load done on time. That is, is the supervisor the only person responsible on the team to decide if the team could meet or not based on the work load? A key decision was made: If the team understood the work load and still decided to meet, that decision would be upheld by management. The supervisor's decision was overruled. The team met and continued to meet its work-load responsibilities. This was a major change in the way decisions had been made regarding what employees would do and the level of responsibility the average employee was given. This was a major step in employee empowerment. It was beyond the traditional participative management approach where employees recommend but supervisors decide.

The teams also had an open invitation to go directly to Deputy Director McRorie should anything be perceived to get in their way of enabling teams to work effectively. It was the institutionalization of the follow-on component to the TPTB process that proved to have exceptionally high payoffs in terms of getting that never-ending commitment to team improvement and breaking down barriers to quality within the organization.

SUMMARY

The follow-on team building effort grew as a result of several factors: (1) The organization was committed to the team-building process as a way of life. (2) The internal organization needed to develop its own internal capability to continue the process with less reliance on the outside facilitator. (3) Leadership from employees within the organization began to emerge when employees themselves wanted to have ownership in keeping the process going. (4) Management in the DS was willing to consign the obligation and responsibility for continuous team building to employees who occupied roles other than those in classic supervisory positions. (5) Supervisors were willing to share power with their team leaders. (6) The union and management were willing to be flexible in the creation of these new roles without becoming prisoners of legalistic procedures between labor and management. (7) The organization sought to optimize the selection of people within the organization to do the job rather than rely on having people merely assigned to the job, but without being either motivated or having the inherent skill to do it well. (8) The outside consultant was given the opportunity to work with management to identify criteria for selecting the people to carry on the team-building processes within the organization and intervene for the team-building consultants, team leaders, and teams themselves when others in the hierarchy were blocking them.

The follow-on component of the TPTB activity has proven to be one of the most effective aspects of PPS. Almost daily, a significant achievement is reported as a result of one of the teams at work. The team leaders, supervisors, and team-building consultants continue to build their skills and commitment to enable those closest to the process to get involved and find new and better ways of doing business.

NOTE

1. The TPTB follow-on component described here was developed through the creative interaction of DS management, organized labor, employees, supervisors, and the external TPTB consultant. Like the TPTB process created in DS, it has served as a role model for others to use. It has been applied basewide as well as in many other public and private organizations nationally.

2. In 1991, a substantial portion of the DS organization was reassigned from the AFLC to the local Defense Logistics Agency (DLA). DLA subsequently abolished the in-house consultants and the TPTB and TQM systems that had worked so well in DS. This points to the vulnerability of TQM when leaders change.

10
Customer-Oriented Leadership: A Model of Supervision

The subject of leadership has great appeal to academicians and practitioners alike. Doctoral programs in schools of business and government have entire courses dedicated to the phenomenon of leadership. Textbooks in management consistently have at least one chapter dedicated to it as well.

Leadership style is a function of the situation (Fielder, 1967; Hersey and Blanchard, 1982; Vroom and Jago, 1974). The style that leaders are encouraged to adopt depends on a variety of factors, usually tied to task and relationship behaviors on the part of the leader, type of work the employee does, the ability and motivation of the subordinate to do the job, and the power of the leader to influence. Generally, the leader is encouraged to modify his or her style to "motivate" the employee to do the job. The underlying assumption in most contingency or situational approaches to leadership is that leaders need to build their repertoire of styles to deal with a multiplicity of contexts and people. The role of the leader in whatever context is to understand the situation and to act appropriately upon it to stimulate employee motivation toward the work objective.

However, what if the employees are already motivated? What if they basically know the job and are able to do the job? What if the leader's assumptions about the subordinate are based on the subordinate being a viable partner on the job, willing and able to learn the job and perform quality work for the customer if enabled to do so? What is the leader's role then?

As the PPS began to develop, it became clear that the emphasis on organizational leadership so well researched in the classic efficiency approach was not necessarily the right focus for the quality approach. The quality approach requires the leader to consider his or her subordinates to be the "customer," too. This would suggest the need for a new model of leadership.

As PPS began to move toward the quality approach through "Tactical Planning and Team Building," it became clear that the assumptions of leadership and the role of the leader in the organization needed changing. Leadership in the classic efficiency approach was not appropriate for leadership in the quality approach.

LEADERSHIP IN THE EFFICIENCY APPROACH

This approach generally promoted a person of "heroic" stature. (See Bradford and Cohen, 1984.) Such a person would be assumed to be smarter, more capable than his or her people. Leaders would be expected to make great decisions, to have dreams or "visions" for those in the unit and the unit as a whole. Also, these leaders would have tremendous power and the authority to control those below them. Such leaders were on management's team. They were in a salaried class by themselves and rewarded differently, being on management's team as opposed to labor's team. This type of leader might be considered to be a "boss" whose directives were to be carried out. Such leaders had the primary authority to sanction their employees. They were encouraged to develop alternative styles of leadership so as to manipulate their employees to peak performance. They relied on external motivators of employee performance. They were students of organizational behavior modification and reinforcement theory.

The consequences of such leaders are many. Most notably leaders who assume such a role encourage passive, dependentlike, behavior on the part of those who are subordinate to them on the job. Their behavior encourages their subordinates to act as though they were the dependent variable in the situation and their supervisors were the independent variable. Followership was a function of leadership. Thus, the very sharing of information, involvement in problem-solving processes, the assumption of responsibility for getting the job done right the first time through teamwork may not be the legitimate objective of the subordinate. Such obligations were owned by those who occupied supervisory positions.

LEADERSHIP IN THE QUALITY APPROACH

In 1987, Gilbert undertook a study to learn about leadership behavior where the quality approach is practiced by the employees themselves. He sought to identify the characteristics of leaders who truly facilitate quality performance in their subordinates. From the eye of the leader's "customer" (the follower), he attempted to capture leader behaviors that stimulate self-initiated followership among members of the leader's team and for the external customer of the group.

He employed a methodology similar to that used by Bass (1985) in his study of leadership. Bernard Bass is one of the eminent leadership scholars in America. However, where Bass focused on the transformational characteristics of leadership (still a heroic orientation), Gilbert sought to learn about leadership from a total quality-oriented approach.

In the quality-oriented approach, the role of the leader is different than in the efficiency-oriented approach. The leader for quality serves as a facilitator of customer-oriented behavior, a developer of the people on the team to encourage their never-ending quest for professional improvement, an empowerer of those closest to the vital work processes, and a champion of the work itself. Such leaders enable their own teams to become self-managed. They are more comfortable with functioning in situations having wider spans of control than those in the past approach where tighter spans were needed to monitor employee performance lest the employees' effectiveness would "drift" from doing what they were supposed to do. They facilitate the intrinsic motivational strengths of the employees themselves toward excellence in job performance. They view their subordinates to be their "customers," and, in being so, they are in constant search to identify ways to respond to their employees' needs. They are partners to both management and labor.

Gilbert (1987, 1990; Gilbert, Collins, and Brenner, 1991) analyzed leadership characteristics from the perspective of the employee and identified twelve leadership characteristics positively associated with employee performance. These characteristics were empirically derived using factorial analysis applications and reliability procedures, with subsequent validation with field observations. His research identified the characteristics of leaders who enabled their subordinates to provide quality work for their customers on the job. He termed his typology "the customer-oriented leader." He identified characteristics of supervisors that excite the intrinsic ability of employees to perform quality work. Further work with the data resulted in an added dimension that was not independent of the twelve factors, but measured the leader as a "team builder." It would also be used in his measurement of leadership abilities in PPS.

Subsequent analyses of the twelve factors of leadership revealed them to fit into three major categories. A description of the dimensions associated with the customer-oriented leader are presented in what follows.

MISSION ACCOMPLISHMENT BEHAVIORS

Forcefulness of Presence

This includes behavior on the part of the leader that is viewed by the subordinate to be forceful, competitive, commanding, charismatic, visionary, and confrontational when necessary.

When it comes to accomplishing the organizational goals, employees need their supervisor to be decisive and forceful, even to the point of being confrontational, when necessary. Effective leaders make it known what is expected and continuously rally others to get the job done. They are not meek or wimpish. Margaret Thatcher, Jesse Jackson, Robert Dole, and Lloyd Bentsen exhibit "forcefulness."

Jim Flaggert of the DS: An Example of Excellence in Forcefulness

Jim Flaggert joined the DS team after PPS was well under way. He joined the team in a senior management position. Whenever that happens, there is animosity and resistance to such a new person by some of those in the old guard who aspired to the position that the new member has assumed. Jim assumed the role of director of training in DS. Soon, he initiated a variety of training programs, including the Job Proficiency Guide (JPG) system, which he presents in the Appendix of this text. For him, the JPG was the right thing to do. Yet to others throughout DS, when first hearing about his proposal, it was another foolish approach. Jim stayed with the task. He kept with the idea and commitment to demonstrate the JPG system was right for the new approach to quality. Within a year, Jim's JPG program was truly endorsed throughout the system. It not only demonstrated itself to be a viable development tool for PPS, but it was subsequently adopted throughout the Air Force Logistics Command. Jim Flaggert's forcefulness was critical to serving his customer as a leader. As a result of Jim's excellent work, he was subsequently promoted to head the Center-wide Human Resources University at MCAFB.

Dependability

Good time management, punctuality, and responsibility are characteristic of leaders who score high in this dimension. Employees need their supervisors to be dependable. Such leaders get back to their subordinates on time, as promised, and consistently. When they fail to demonstrate dependability, it gives a clear signal that the employees' work is less important to the supervisor than other things. It places a lowered priority on the work of the employees themselves. It communicates the message, "I don't care so much about this," and may lead to employee disappointment and discouragement. During the Iraqi occupation of Kuwait, for the Iraqi soldiers at the front lines who failed to get food and water and basic supplies, their leader, Saddam Hussein was not thought to be dependable.

Colonel David Naehring of DS: An Example of Excellence in Dependability

Colonel David Naehring, the Director of DS, demonstrated excellence in dependability. Without fanfare, without reminding, he constantly demonstrated follow-through with his commitments to his teams and the individuals both above and below him in the organizational hierarchy whom he viewed to be his customers. During the three-year life of the PPS program, prior to reorganization and the handoff to new project leadership, Col. Naehring had exceptional demands on his time. Yet, even in those tough and turbulent times, he continued to get back, to follow through, and to deliver on his commitments made to others, no matter what their station was in the system—hourly/salaried; military/civilian; supervisor/nonsupervisor; male/female; general or airman. A handshake with him was equivalent to a binding contract—he delivered.

Industriousness

Willingness to work hard, to make personal sacrifice for the job, and to work longer hours than most are examples of this dimension.

Leaders just don't show up, they model industriousness, the will to go beyond expectation to get the job done, consistently. They inspire their people through their own hard work and effort. Secretary of State James Baker models industriousness very well. When the United Nations Security Council support was needed to help America and its allies drive Iraq out of Kuwait, Secretary Baker traveled tirelessly around the world, meeting with heads of state of other nations to obtain their support for a U.N. resolution against Iraq. Since Operation Desert Storm, Baker continued to rally support for a Middle East peace process.

Contrarily, during the Iraqi invasion of Kuwait and the United States's initial involvement in that crisis, President George Bush remained on vacation at his home in Kennebunkport. Although his was not a real vacation, the "appearance" that he was there just fishing and golfing when the rest of the nation was asked to get behind the buildup in Saudi Arabia tended to reduce Bush's leadership. At that time, the appearance of his not working "turned off" some of the people in America. Later, President Bush reversed that misperception about his lack of industriousness with his absolute forcefulness and resolve to free Kuwait, which he did. He demonstrated excellence in industriousness and the next dimension of leadership, authoritativeness.

Ed Slover and Eileen Smith of DS: Examples of Excellence in Industriousness

Ed Slover and Eileen Smith are two leaders in DS who demonstrate industriousness. They willingly do what they ask members of their own teams to do.

Ed Slover has a "can-do" attitude about his work and the work of his team. He voluntarily puts in long hours to get the job done, and it is not uncommon for him to come in over the weekend on his own time if members of his team are asked to work overtime on a given mission. He doesn't "have" to work, he "gets" to work, and that attitude has earned him a good reputation as a leader among those who work for him. Working on his team is like playing in a ball game—from his viewpoint, everyday is another opportunity to go beyond expectation on the job and win through service to his team's customers.

Eileen Smith loves her work. She was one of the very first supervisors to truly demonstrate enthusiasm about the new approach to leadership where her employees were to be considered as valuable customers; she was to "delight" them while enabling them to perform better than ever before. During the project life, several major changes in technology were introduced. These major innovations required massive systems' redesign and extraordinary effort to address the needs of people having to face change. Eileen seemed to always be on the transition team in charge of major new approaches being introduced. She had an incredible capacity for work.

She started at the bottom of the organization many years ago. Today, she is the highest ranking female in the DS system. She is also a widely respected leader, and she has strong support of those within her leadership realm. She is an example of industriousness excellence. Like Ed Slover, she never asks others to do what she wouldn't first do herself.

Authoritativeness

Making decisions in an open, credible manner, involving others and getting the facts before making a decision, and respect for one's ability to lead are examples of this characteristic.

A supervisor's employees need to think the supervisor knows the business and makes sound decisions. If a leader is perceived to be technically unqualified and ill-informed, he or she will score low here. When ill-informed decisions are made by leaders, the employees who have to implement such decisions will do so half heartedly, as they know the decisions to be unsound. This was a major strategy with the U.S. led worldwide condemnation of Saddam Hussein following the Kuwait invasion. If the people in Iraq lost confidence in their leadership, they would not support the leader.

Secretary of Defense, Richard B. Cheney, distinguished himself as an authoritative leader during Operation Desert Storm, as did General Colin L. Powell and General H. Norman Schwarzkopf. These leaders appeared to know what they were talking about in terms of the war.

Janet Aguilar and Kay Abel of DS: Examples of Excellence in Authoritativeness

Both Janet Aguilar and Kay Abel are very knowledgeable of the fields in which they lead. They are viewed as expert consultants by the people who work for them. Rather than telling their people what to do, they manage their people in such a way that the people consult with them, willingly seek their guidance, ideas, and recommendations. Both of these excellent leaders have credibility through their having had experience in the workplace, their expert knowledge, and willingness to learn from their people. Unlike some experts who are one-way information givers, Janet and Kay are information processors with the people with whom they work.

EMPOWERMENT BEHAVIORS

Calming Influence and Attentiveness

Keeping one's head when those around him or her have lost theirs exemplifies this quality of leadership. This dimension identifies the extent to which a leader is relaxed, listens attentively to others, and responds to situations in a reasonable and assuring manner.

Supervisors need to listen to their people so they can learn about the things that are in the way of their subordinates doing their jobs. Supervisors who listen enable their employees to become engaged in the problem-solving process that is essential between coach and player. When supervisors take time to listen without getting "wired up" themselves, they "calm the waters" for their employees and, by doing so, enable the employees to gain control of the situation that has unsettled them or made them feel fear.

When leaders get unnerved by the information brought to them by their own employees, it excites the employees; they become threatened and, by doing so, become fearful. Fearful people don't take risks; they fail to go beyond expectation because they may face retribution. Leaders need to give their people time to express their concerns without the supervisor getting overly involved in the situation. Such leaders are calm when others are losing their heads. Great spiritual leaders such as Jesus and Mahatma Gandhi tend to be excellent examples of this leadership characteristic.

Glen Berlo and Patty Ingram of DS: Examples of Excellence in Calming Influence

Glen Berlo is a DS manager with extraordinary patience and interest in other people. He is the type of leader people feel they can come to when there is a problem. What makes Glen so exceptional when compared to others is that he does not come to quick conclusions or judgments about the situation being presented to him by others. He looks people in the eye, shows genuine concern (as though he is truly trusting of the person talking to him), and takes time to let the person give the whole story. He is more than a listener; he calms the situation and builds confidence in the other as he listens. He does not let the other's emotions become his own.

Patty Ingram is a supervisor in DST. She has an exceptional ability to listen to others as though they were saying something very important and she wanted to understand because she values their viewpoints. In the TPTB workshops, she consistently demonstrated an ability to listen to the members of her team as well as to her internal customers and suppliers.

Patty is quiet, yet she is strong. She never needs to say, "I understand," for her taking time to listen and respond back in her own words tells the other person she understands. She is a model of excellence in attentiveness and calming influence for others who may be unnerved by their own situations when coming to her to talk.

Delegation

This dimension identifies the extent to which a leader assigns work and leaves the subordinate alone to do the job. Through the practice of delegation, leaders enable the individuals and teams reporting to them to share responsibility with them for getting the job done.

Customer-oriented leaders delegate both authority and accountability, and, by doing so, demonstrate the trust and respect that encourages greatness in others. They avoid the temptation to overrule their subordinates by insisting that their subordinates apply the leader's own idiosyncratic choices of style or preference. They give their people room to take responsibility and to assume ownership of their own work. Rather than focusing on the process of work performance, quality-driven leaders join with their people to get results. They do not "micromanage" their employees.

"Give a man a fish and he eats for a day, but teach a man to fish and he eats for the rest of his life," depicts another important leadership behavior. Your people need you to give them room to learn and be held responsible to do their part of the work process. When you micromanage, your people react by becoming less responsible and more dependent—just the opposite of what you want them to be.

Frank Mason of the DS: An Example of Excellence in Delegation

Frank Mason believes in his people. During the first three years of PPS, Frank headed two different divisions—DSF and DSM. In both leadership situations, he distinguished himself by gaining the respect of his people while the organizations that he directed improved their performance.

Frank has an unflinching belief that experienced members of the work force basically know how to do the job and want to do a good job if treated as though that were true. Under his leadership emerged the team-building consultants positions that placed a lot of responsibility on hourly worker-type employees who, in the classic, efficiency-oriented system of the past, were not trusted to do their work unless controlled by a supervisor armed with sanctions to exercise when they did something wrong. Also, unless proven wrong by the group itself, he believed the members of a group, having common goals and a sense of professionalism, would be capable of self-management.

Under the leadership of Frank Mason, the experiment in self-managed work groups in DS was initiated. He didn't just permit them, he encouraged them. He facilitated them; he did not supervise them. As a representative from management working with the AFGE labor union, both he and the union were able to foster a working relationship that proved to be more of a partnership than the adversarial relationship that had been the case in the past. Frank Mason is one of many leaders in the DS who demonstrated excellence in delegation and as a result was able to increase performance and enable the organization to move further toward the quality approach.

Followership

Leaders are followers, too. A leader scoring high here would tend to communicate enthusiasm for the organization, its policies, and its leadership, and demonstrate pride and personal accountability to his or her own leadership. Followership does not mean "blind obedience" to a corrupt leader or system. Rather, this dimension of empowerment captures the extent to which the leader communicates respect for the very leadership and organization that the subordinate feels obliged to serve.

Leaders have three key roles: They lead others; they serve on a team with their peers; and they follow their own leaders. This category is a measure of their followership on their own leader's team. Good leaders model followership behavior toward their own leaders. They are advocates of their own supervisors' goals and objectives. They constantly demonstrate loyalty and pride toward their own organization. When leaders fail as followers, when they are not on their own leader's team, it creates a sense of hopelessness among their own subordinates.

Leaders who demonstrate poor followership are perceived by their subordinates to be undermining the system that the subordinates want to serve. Such leaders do not constructively confront issues with their own management. Rather, they "whisper" or "rumor" about them to their own subordinates. Such behavior takes away the empowering effect that comes with hope in the people who work for such leaders. When a leader demonstrates his or her support for the goals of the organization, and respect for his or her own boss, it excites the loyalty and pride of those who work for such a leader. It inspires people to take risks and to pitch in wherever needed because such service to the organization is merited.

People would rather work for leaders having positive followership characteristics like the late Hubert Humphrey who was always positive about America and the value of his own leadership, Congress, and the courts. He looked at the American system and called it "good." They do not like working for leaders who are on a constant search to find fault with their own immediate supervisors and then campaign to get their employees involved in the fracas. When leaders do not respect the system they are paid to serve, they can choose to work constructively to change it, as did co-author Nelson with his development of PPS, or they can opt to get out of the system and create their own following with regard to any system they want to propose, for example, George Washington. However, when one works for an organization, takes pay to support its purposes, and is in charge of others who are loyal to the organization's purposes, such a leader's subordinates would prefer their leader to assume a positive, trustworthy attitude toward the system. It is more difficult for employees to give their best toward customer service when their own leader is trying to undermine their system through bad talk.

Colene Krum of DS: An Example of Excellence in Followership

Colene Krum is a member of the PPS design team. She was there from the start. Although the very nature of the project challenged management's way of doing things (the efficiency-oriented approach), Colene conducted herself in such a way as to communicate pride in the organization and the people in leadership positions there.

As the major contact person between the outside team-building consultant (Gilbert) and the leadership of DS and PPS, Colene was the organization's translator. She was the person who had to make the changes, give the briefings, and follow up when others had failed. When others had dropped the ball, she was the one who picked it up and carried it. In doing so, she received support from others in what was to take place. She championed her leadership and the PPS effort, rather than heralding others' "blemishes" or misdeeds. Had it not been for her, the team-building efforts reported in Chapters 8 and 9 would not have been accomplished. She played a vital role in building on the strengths of the organizational policies and people that were to be enhanced through team building. Her supportive interpretations of others' fears and misgivings with PPS and its invitation for all DS employees to participate as partners (enlarging their roles to get beyond mere participative management) was irreplacable. Her persistent, unshakable positive followership for the organization and her leadership made a major difference in the PPS demonstration.

Straightforwardness

This identifies the extent to which a leader is candid, telling it like it is, and does not get involved in office "game playing."

This relates to the supervisor's level of candor, the extent to which the leader is viewed to be giving straight information so the employee can be in further control of his or her own situation at work. Leaders not rated high here may be more involved in organizational "politics" than others. They may tend to obfuscate information rather than share information with their people, factually and in an open and forthright manner. Harry Truman would probably score high here, whereas Henry VIII's wives would not rate old Henry to have been quite as candid. The first lady, Barbara Bush, seems to be especially excellent in her ability to appear to the American people as being straightforward as does Secretary of Defense, Richard B. Cheney.

Carl McRorie of DS: An Example of Excellence in Straightforwardness

Carl McRorie, the Deputy Director of DS, is straightforward. He is forthright when speaking to others. He tells it like it is rather than masking things in innuendo or metaphor. In the highly charged political environment in which PPS was put to the test, Carl did not once demonstrate self-serving behavior—he did not use the situation to build his own empire even though others in organizations outside DS were building theirs while directly plagiarizing his and his organization's work. With the exception of personnel issues, where he was bound by institutional confidentiality, Carl would speak up forthrightly and tell people what he was observing. He not only failed to engage in interpersonal "game playing," he would not tolerate it. He was respected for his forthright approach. When he differed with others, he generally did so while communicating respect for the other person.

During the first three years of PPS, several times others from within or outside DS would try to undermine Carl—typical bureaucratic power plays. When Carl would hear of it, he did not respond in kind. He addressed the issues without engaging in denigrating speculation or behavior toward those who were doing it to him. Carl's openness enabled people who worked for him to trust that he would tell them the truth. For those under Carl's leadership, his straightforwardness enabled them to have more confidence that the many changes occurring around them would not harm them. It reduced their fear rather than add fuel to their fires of speculation.

RELATIONSHIP BEHAVIORS

Partnership

Included here are characteristics that suggest the leader cares about the subordinate's welfare, tells others about the good qualities of the subordinate, and is sincerely interested in the subordinate as a person. Such a leader demonstrates an interest in the employee's long-term career success.

Leaders scoring high here demonstrate a commitment to the development of each employee on their team. Such leaders behave as partners and coaches for their employees. They are viewed as "sponsors," "advocates," and "ambassadors" of those on their team. This is a critical behavioral characteristic of "customer-oriented" leadership. Leaders and followers do not work well together if they are not on the same team.

John Berger and Gary Thompson of DS: Examples of Excellence in Partnership

During the TPTB sessions, John Berger served as a role model in partnership for other supervisors to observe. Often, supervisors did not know how to listen to their people. They felt as though they would lose control of the situation if the tables were turned and they were to listen to their people and work for them as though the people on their teams were among their most important customers. By watching John work with his team, other supervisors came to understand and respect the power they gain from becoming partners with their team members. For that reason, John was used in the TPTB process as a positive role model for other supervisors to emulate.

John respected the members of his team and worked with them to accomplish their objectives. He took a personal interest in the people in his work unit. He listened to them, he advocated for them, he worked for them.

Gary Thompson's entire career has been spent in DS. He never forgot what it was like to sweep the warehouse floor or uncrate a heavy box, or tear down a row of bins and move them. As a leader in PPS, he developed his ability to treat the people within his unit as his partners. He did not separate himself from them because he had moved further up the organizational ladder than they. When they had a problem, it was his problem, too. He worked behind the scenes to help them overcome the obstacles that were in their way. He demonstrated a personal interest in his people and would speak up and take on policies that would inadvertently demean those who worked the "floor" in DS. As he further practiced his partnership with his employees, they gave more to the system.

Friend

This refers to the extent to which the supervisor and subordinate are personal friends as well as colleagues, which may even include socialization off hours— getting together after work and sharing things with one another's family.

It is a measure of the extent to which a leader takes personal interest in the welfare of his or her employees and their families. It is the quality of relationship that instills extraordinary protective performance toward the leader by the employee or subordinate—even to the extent of an employee giving up his or her own career (or life) to protect the leader.

When a leader is perceived by the worker to be unfriendly, the employee will more likely go the extra mile to sabotage the leader's initiatives. Just as in previous wars, some military leaders were "fragged" (blown up intentionally by their own people) because of the personal animosity the soldiers had for their leaders; so, too, does it happen in our own organizations. Instead of using fragmentary weapons to destroy their leaders, bureaucrats frag their leaders by their deliberate failure to support their supervisors' initiatives.

Ginger Champaigne of DS: An Example of Excellence in the Dimension of Friend

Ginger is not just a supervisor, she is a leader who takes a personal interest in each of her employees. She remembers birthdays, special events, and brings them little things to share her appreciation of them. She doesn't do this because it is what has been suggested in a textbook. She does it because she has a genuine interest in the men and women who work for her—even taking an interest in the children, spouses or significant others outside their immediate families. She doesn't pry into the private lives of her people; she shares life with them—hers and theirs. When Ginger has a need of them, they don't "slow roll" her or complain, they help Ginger out.

Enjoyableness

Sharing humor, having fun together, and keeping good cheer among those with whom one leads are captured in this dimension.

Charles Dickens captured the antithesis of the enjoyable leader in his character,

Scrooge. People don't like to work for a Scrooge, a person who never smiles, is tense, and doesn't share humor with his people. Enjoyable leaders tend to use humor to reduce tension for those who work for them. Their use of humor emotionally bonds them with their subordinates. Leaders who score high in this dimension are thought to be very pleasant and enjoyable to be around.

In the national election for the presidency of the United States, George Bush was able to demonstrate his "enjoyableness," whereas others like Jesse Jackson and Michael Dukakis were not. Even in tough times, leaders can be enjoyable. This was demonstrated by General Colin L. Powell during Operation Desert Storm, the war to free Kuwait. His one liners facilitated America's confidence in him and the military.

Buss Gehring of DS: An Example of Excellence in Enjoyability

Mention the name of Buss Gehring and you generally get a smile from the other person. Whether at a coffee break in the morning or a social event, Buss Gehring's table is never empty—people seek him out to keep them company. He has an ability to cheer others up, especially with his humorous interpretations of events, stories, and jokes. He also invites the humor in others to come out.

When situations have been tense during team-building sessions and Buss was there, he would use his humor to cut through the tension and get to the basic issues in a manner that lubricated the problem-solving process rather than impeded it. Buss's smile and quick mind, and ready recall of funny stories, help to make work more enjoyable for others. Buss was not the office "clown." He demonstrated high industry and commitment to the job. His use of humor, his enjoyableness, provided the people in DS release from tension and new, more positive perspectives about situations confronting them. Buss's humor helped others bond together with him to get the job done.

Organizational Outreach

Getting along with others beyond the work group, networking professionally, and participating in company-sponsored activities are characteristic of leaders who score high in this factor.

Building one's relationships beyond the team is very important. Leaders who have a lot of contacts, those who have a strong professional network, tend to be better able to support their people than those who do not. Employees would rather work for someone who has a good reputation outside the immediate work environment than is either not known or has a poor reputation. Leaders need to have a strong network that brings added strength and reputation to their teams.

John Salas of AFGE: An Example of Excellence in Organizational Outreach

John Salas is President of AFGE Local Union 1857 at Sacramento. He was the chief negotiator for labor in PPS at MCAFB. His outreach is not only basewide, it is nationwide, with management and labor leaders alike, as well as rank-and-file employees. He has sound links to congressional leaders and has built a tight bond with successive leaders of the ALC.

When serious challenges were made to PPS, John Salas was able to build on his excellent network of leaders to continue the support of the program. Without his leadership and the good rapport he has developed with leaders throughout the DOD, OPM, and Congress, the project would not have been demonstrated.

John Salas was willing to risk himself and his local union when he supported PPS in its formulation stage. Today, he continues to be a major architect in continuous improvement of the project.

Team Builder

Although not independent of the twelve other dimensions presented before, a Quartimax factor-analysis procedure did identify an added dimension of leadership—team builder. It includes how the leader works with all others on the team rather than just the subordinate responding to the questionnaire.

There is no one great team builder in PPS; the entire organization has demonstrated excellence in this regard. However, if one were to identify extraordinary performance in enabling the PPS team to work, the American Federation of Government Employees (AFGE) local number 1878 at MCAFB must be recognized for its willingness to not only approve of the PPS experiment, but to take a leadership role in it by promoting and advocating the team approach. The union has attended TPTB sessions and taken leadership roles in enabling the work force to be team players.

Each of the previous leadership characteristics was found to be significantly associated with performance in a national sample of over 1,400 employees by the MEDi research team—the higher the rating on each dimension, the better the subordinates' performance.

ANALYSIS OF CUSTOMER-ORIENTED LEADERSHIP IN PPS, 1988

In 1988, a random sample of 25 percent of the DS work force was confidentially surveyed by Gilbert using MEDi's Leadership Effectiveness Assessment (LEA) in an effort to learn about leadership performance organizationwide (Gilbert, 1988). With the exception of the leadership characteristic termed "organizational outreach," leadership performance on all thirteen dimensions was found to be associated with the subordinates' overall positive rating of their leaders and the employees' productivity. The "organizational outreach" dimension was mildly associated with effectiveness ($p = 0.06$). Thus, the higher the leader's performance on these dimensions, the better the subordinates' morale and performance on the job.

First, the data were analyzed in terms of possible association between the ratings leaders received on the thirteen dimensions and the overall rating of the leader by the subordinates. The leadership dimensions were then rank ordered, comparing one to the others in terms of the strength of association with the subordinates' overall satisfaction with their leadership.

Relative Importance of Each Dimension

The rankings, in terms of strength of association with overall leadership effectiveness from the customer-oriented perspective, were found to be as follows:

 1. Team builder
 2. Partner
 3. Authoritative
 4. Straightforward
 5. Industrious
 6. Calming influence
 7. Enjoyableness
 8. Followership
 9. Forceful
10. Dependable
11. Friend
12. Delegator
13. Organizational outreach

These findings suggested that leaders in PPS who were team builders had partnerships with their people, were authoritative, straightforward, worked hard, and listened to their people, were most effective from the "quality" perspective in PPS. These characteristics were to be encouraged the most throughout the PPS demonstration.

Relative Leader Effectiveness in PPS When Compared to Other Air Force Logisticians

When compared with other MEDi samples of Air Force logistics leaders using the LEA, the PPS leadership scored high in some areas and low in others. Using a pooled analysis of variance statistical procedure and z score conversions, the ratings of the DS leaders were compared to a national sample of government leaders on file with MEDi. The DS leaders were higher than average in enjoyableness (99 percent), straightforwardness (92 percent), calming influence (80 percent), followership (79 percent), authoritative (75 percent), and forceful (71 percent). They were about average in organizational outreach (58 percent), team builder (53 percent), and friend (47 percent). They were below average in industrious (32 percent), partner (29 percent), and dependable (2 percent) (Gilbert, 1988).

For PPS to make a difference, the leadership in DS would have to improve—especially in partnership, as this was a very highly ranked leader characteristic associated with the quality approach and the DS group was relatively low in it. Also, the PPS leadership needed to focus more directly on improving their dependability and industriousness, as well.

Politics Was the Key Leader Behavior Associated with Promotions in the Past System

When the leaders' rates of promotion were analyzed in terms of the leadership ratings the supervisors received from their subordinates, it was revealed that a negative correlation was found between the supervisors' ratings in most of the thirteen leader dimensions analyzed. That is, good leaders from the eyes of their subordinates were being promoted significantly slower than those poor leaders. The only positive relationship identified between the leader's rate of promotion within the DS system and leadership scores was in organizational outreach. When a leader was particularly high in that dimension, the individual would more likely be promoted faster in the old system than others. In other words, the data suggested that the more one "politicked" with others outside his or her immediate work group, the more likely that person would be promoted. This is especially insightful as that same measure of leader effectiveness was the only one of the thirteen measures that was NOT associated with positive subordinate performance.

The MEDi data suggested leaders in the old system were more likely to be promoted based on who they knew rather than their effectiveness in working with their people in teams and in partnership to get the job done. The MEDi data revealed these results were not typical. Rather, they were unique to the DS system that gave rise to PPS.

As a result of these findings, the "Tactical Planning and Team Building" (TPTB) effort became even more important to the overall PPS project, for it intentionally provided the supervisors the opportunity to become better team builders and partners with their people. Thus, partnership, team building, and skills in authoritativeness, listening, and behaving in a more straightforward manner were systematically emphasized during the TPTB efforts that continued for the next two years in PPS. Every supervisor was exposed to the TPTB process at least twice during the PPS demonstration with Gilbert. They learned to behave as partners in problem solving and team performance with their own people and other customers and suppliers with whom their teams interacted.

LEADERSHIP IMPROVEMENTS: A SECOND ASSESSMENT TWO YEARS LATER

Two empirical assessments were conducted regarding change in the quality of leadership in the DS. RAND, the official "evaluator" of PPS, and MEDi each

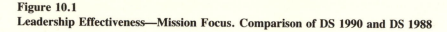

Figure 10.1
Leadership Effectiveness—Mission Focus. Comparison of DS 1990 and DS 1988

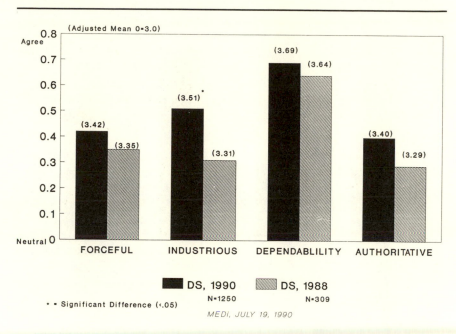

conducted analyses regarding the effectiveness of the leadership within DS. Both RAND and MEDi used employee surveys to gain information about employee attitudes about their work situations and their supervision.

RAND (1990) found the changes in attitude within DS at Sacramento to be significantly improved over attitude changes in like organizations (control groups) at other Air Force Logistics Centers. Specifically, they found the "general supervision and direction," "group functioning," "open-group process," and "satisfaction with supervisor/work unit" to be significantly more improved in DS at the Sacramento ALC than elsewhere.

In 1990, MEDi conducted a second organizationwide survey of employee ratings of their supervisors using the LEA that had been administered to a sample of 25 percent of the DS population two years ago. MEDi's second-year assessment queried all DS employees. It identified improvements in leader performance in DS in each of the thirteen dimensions associated with MEDi's "customer-oriented leader."

Figures 10.1, 10.2, and 10.3 reveal the relative leadership ratings employees in DS assigned their direct supervisors, using the LEA in April 1988 and June 1990. Those dimensions assigned an asterisk indicate a statistically significant difference in scores from 1988 to 1990 based on applications of analysis of variance procedures. In every dimension, the overall subordinates' assessments showed improvement from 1988 to 1990. Note: The RAND analysis linked these improvements with team building being stressed in day-to-day operations, sup-

Figure 10.2
Leadership Effectiveness—Empowerment. Comparison of DS 1990 and DS 1988

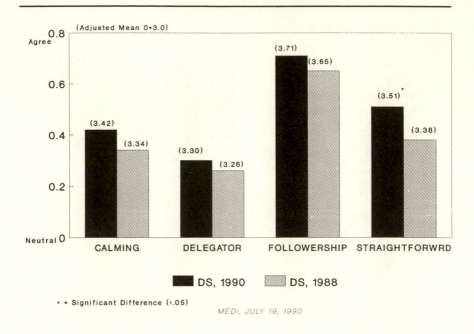

port for team building from the top down, open group process, and co-worker interactions.

Especially high improvements were identified from the first survey MEDi conducted in 1988 and the second survey administered by MEDi in 1990 in "industriousness," "straightforwardness," "partnership," "friend," organizational outreach," and "team builder." Because the first survey targeted "partnership," "friend," and industriousness" as particular leadership weaknesses, and the TPTB program was revised to improve leadership throughout the organization in these areas, the results are particularly important. Such results would seem to support the appropriateness of the organizational development and CSS interventions that had been implemented in PPS for the DS.

At the time the second MEDi survey was administered, practically all of the supervisors and most of the people in their units had been trained in TPTB, the TQM college, and EPM, and were involved in ongoing team-building follow-on efforts.

The leadership within DS experienced substantial gains in making the transformation to the quality approach as a result of the interventions provided it through PPS.

In the next chapter, we will introduce the essential element to the quality approach to doing business—self-initiated followership. This is a unique focus on organizational behavior. It is essential to the quality approach. Every employee

Figure 10.3
Leadership Effectiveness—Relations. Comparison of DS 1990 and DS 1988

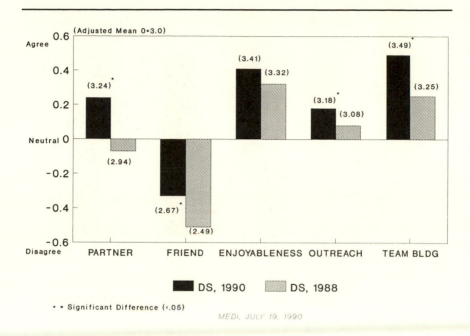

needs to gain followership skills in order to demonstrate customer-oriented behavior.

REFERENCES

Bass, B. M. (1985). *Leadership and Performance Beyond Expectations*. New York: The Free Press.

Bradford, D. L., and Cohen, A. R. (1984). *Managing for Excellence: The Guide to Developing High Performance in Contemporary Organizations*. New York: Wiley.

Fiedler, F. E. (1967). *A Theory of Leadership Effectiveness*. New York: McGraw-Hill.

Gilbert, G. R. (1987). *Leadership Effectiveness Assessment*. Boca Raton, FL: Management Education and Development, Inc.

————. (1988). *Leadership Effectiveness Within the Directorate of Distribution at MCAFB*. Boca Raton, FL: Management Education and Development, Inc.

————. (1990). "How to Be a Customer-Oriented Supervisor." *Government Executive* (February): 54.

Gilbert, G. R., Collins, R. W., and Brenner, R. (1991). "Age and Leadership Effectiveness: From the Perception of the Follower." *Human Resource Management Journal* (August).

Hersey, P., and Blanchard, K. (1982). *Management of Organizational Behavior,* 4th ed. Englewood Cliffs, NJ: Prentice Hall.

RAND Corporation (1990). ''Pacer Share Demonstration Project: Preliminary Second
     Year Results.'' June, Vugraphs –5.
Vroom, V. H., and Jago, A. G. (1974). ''Decision Making as a Social Process: Normative
     and Descriptive Models of Leader Behavior.'' *Decision Sciences 5* (October):
     743–769.

11

Self-Initiated Followership: The Essence of Quality and Customer Service

The quality approach is founded on customer orientation: providing the very best service or product one can deliver to the customer so the customer wins. It means preparing what your customer wants and needs, on time, in support of the customer's schedule. It means follow up to assure the customer succeeds over time and for the long run. It also means never-ending, continuous self-improvement. It means providing the customer with what the customer wants and needs the first time and every time, with minimal error or variance from expectation.

The classic efficiency model of management relies on special "first-class men" (and women) to lead people. In that model, such leaders are the visionaries, the charismatics, the motivators, the best and the brightest, who guide others less able than they to find the way. They are the decision makers and problem solvers.

In the 1980s, American business and government gurus wrote about great leaders and their importance as though they had a romance with the role of leadership itself (Meindl et al., 1985). The flirtation with heroic leaders in the 1980s diverted many observers of organizational behavior from noticing other important aspects of personal and organizational excellence. Many of the most widely published and best-selling books in management were written about leadership of "heroic" proportion. Through them we were introduced to "super" leaders like Lee Iacocca of Chrysler and Donald Trump, a "top-gun" negotiator who, through his deal making, could lead companies to the top. Blanchard and Johnson (1981) boiled the heroic task of the leadership down to sixty seconds of activity through their "one minute manager." Bennis and Nanus (1985) focused management's attention of visionary leadership as a strategy for taking charge. Indeed, great leadership was given extraordinary credit for the success of companies, nations, and teams.

For these and other champions of performance excellence in the 1980s, the visionary leader, able to change his or her style as fluidly as a running back in the National Football League when in open field, had become the "hero" for all in American industry to emulate. "Celebrity-type" leadership makes sense in the classic efficiency model of management where power is heavily placed at the top. As Bradford and Cohen (1984) have so aptly described, heroic leaders are needed by despondent people, people who are not able to think or act for themselves.

But what about the rest of the labor force, the men and women on the floor, in the factory, at the counter, taking the orders as they come in? What are they able to do on their own? Do they really need heroes at the top who are able to modify their leadership styles at the instant the subordinate's behavior calls for it; practice "one minute management" rewards and reprimands at the skip of a misdeed or accomplishment to get those in their work force to do quality work for their customer? No, they do not. Adults placed in jobs for which they are well suited, trained to do the job, given the necessary support in terms of equipment and supplies, and provided the time necessary to communicate with their customers are able to demonstrate excellence in customer behavior on their own.

As long as the responsibility for quality is centered on heroic leadership, the system will fail. For systemwide quality to take place, the responsibility and opportunity for quality must rest with each individual employee. We must put the responsibility squarely in the hands of the employees themselves, give them the support to do the job, and then watch them take the ball for quality (Gilbert, 1990).

THE EMPOWERED EMPLOYEE

In the quality approach, every employee is involved in the design and implementation of excellence in customer care. In such a model, it is the employee on the line, in the production process, in the office operations, and at the counter who is the "hero."

The quality approach assumes the people closest to the process know what the problems are to getting quality to the customer. They have good ideas about how to improve things so they can do their jobs better. They are encouraged to discuss them and be heard by others with whom they work, and they are able to improve things in collaboration with others on their teams. They do not need heroic leaders to solve their problems. They are partners in problem solving with their customers, suppliers, and others on their teams who can help.

But how then do you get employees to take initiative? How do you get them to demonstrate dependability and act with such attentiveness that they will become their customer's choice? To get the responsibility for personal excellence in customer service in the "bellies" of the employee, the employee needs to be given the expectation and encouragement to take command of the situation for the customer on his or her own. Rather than leadership, the emphasis needs to be on followership. That is, dedicating one's self to helping others accomplish their goals, one becomes the winner over the long term, for he or she will be the customer's choice in the future.

SELF-INITIATED FOLLOWERSHIP DEFINED

After many years of research, studying heroes of mythical proportion in a multiplicity of languages and times, crossing multiple cultures, Joseph Campbell (1988) found that heroes and celebrities differ. Like Donald Trump, celebrities make great names for themselves. Such is the way of the celebrity. However, as Bill Moyer reports, Campbell found that true heroes are different. They never distinguish themselves from those they serve. Rather, those whom they serve distinguish them. And this is the case of all heroes of all cultures.

"HHH Airport" in Minneapolis was never named by Hubert H. Humphrey after himself; those he served named it after him. Most every major city in the United States has a Martin Luther King Boulevard. Reverend King did not name those streets after himself; the people named them after him. Though great leaders, both Humphrey and King were exceptional followers. They were of service to others.

The practice of followership does not require celebrity status. Each individual has the opportunity to practice it with every contact they have with others whom they would term their "customer." While followership is most commonly identified as the counterpart to leadership, it is more than that. It transcends the role of the leader. It is self-initiated behavior that enables others to reach their own potential and goals.

Followership for the customer does not imply selective interpretation on the part of the employee regarding the definition of one's customer. It means all people in need of the employee's services. It not only means the customer representing the public that is external to the system, it also includes those within the organization who represent other units who have needs of the employee's services. It includes others within the employee's own work team. It also means that your supervisor is your customer, too. There is no room for double standards with regard to this in the system that is dedicated to total quality. Everyone is to be treated as one's customer and merits the very best service one can give. For further explication of followership as it pertains to customer-focused quality service, see Gilbert (1991).

Following over a decade of research, Gilbert identified eight characteristics of outstanding followership behavior on the job. He interviewed thousands of executives, managers and supervisors. He then surveyed 939 supervisors in government and industry to identify key followership behaviors on the job. He identified eight empirically derived dimensions of customer followership, and then, in subsequent research, found the better one demonstrates these behaviors on the job, the more likely the person becomes the customer's choice. These behaviors can be influenced by both the customer and the employee. A "bad" customer (boss, fellow worker, client, patient, or patron) does not necessarily have to negatively affect followership. Even in tough times, a person dedicated to followership excellence can be outstanding. The responsibility for top-followership performance rests in the hands of the employee, not the supervisor, executive, or discourteous patron. (See Gilbert and Hyde, 1988; Gilbert and Whiteside, 1988; Gilbert, 1990.)

When the behaviors are not demonstrated, the employee fails his or her customer. Here are the eight characteristics of followership behavior that are essential to one's "customer."

Partnership

Quality-oriented followers create a partnership relationship with their customers and suppliers. They assimilate the goals and objectives of their customers as though they were their own. They demonstrate loyalty to the customer. They build their customer up, not tear them down. They are their customer's ambassador and business agent.

Many employees (like the young lady discussed in Chapter 8, who said aloud at the start of a team-building session that her boss was a "paranoid schizophrenic who needed long-term care") have not envisioned themselves to view their supervisors as though they were their customers. They have not learned to demonstrate partnership behaviors for their own leaders. It is because they were not sufficiently empowered in their own organization to assume the responsibility of a partner with those in the organizational hierarchy.

Joe Prater of DS, An Example of Excellence in Partnership

When Joe Prater, a trucker, was required to attend his first "Tactical Planning and Team Building" session, he was reluctant (see his personal story in the Appendixes). After having had nine years experience in the old DS system, he was leery of anything "new" management had in mind for him. He had attended training in the past and, like many others in DS, had found it to be a waste of time. Being forced to attend, he sat through the first day with Lee Tefetiller, the lead worker in his work unit, and others in his group. Soon Joe became hooked on the process and the invitation to become more customer-oriented. Both Lee and Joe demonstrated exceptional ability to provide quality through their own team play and service to their customers. Soon management began to take notice of the excellent things Lee and Joe and other members of their team were doing. They were "behaving" the quality model.

Both Lee and Joe were called upon to tell other managers and other work units about their approach to actually making team building work back on the job. Joe was careful not to upstage Lee. When speaking before top-level managers and influential outsiders who were desperate to have a Joe Prater-type on their own teams, he gave Lee the credit for being the team leader and Lee had earned the credit Joe gave him. Joe's demonstration of partnership with Lee continues today. First, Lee became a team-building consultant and later Joe joined the consultant team in PPS. Lee's being given the chance first was the way Joe wanted it, because for Joe, Lee was his lead man, and Joe was a member of Lee's team.

Motivation

The behavior identified here is about one's attitude toward doing the work, providing the service that is needed by the customer. A person rated high in this characteristic of self-initiated followership would have a "can-do" attitude and demonstrate enthusiasm when undertaking the tasks associated with providing the service. When people reflect high motivation, they are generally valued more by their customer.

Some people on the job nag about the work they do. They take their work for granted. This is especially true when working in a classic, efficiency-oriented system where the problem solving and decision making are done by management FOR the employees. Over time, some employees learn to demonstrate a negative attitude about work, they slow their walk, they work to get by rather than to delight their customers. Those who are eager to do the work for their customers are most prized and respected. As one's supervisor is a "customer," it is important to demonstrate high motivation about the work that one does as an extension of the supervisor's work effort.

Princess Putney of DS, An Example of Excellence in Motivation

Princess Putney worked as a packer in the warehouse. A single parent solely responsible to raise five children on her own, she had her hands full. However, she volunteered to participate in every event that offered her a chance to be of assistance to others and to further the quality approach in PPS. When an educational video tape was needed by management for the purposes of educating others with whom she worked, Princess volunteered to do the job. She worked beyond normal working hours for days on end without any demands for added compensation. Her contributions to the quality approach soon were so widely recognized that she was selected by her management to become an in-house team-building consultant.

In her division, DST, she was the only team consultant, whereas some other organizations had five or more. Clearly, she had an overload of work. She could have built a good case for herself regarding management's "unfair practices" toward her. However, she never complained about the excessive work load, for she viewed her work to be an opportunity, and she appreciated the opportunity her tremendous work load offered her to be of assistance to others. Princess Putney demonstrated motivation as a follower for her customers in DST. Because of her enthusiasm for getting the job done, she has been called upon by her management to consult with other organizations beyond DS who are attempting to jump-start their own team-building efforts.

Technical Competence

It is not enough to be able to perform your work, but to be a quality worker, one must be eager to master new skills and acquire knowledge to remain an expert in the eyes of the customer. Persons who rate high in technical competence would be viewed to be especially able in the field in which they work—they would be perceived to know their business. They would be regarded as a "consultant" in terms of the type of work they do.

To do the job for the customer, one needs to be able to do the job right the first time and not have to delay the customer by costly rework. Supervisors value employees who know their stuff and can be counted on to do the job right and to be a coach to others on the team.

Jim Rollins of DS, An Example of Excellence in Technical Competence

Jim Rollins is a quiet man. He is not likely to be noticed first when one walks into a room. He does not push himself on others. However, he is on constant alert to learn about new ways to do things so he can lend technical assistance to his team and organization. When the in-house team-building consultant role was first developed in DSF, Jim put together a computerized system to track the commitments made of every individual and group (team-building stage 10, Chapter 8). He then took responsibility to track performance and remind people what they had obligated themselves to do. He didn't use his superior technical skills to upstage others. Rather, he used his technical skills to enable others to accomplish their goals. Jim is an example of a person who, through self-initiated followership, developed his technical competence and used it in PPS to advance quality to the customer.

Dependability

Customers want to be able to count on their supplier to be on time. Dependability is another side of the word "integrity" from the customer's perspective. They can trust those who keep their commitments.

Supervisors value employees who can be counted on to be at work on time, attend meetings, and satisfy their obligations as agreed. A supplier that fails to deliver the goods on time is a supplier that is not valued by the customer. One's obligation to his or her supervisor includes good time management.

Lee Tefertiller of DS, An Example of Excellence in Dependability

Lee's word is his obligation. When he shakes your hand, you know you have a deal. His sense of obligation and dependability resulted in his own self-initiated followup to see that the promises he and others on his team made to their customers through the TPTB program were actually carried out.

Lee keeps a list of things he has committed to do for others and he keeps it up to date as he progressively attends to his promises. When Lee finds himself unable to deliver on a promise, he gets back with the person with whom he is obligated and lets them know about the possible delay in his delivery and solicits the help of others before he finds himself failing to deliver to his customer on time.

When the management in DS was looking for someone to assume the role of an in-house team-building follow-on consultant (see Chapter 9), Lee was among the very first chosen. He has demonstrated an exceptional ability to get the job done. The trust that he has earned from others as a result of his dependability has helped PPS, his customers, and himself.

Professional Comportment

This refers to the manner in which the employee presents himself or herself in terms of manners, dress, courtesy, speech, language, cleanliness, tact, and diplomacy. A waiter who is unkempt can turn the customer off very quickly, just as can a person behind the desk at a motel, hospital, registrar, or reception area. When we work for another, we are an extension of that person's values. It is the obligation of the follower to project respect for the customer's values.

The customer-oriented employee will pay close attention to the values of his or her supervisor, organization as a whole, and external customers. It is the follower's obligation to dress and carry him or herself in such a way as to not excite the prejudice that the customer may have regarding proper conduct. This is a measure of quality performance that is rarely discussed as a performance issue at work. However, it was found to be very important in terms of predicting one's promotability in the DS system.

Barry Monroe of DS, An Example of Professional Comportment Excellence

Barry Monroe, a retired veteran, works for the DSS division director as a secretary. He is widely respected if not just plain revered by others who know him. The reason for his having such respect is the quality of his personal presence.

He dresses in a manner that brings respect to his team. His demeanor on the telephone is always pleasant and communicates he is working for the person on the other end. His tact and diplomacy set the tone for those around him. People look forward to working with him, because they consider him to be highly professional. He builds people up rather than puts them down. His very presence is felt by others attending a meeting with him through the highly professional conduct he displays. Every time he answers the phone in his office, the caller feels his attentiveness and good spirit.

Sense of Humor

Customers value pleasant suppliers. To be customer-oriented, employees need to demonstrate good cheer, smile, and share humor. Notice television commercials. Some are almost entirely humorous. Humor bonds people together. One never shares humor with someone whom he or she is at odds. They may share humor with others about the person, but they do not share humor WITH the person.

Humor makes people feel good. Customers want to feel good, and every employee has the power through his or her humor to give them a shot of happiness at every contact. Also, supervisors, as customers, do not want a "grouch" on the team. Grouches make them feel bad and, as a result, leaders tend to avoid them. On the other hand, people who are enjoyable make leaders feel good. The customer-driven employee is an enjoyable person for his or her supervisors and other customers.

Although not all people are natural comedians, and not all have a good smile, everyone has the opportunity to let his or her customers know they are valued through the sharing of humor.

Brenda Sturdevant of DS, An Example of Excellence in Humor

Brenda Sturdevant is a pleasure! She has a smile that lights up the room. In the three years she worked in the PPS design team, she never failed to give the customer a smile—her smile was contagious. She even delights others by laughing at their jokes when, at times, anyone else would have had to strain to patiently wait for a fizzled punch line. Many a time in the life of the project her good cheer helped keep potentially devastatingly tense situations in check for her customers. By keeping her customers in humor, she enabled them to retain a positive attitude toward managing tough situations. Through her humor, she built teams. When the DS team-builders group chose to put together a short video on quality, they included Brenda as one of about twenty-five employees having star roles. In that video, they capture Brenda at her desk with her best smile. Having people like Brenda around makes life a pleasure for the customer.

Positive Working Relations and Team Play

Some employees are particularly negative about others. They tell their customers about the wrong things people do rather than the right things they do. They "stir the pot" and engage in backstabbing. By doing so, they challenge the confidence their customers have in the service or products they are getting. They cloud the quality of the product by raising issues about the quality of the people doing the work.

Supervisors, as customers, are threatened when employees engage in dysfunctional organizational games with one another. Employees who arouse their insecurities and create tension in others are not highly valued. Sharing the good things with others, being a team player, demonstrates the qualities customers want of their suppliers.

Dalene Clausen of DS, An Example of Excellence in Positive Working Relations with Others

Dalene Clausen, a lead worker who was placed in the position of supervisor without a pay raise and title to accompany it, is a positive problem solver. She helps find the positive in others' needs. She doesn't engage in deciding who is right and who is wrong in conflict situations—be they hers or those of others on her team. When she and her work unit were first involved in TPTB, it became very evident that the members of her team worked very well together. As their leader, she was their role model. Unlike other teams that chose to select someone other than their supervisor for the role of team leader, her team chose Dalene because, as their supervisor, the team members felt that she was on their team.

Near the end of the third project year, Dalene was assigned to become an in-house team-building consultant. At the time of this assignment, she was an unknown. The other members did not know her, and they had formed themselves into a team. Thus, to them, she was an outsider. Yet, only after a month or so, she was elected leader of the in-house team-building consultants by the consultants themselves. In a very short time, she demonstrated her ability to be a positive, affirming force for others. She is especially able to capture the positive qualities in others and to educate others about them.

Speaking Up

At times, the customers may not have all the facts. They need to know what you know about a situation so they do not make a bad decision. They need you to speak up and share what you know so they can remain in control of their situation. Some people are hesitant to speak up to their customers and let them know that they are about to make a mistake. When you withhold information from your customer, you are failing that customer at the same time.

As the employee's customer, supervisors value those who speak up and keep them in control of their work situations. When speaking up, it is important that you do so without creating fear or insecurity for the customer. A lot of employees do not know that they threaten their supervisors when they speak up in a manner that is aggressive or if they withhold information. Employees need to speak up and educate their supervisors with as much respect as they would expect of a first-rate waiter in a restaurant when they are about to order a meal that is not really that good.

Don Harlan of DS, An Example of Excellence in Speaking Up

Don Harlan is a manager within DS. He, like all other supervisors in PPS, attended the TPTB sessions. Don was not comfortable with one approach the TPTB workshop facilitator had been taking. Don called the workshop facilitator and asked if the two could sit down and discuss his concerns.

In a comfortable setting, Harlan presented his concerns, and, as a result, the facilitator was able to adjust his program to make it more effective for all future supervisors and their teams who would attend the TPTB workshops. The difference between Harlan and the other individuals who felt uncomfortable with the same process is that Harlan spoke up and shared his information in such a way that it invited creative problem solving and continued team play between he and the facilitator. It seems others had concerns like Harlan, but didn't share it with the person who could best use it. Harlan did.

Don Harlan demonstrated the ability to speak up in order to keep another in control of the situation. Following that initial review of his concerns, Don continued to share his ideas with the facilitator, and, as a result, the facilitator was able to improve his service to Harlan and the rest of the DS organization. To be forthcoming and direct with another is a key followership characteristic. And when so doing, it is also critical that it be done in a manner that builds on the partnership with the other without inviting the other to feel the need to be defensive or protective personally.

FOLLOWERSHIP AND PPS

Early in the second program year, a survey was taken to determine the level of followership within DS. In 1989, 497 randomly sampled employees were rated by their supervisors using MEDi's Followership Effectiveness Assessment (FEA) (Gilbert, 1987). About one-third of the organization had already been involved in followership training.

When compared to a sample of employees in all other AFLC organizations, the DS employees tended to rate better in followership in six of eight categories. They were especially higher than their AFLC counterparts in positive working relations, partnership, motivation, and speaking up. They were considerably lower than their counterparts in dependability; their supervisors were also found to be lower in this dimension of followership.

Analyses by MEDi determined the followership dimensions discussed before were directly associated with "best" performers in DS. The MEDi study revealed stronger association between measured followership performance and the actual job performance than past performance appraisal ratings and actual job performance. In fact, some employees who were rated to be extremely low in true job performance followership had correspondingly been given exceptionally high numerical ratings on their performance appraisals by the same supervisors (Gilbert, 1989).

Such inconsistencies in supervisors' ratings of their people were found to make sense in terms of the old CSS, which Nelson describes in Chapter 3. In the old system, the employee having had such high performance ratings would be eligible for promotion (and relocation—the real objective of the unsatisfied supervisor). Thus, the old system with its practice of performance appraisal was not found to be as good a predictor of the high performers in DS as the developmentally oriented FEA, which identified comparative strengths and weaknesses of subordinates in eight key dimensions of customer-oriented behavior.

The ratings individuals received in past performance appraisals were not considered by the employees themselves to be valid indicators of employee performance. Most employees and supervisors understood the game that went on with their use. In addition to inflating scores to move someone out of a supervisor's unit, the ratings attributed to a subordinate by the supervisor in the former appraisal system would also be based on whose time had come up for an extra special rating. High ratings would sometimes justify added pay or promotion to another step increase in the old system. Even though an employee may have merited an outstanding rating, it may not have been that employee's turn to get a high rating. It seems the supervisors had to work within an unstated, but real, quota system that detailed the number of outstanding ratings they could give to their employees. They were obliged to adhere to such quotas, and they did. Everyone knew the unspoken game in the old system. Like other things in their bureaucratic workplace, although they didn't like the practice, they lived with it, however dishonest it was.

The information about the weak association between performance appraisal and true perception about employee performance on the part of the supervisor tended to support the PPS assumption that performance appraisals were more disruptive than helpful and merited their suspension. If the association between numerical performance ratings and actual perceived ratings of employees by their supervisors is as weak in other federal agencies as was found to be the case in DS, a substantial waste of resources, time, and effort exists within the present performance-appraisal system in the federal government and merits correction.

At the time of the organizationwide followership survey in DS, the DS organization consisted of the office of the director and five other divisions. Three of the five divisions were involved in direct services or production-type work. Two others were involved in more specialized staff-services-type work. Consistently, the two divisions involved in staff services scored lower than those involved in production. The application of statistical procedures revealed the differences found to be highly significant. In the case of positive working relations, the staff organization responsible for quality assurance in the traditional organization not only was significantly lower than other DS organizations, the employees in that organization were rated below the neutral point in terms of their working in a positive manner together. In that organization, the supervisors tended to disagree with the statements suggesting the employees worked well together as a team.

As a result of the findings from the survey, greater emphasis was placed on self-initiated followership at every level in the organization. Followership became a household word in the PPS lexicon. The TPTB program was modified to place greater emphasis on it as a concept and job performance skill.

Followership as the Key to the Transformation to the Quality Approach

Key to the success of PPS would be the ability of the entire work force to view others as their own customers, to become dedicated to customer service, and to demonstrate self-initiated followership at every level. Also, heroic behavior would have to be redefined from superhuman, first-class leaders to individuals and groups that go beyond expectation on the job for their customers.

Every employee in DS was trained by the outside consultant in self-initiated followership. Each employee received the same "treatment" in skill development. He or she came to understand the same language and cultural role expectations regarding customer service and the opportunity to excel regardless of others or the system. Through TPTB, all employees were given the opportunity to hear from their customers (including their supervisors and subordinates) and respond in a manner that enabled their customers to further accomplish their goals and objectives. Also, all employees in DS were given the opportunity to be treated by their fellow workers and supervisors as customers and to experience the power that comes from practicing followership. As the program moved forward, as time went by, the practice of followership began to take hold. Individuals and small work groups began to initiate more positive service to others. Work groups began to demonstrate their ability to be self-managed.

Misgivings About Followership

To assume a positive followership role, one needs to believe that he or she has something of value to give. Some workers were so despondent, they had given up hope to such an extent that they no longer recognized the value they had to offer others. To them, they chose to keep the focus on others, especially management and their supervisors, regarding what others were not doing rather than assume responsibility themselves. For many in DS, followership behavior was never independent of the customer. If the customer did not live up to one's rules, then the employee would not be helpful. This way of thinking, though understandable, has no place in the quality approach. Top followership behavior can become so strong that it can be practiced *independently* of the customer's behavior.

The term followership tends to indicate a passive, compliant role—as though a person is inferior or nonassertive. However, as people were educated in it, as they were given the opportunity to experiment with it, and to behave it, they generally learned to like it. It brought respect to them from others as well as from themselves—self-respect.

Followership began to be recognized for what it is—a gift to others. As people began to give one another the gifts of service and respect, they began to be more concerned and dedicated to quality. It was a driving force behind the success of PPS. Without it, sustained customer-oriented behavior could not be realized.

In the TPTB program, each employee was given the opportunity to demonstrate customer-oriented followership to others having needs of them. When individuals undertook the role of the follower for the customer through their own self-initiation, "magic" occurred. They gave of themselves to satisfy the needs of their customers. As a result, cooperation and collaboration began to become contagious. As evidenced by the RAND Corporation findings, DS had made more positive strides at team play than employees in comparison groups throughout the AFLC who had not been given the followership training or invitation to practice it with their supervisors and counterparts (RAND, 1990).

SUMMARY

Followership is an assertive, self-affirming behavior that is essential to customer service and the quality approach. It is something that management can encourage but can only occur from one's own intrinsic will to act.

The next chapter introduces two training and development efforts that emerged organically following the development of PPS. The DS organization created its own college and its own division to enhance the skill levels and general competence of its work force.

REFERENCES

Bennis, W., and Nanus, B. (1985). *Leaders: The Strategies for Taking Charge*. New York: Harper and Row.

Blanchard, K., and Johnson, S. (1981). *The One Minute Manager*. New York: Morrow.

Bradford, D. L., and Cohen, A. R. (1984). *Managing for Excellence: The Guide to Developing High Performance in Contemporary Organizations*. New York: Wiley.

Campbell, J., with Moyers, B. (1988). *The Power of Myth*. New York: Doubleday.

Gilbert, G. R. (1987). *Followership Effectiveness Assessment*. Boca Raton, FL: Management Education and Development, Inc.

Gilbert, G. R. (1989). *Managing for Quality in the Directorate of Distribution, McClellan Air Force Base: A Review of Quality Practices and Followership Performance in the Directorate*. Boca Raton, FL: Management Education and Development, Inc.

Gilbert, G. R. (1990). "Effective Leaders Must be Good Followers Too." *Government Executive* (June): 58.

Gilbert, G. R. (1990). "Jump-Start Your Team For Quality," *Government Executive* (November): 54.

Gilbert, G. R. (1991). *The TQS Factor and You: Learn to Lead Yourself, Manage Your Boss, Delight Your Customer*. Boca Raton, FL: Business Performance Publications.

Gilbert, G. R., and Hyde, A. C. (1988). "Followership and the Federal Worker." *Public Administration Review* 48 (November–December): 962–968.

Gilbert, G. R., and Whiteside, C. W. (1988). "Performance Appraisal and Followership: An Analysis of the Officer on the Boss/Subordinate Team." *Journal of Police Science and Administration* 16 (1): 39–40.

Meindl, J. R., Ehrlich, S. B., and Dukerich, J. M. (1985). "The Romance of Leadership." *Administrative Science Quarterly* 30 (March): 49–52.

RAND Corporation (1990). "Pacer Share Demonstration Project: Preliminary Second Year Results." June, Vugraphs −5.

12

Essential Process Management

INTRODUCTION

The purpose of this chapter is to provide an overview of structured process analysis and statistical process-control techniques that were applied in PPS. They are technical problem-solving tools most commonly associated with TQM. However, we have attempted to present them as an overview and in nontechnical language. Note: For a more in-depth understanding of the material covered here, the interested reader can refer to DeMarco (1978), Yourdon (1975), Yourdon and Constantine (1976), McMenamin and Palmer (1984), and Ishikawa (1986).

Essential Process Management (EPM): The Beginnings

One of the most difficult problems confronting any organization moving into the new quality model is that of analyzing its current operations and processes. Over the years, many organizations have attempted to do this using existing tools. These tools, especially in the world of process flow charting, have frequently centered on the use of the American National Standards Institute (ANSI) flow charting techniques. Such flow-charting techniques attempt to model how a current process operates or how a future process might be designed to improve that operation. However, they are too simplistic.

In the early 1970s, a movement began in the field of data automation that was to change all such process analyses. This was the move to structured systems analysis and design. Pioneered by such people as Ed Yourdon (1975) and Tom DeMarco (1978), and many others in this country, they developed a means of analyzing a process that would serve to revolutionize computer design and implementation. These were the tools that came to be known as the tools of structured analysis and design.

In the mid- and late 1970s, co-author Nelson was introduced to them as he served as program integration chief for the design of a major computer system being developed by the U.S. Air Force for one of its allies. By the early 1980s, during the implementation of the first Quality Circle movement at Sacramento, Nelson and the DS Quality Circle facilitators began to expand the use of the analysis technique to allow teams to analyze and improve every aspect of their operations.

It was during this time that the process came to be called Essential Process Management (EPM). This name was derived not only from the structured technique work of the early pioneers like DeMarco, but especially through the follow-on work of McMenamin and Palmer (1984) in their landmark work in essential analysis. McMenamin and Palmer noted that the basis for difficulty, and lack of consistency in any system (which we now equate to variance or a lack of quality), was due to not understanding the "essence" of a system.

Putting this in slightly different language, and giving an example of what we mean, let us examine a situation that is common to all walks of life: the delivery of groceries to a home. Given the ideal world, that of a perfect technology, we might envision the following:

1. It is morning. The customer/consumer opens the refrigerator and takes the container of milk from the refrigerator.

2. Finishing the milk that is in the container, the customer/consumer discards the milk container in the trash.

3. That discarding, coupled with the non-replacement of the container in the refrigerator, sends an electronic signal to the dairy that tells the dairy that the customer is in need of more milk.

4. By using "matter transmission," a new container of milk "appears" in the refrigerator of the customer/consumer.

This would be a perfect technology, with the consumer never having to take any other action. This would be the essence of the replacement of foodstuffs for the customer/consumer and could be envisioned to include all necessary foodstuffs. However, we do not have a perfect technology, and, further, because we have a need for the exchange of finances, transportation, advertising, and the like, the essential system is not present. The need is the same, that is, the need to replace milk, but given the existing sociopolitical structure and existing technology, many, many other steps are going to be required; one example might be:

1. On finishing the milk, the customer/consumer must add milk to the shopping list (if it can be found).

2. The consumer with the shopping list must be taken by some means of transportation to the local shopping point, be it store, supermarket, or whatever.

3. The consumer must physically locate the milk in the shopping center and take it to a checkout counter.

4. On checking out the milk, the customer/consumer will be involved in a financial transaction for the payment of that milk.

5. The customer/consumer must again attain some means of transportation to return the milk to the home to be placed in the refrigerator for subsequent use.

Of course, there are all types of other spin-offs from this. If that method of transportation involves a car, we are involved with the purchase, refueling, and maintenance of the vehicle, its safeguarding during the night, the necessity for a parking place or a driveway or a garage, etc., ad infinitum.

Thus, because we do not have the perfect technology in place, we see a tremendous escalation in the steps and complexity required to bring milk to the home for the use of the customer/consumer.

The problem lies in this: at a given point in time, a decision was made by the customer/consumer to choose a specific means to move to the point of purchase, to pay for the purchase, and to return the purchase to the home. That time-bound decision involved the choices of certain technologies (e.g., a car, a bus, a bicycle) and the choice of certain sociopolitical means to record information on a shopping list (on paper or on a computer), to transport himself or herself to the shopping location, to combine or not to combine that trip with the purchase of other materials, to the sociopolitical decision of the means and manner of payment (check, cash, credit card, etc.) and all of the other things that the reader can envision surrounding that.

Quality problems can become readily apparent when we realize that the insertion of every single additional technology and sociopolitical step has the possibility of error. These additions multiply radically across the system and thereby enhance the probability of error. Further, the addition of every technological choice and concurrent sociopolitical factors increases the complexity of the operation, and increases its cost. This is a radically different view of systems than is presented in conventional systems analysis. It is much more complex and dynamic.

EPM is a view of a system that encompasses not only the normally analyzed and documented inputs and outputs, but also accounts for the sociopolitical, that is, the human side, and the technological inputs and outputs. Additionally, it acknowledges that every process/system has sociopolitical and technological impacts on the surrounding environment. It begins to meet the criterion of Deming in his writings on profound knowledge, because it gives recognition to a system wherein the interrelationships between the various facets of any one single process and/or system with all other processes and systems are identified and documented.

EPM entails three phases of analysis. The first phase of EPM is known as Essential Process Analysis (EPA).

It makes use of only four graphic symbols to illustrate the total complexity of a system. (When these four are compared to the use of sixteen-plus symbols in conventional ANSI flow chart analysis, they are absolutely simple:)

1. Rectangles that identify those elements of the overall system that we do not intend to analyze. These rectangles stand for external suppliers and external customers of the system.

2. Circles, sometimes referred to as bubbles, that identify the system processes, that is, the processes that turn inputs into outputs.

3. Arrows that are used to show the flow of whatever is moving in the system, both external and internal to the system.

4. Straight lines that are used to symbolize "resting places" in the system. These can symbolize anything from a warehouse used for storage to a computer memory bank used to store information. By storage, we refer to a place where anything is waiting/pausing for future processing and/or use by the system under analysis.

For further detailed writings on this, the reader is referred to the works of McMenamin and Palmer (1984) and DeMarco (1978).

After the visual depiction of the system in a diagrammatic manner called the process-flow diagram (PFD), the EPM/EPA technique proceeds to define all of the elements that make up the flows of the processes and whatever is in storage in the process. This is done by means of what is called a data dictionary (DD). The data dictionary is very precise in the manner in which it approaches how a process flow or file element is defined. From the application of EPA, quality control can be placed in the hands of the person closest to the process who receives or issues a product, or service, for it states precisely what is expected and what exists from point to point in the process flow. Thus, through EPA, at any point in a process flow, an employee using the tool can tell what exists and what is missing. Furthermore, it provides a training outline for the process, wherein the trainee can learn the basic inputs and/or outputs associated with the item or service of concern.

In its totality, the EPM documentation is designed to replace all existing documentation in an organization from its basic regulations to job descriptions, and even to training plans for the individuals occupying the jobs. The process-flow diagrams used in EPM, with the "bubbles and arrows," visually depict the total process, including all of the inputs and outputs through every single step of the operation. The data dictionary defines each of the inputs and outputs in a totally unique manner, that is, not only as a description of what is required in each job, but as an internal quality control that incorporates self-management of each process and its relationship to the voice of the customer.

Let's see how the *voice of the customer* gets introduced through EPM by the use of a hardware store example. Let us suppose a customer has requested a "drill" and that the process involved is a hardware store. From the perspective of the hardware store (the process), the output arrow indicates the customer is delivered a drill. Before we are done, the initial naming of that process is to output a "drill" to the customer. Through EPM, the output is distilled down to the fact that it is a specific drill bit wanted by a customer and is related to the length of the drill, the specific size of the chuck of the power drill, and the diameter of the drill itself. Tentative investigation and refinement through the EPM techniques reveal that the customer is not there at all to buy a drill, but is in fact there to purchase the ability to make a hole in some material. This further refines itself into the renaming of the output arrow to the customer as a "one-quarter-inch hole."

This is entirely different than the original concept of what the customer was there to buy, that is, the customer was not there to buy a drill bit, the customer was there to buy a "hole." This allows us, therefore, to redefine the entire nature of the subprocesses. It is not to provide the customer a drill bit, but to provide the customer with a hole. This allows us the continuing unique advantage of seeing the job not as delivering an existing technology to support the customer, but delivering a never-ending series of improvements of technologies in supporting the customer. Our existing technology may require that it be delivered in the point of a standard drill bit, but then it may evolve to allow the delivery of a laser that would be capable of delivering the same product, that is, the hole to the customer. Contrast this approach to delivering a product or service to a customer via the "old" way of thinking. There the one-quarter-inch drill is a given, and the analytic approach used focuses on efficiency within the process but not in the ultimate results for the customer. The ANSI approach would not allow the shift of technology and/or sociopolitical situation, the moving from the delivery of a drill bit to a laser to whatever might be able to provide this customer with the hole that he or she, in fact, seeks to obtain from the supplier. But the EPA approach forces this type of thinking and analysis.

EPA continues downward, subitem by subitem, subprocess by subprocess, until "the bottom" is reached. By this terminology, we mean until the basic task level of the multiple tasks that are combined to make up a process is reached. On the EPA flow diagram, this can be actually seen when the process illustrated has no more than two to four inputs and outputs. In addition, the definition of those inputs and outputs (and/or file references) contains terms that are fundamentally self-defining, that is, do not themselves consist of elements that have multiple levels of further defined terms.

You might start off, for example, with a general process of some complexity such as to develop the essential-process-analysis documentation for Company X. We then proceed on down, utilizing the techniques of EPA as noted before, until we have reached the bottom-level taskings of the multiple people who work in Company X. The bottom-level process might be designated as "type draft letter." Inputs and outputs could read: "Input: handwritten draft letter. Output: typed draft letter. File access: to a spelling dictionary."

This would be a bottom-level process and would now be ready to be analyzed according to the next step of EPM, Essential Quality Analysis (EQA). A first-hand example of the benefits of EPA as perceived by a first-line supervisor (Connie Fullmer) can be found in the Appendix.

Figure 12.1
The Deming/Shewart Cycle (frequently referred to by its acronym: as the P-D-C-A cycle)

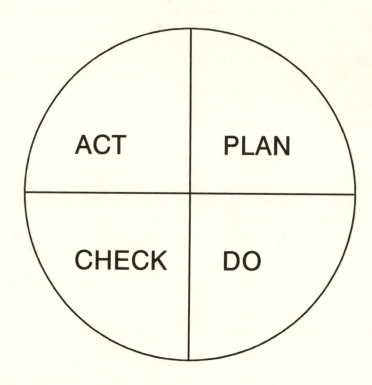

Essential Quality Analysis (EQA)

This section in the analysis of our overall process incorporates the initial four steps of never-ending improvement as developed by Walter Shewhart in the 1920s (Deming, 1986). Over time, due to the popularization of this technique of analyzing processes, and due to Deming's improvement on the basic Shewhart process, this approach to never-ending improvement in every single process or task has come to be known as the "Deming Cycle." The Deming/Shewhart Cycle, see Figure 12.1, is based on the concept that each job can be broken into four basic steps: The *planning* step; the *doing* step; the *checking* step; and lastly, the *act* to improve step. This cycle is viewed as a series in which one first plans the action, then one does the action, then one checks it against the plan, and then one acts to improve the overall process. Over time, especially in Japan, this Deming Cycle came to be enhanced to include several other elements. These are described by Masaaki Imai (1988) as also incorporating the critical step of standardization. The cycle, therefore, is viewed as somewhat more dynamic than the original Deming Cycle. In PPS, this enhancement by Imai was yet insufficient to allow for never-ending improvement in every function of the workplace.

To enhance incorporation of the never-ending improvement cycle by every person in every single task and every single job, the techniques of EPA, described before, were therefore added to the Deming/Shewhart Cycle with the resulting development of an interactive, real-time model of any task that would show the total flow of the process including its relationship to the input/output process. Additionally, by utilizing the technique of the process-flow diagrams, as also described before, the actual sequential flow and process of the substeps of any task were incorporated in a visual depiction understandable by nearly everyone.

If we take the basic previously described process of producing the typed draft, we would note that this bottom-level process would be viewed under EQA as being able to be taken down one more level. That level would include a visual depiction of the never-ending improvement steps: first, as described and incorporated by Deming, Shewhart, Imai, and others; then adding the essential link to the outside world of providing for the essential support, and obtaining resources necessary, to accomplish the four taskings of plan, do, check, and act (P–D–C–A) to improve.

With a slight change of terminology a five-step modified cycle was developed and used in PPS to incorporate to "plan the process," "do the process," "check the process against the plan," "assess the process for improvement" and provide "support to the process elements." Figure 12.2 shows the dynamic flow (arrows) of never-ending improvement of the processes (circles) as follows. A plan is developed (process 1.0) and used to do a process (process 2.0). This process produces data that are compared with the plan (process 3.0) to identify variances. These variances are used to develop process improvements (process 4.0) that will cause an update of the plan and necessary responses for all this are obtained by process 5.0. From this, the PPS analyst and others that used the technique naturally developed the acronym of P–D–C–A–S even as the original Deming/Shewhart cycle came to be known as P–D–C–A.

Additional flow-chart interfaces with the outside world were then added. They accounted for direction received from outside, for example, management direction to an individual worker, or headquarters direction to an individual organization, and the process flow of requiring a person to seek coordination and/or authorization from the outside world. This enhanced flow chart is recognized within PPS as the full EQA flow-process cycle.

To apply this to our "bottom-level process" example, the basic draft correspondence process would be able to be reduced down to five sequential subprocesses using the P–D–C–A–S model. Plan: how to type that draft. Do: receive and type it. Check: check the typing process against the plan to see if it was done according to the plan and identify any variance from the plan. Assess: assess the variance, be it a qualitative or quantitative assessment to determine if the process is in control and if not how to bring it into control. Support: if it is in control, how to change the process to better improve it and the process to

Figure 12.2
The Revised Deming/Shewart Cycle EQA Process Flow Diagram

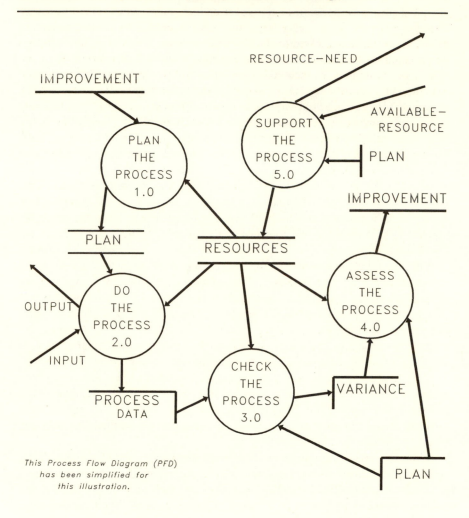

This Process Flow Diagram (PFD)
has been simplified for
this illustration.

obtain the required support to produce the typed draft, to do the planning, do the checking, do the assessing, etc.

Although not every process has been so flowed, many members of the work force have been trained to do so, and they are using such techniques to pinpoint causes for variation and identifying ways for improvement. Thus, in every process, they incorporate an almost self-learning mode to allow the individual to gain control of his or her own work and to work either alone or with others for its improvement (others when there is more than one person performing the same tasks or where teams have been created).

From the process-flow diagram of the EQA, and the previous description, it is apparent that one of the most critical elements of the entire EPM approach is the *plan*. The plan is viewed as the heart and soul of the entire improvement process. The plan gives the rationale for the performance that tells how to do the checks, guides the assessment for improvement, and determines how specifically the support is going to be obtained for the entire EPM/EQA improvement process.

It is in the approach to what a plan is that EPM veers sharply from other conventional system-analysis approaches. And this is true whether we are talking of General Motors or Japanese approaches to business planning. The heart of every plan is viewed as the incorporation of six elements. A plan must consist of the identification of the following:

1. The Who, that is, who is the agent that is to perform the action? What talents, skills, and competencies are required?

2. The What of the process, that is, the identification of the principal steps in broad terms that are accomplished by the process to produce the output.

3. The Why of the process, which is the link with the external customer and validates the reason for the process in the first place.

4. The Where of the process, which is the identification of the geographic/physical location of process performance.

5. The When of the process, which identifies the total timing of the process including all of its substeps and timing sequence.

6. The How of the process, which is a detailed description to be followed by the person actually doing the action and which will enable the output of the process to be accomplished in quality terms, that is, with minimal variance every single time.

In EQA, this is developed far beyond the basic concepts of Imai (1986) and Mizuno (1988).

To enhance the communication of this plan, the EQA process uses a modified version of the fishbone, or cause-and-effect, diagram as taught in the Seven Basic Tools of Statistical Process Control (Imai, 1986), commonly called the Ishikawa fishbone diagram (see Figure 12.3) because it was developed by Dr. Kaoru Ishikawa in the late 1950s and early 1960s in Japan. The standard Ishikawa diagram, however, uses brainstorming to fill out the various legs that lead to the cause-and-effect relationship between the process being analyzed and what contributes to that process, or problem/process analysis. In problem analysis, the EQA approach uses the same identification and identical content of each leg every time. Hence, in EQA terminology, it is usually referred to as a Standardized Cause and Effect Diagram (SCED). See Figure 12.4.

This SCED, identifying the who, what, why, where, when, and how for each and every single step is laid out for each of the P–D–C–A–S elements. Thus, for any single process such as our "produce typed draft" example, we would

Figure 12.3
The Ishikawa Fishbone Diagram with a Standardized Who, What, Why, Where, When, and How Format for any Process

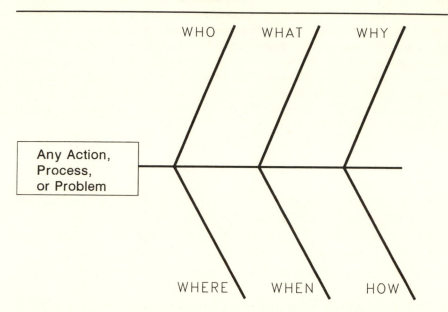

have the five steps of plan, do, check, act, and support and the six elements of the SCED, the who, what, why, where, when, and how for each of those five.

Many will view the provision of thirty elements (P–D–C–A–S times the five "W's" and an "H") to be excessive for simple processes. It is this belief that leads to variance and lack of quality.

The goal of the EQA analysis is to allow for the production of one document consisting of the original process-flow diagram, the data dictionary, and then the EQA behind every bottom-level process, the P–D–C–A–S within each bottom-level process, and, finally, the SCED behind each of the P–D–C–A–S elements as a total systems documentation. It is designed to replace all other policies, procedures, training, and job-description documents. This reaches the goals of standardization as described by Imai (1986), while incorporating the other elements (e.g., the five W's and an H) and while avoiding the variance that is built into the normal Ishikawa diagram and brainstorming process.

In actual test applications, Nelson has found it to provide the foundation for an organization to do the following:

(a) build a uniform approach to training and job standardization for all personnel in an organization;

(b) allow for improved communications between organizations based on the use of common flow techniques and common terminology as found in the data dictionary, along with standardized planning elements as found in the P–D–C–A–S/SCED, and form

Figure 12.4
Standardized Cause and Effect Diagram (SCED) for the EQA P-D-C-A-S Cycle

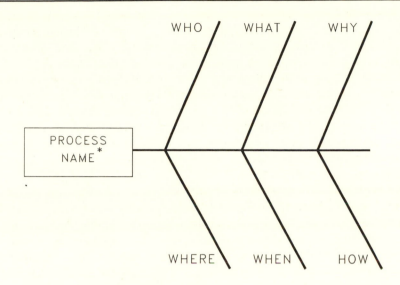

*A Standardized Cause & Effect Diagram (SCED)
is prepared for each process, i.e., one for
the "Plan," one for the "Do," one for
the "Check," one for the "Assess," and
one for the "Support" process.

the basis then for collaborative efforts in never-ending improvement in every single process and in every single job.

A brief commentary on the value of EQA by a DS analyst, Willie Nesbit, can be found in the Appendixes.

Statistical Process Control (SPC)

We have thus described the first two steps of EPM, that is, the analysis of processes for value added through the EPA technique and the standardization of processes and the incorporation of never-ending improvement in all elements through EQA. We are now ready to approach the next leg of essential process management, Statistical Process Control (SPC).

In EPM, it is not until this latter stage that SPC is normally considered for use. In EPM, the alignment of processes for value added to the external customer and their initial qualitative standardization as (P–D–C–A–S and SCED) must be accomplished prior to quantitative standardization as effected through Statistical Process Control (SPC).

If an organization initiates process improvement based on SPC as a first effort, it will inevitably wind up improving processes that should not even be there. And this, of course, causes a situation that makes it far more difficult to eliminate unneeded processes because the company/organization invested time, effort, and money to improve such process, and, as a result, has placed value in it.

An additional benefit in waiting until this level of analysis is completed before starting SPC is that within the data dictionary every single possible variable and attribute of the process that could be measured has been identified. Thus, once the plan is in place and the data dictionary has been defined, individual and team efforts can now be focused on implementing the necessary techniques to bring processes that are already known to add value into Statistical Process Control, and, thus, prepare them for the next level of improvement effort.

In a sense, the SPC effort can be viewed as a direct follow-on and as part of the EQA effort. When we look at a process, we will usually begin with the check process, not the plan, because we are going to be applying this to existing operations. Were it new operations starting off for the first time we would, of course, start with the "P," or plan, element. However, most organizations already in existence will start with the "C," or check, to see what is the existing state of the process. This check will usually reveal (in the test organization, we found it to be 99 percent true) that the first missing element identified by a check is that there is no plan. Not only is there no plan in the sense of the SCED, there is no plan in the sense of any of the EPM/EPA/EQA elements.

The first level of effort then is to begin with the process analysis (incorporating the voice of the customer across all the processes) and thus assure that we are dealing with value-added processes to begin with. Only once this has been done can one proceed with the next level of effort, to improve the value and the quality of those remaining processes.

We are not going to go into an in depth explanation of the tools and techniques of SPC within this text. There are many excellent texts on the subject that can be found. SPC consists of a series of steps:

Data collection

Pareto analysis

Histograms (though of limited use)

Run charts

Correlation charts

Control charts

Deming has raised a serious concern about various statistical applications commonly used.

Analysis of variance, t-tests, confidence intervals, and other statistical techniques commonly used by quantitative analysts are inappropriate because they provide no basis for prediction. Furthermore, such applications bury the information contained in the order of production. Most if not all computer packages for analysis of data, as they are commonly termed, provide flagrant examples of inefficiency. (Deming, 1986, p. 132)

For those truly interested in the application of classic TQM statistical methodology, we limit our recommendation of statistical texts to the works of Deming (1986), Ishikawa (1986), and Nelson (1985).

Use of Control Charts

Probably the most valuable tool within the tool kit of SPC is the control chart itself. It allows individual workers and/or work teams to identify problems that occur in both production and administrative processes that are caused by the system and/or events outside the system. Such applications effect rapid improvement of the quality delivered to the customer. Used in the board room or at upper staff levels, control charts allow management to avoid the critical action called "tampering," that is, taking action on an individual variance when the problem is the system itself, or its opposite, not taking action on an individual variance and assuming it is the system at work when in fact it is a cause outside the system.

Management not knowing these things can only increase the variance and decrease the quality of the output of any process and or system. This is graphically illustrated by not only Deming in his work, but by Nelson (1985) in a video tape series.

We will not explore further the development and exploration of these tools in this text because the purpose of this chapter is merely an exposition of the tools used by PPS in effecting organizational and process change. Reference to the texts cited provides an adequate basis for individual exploration and practical application.

SUMMARY

This chapter introduces a key approach to analyzing socio-technical processes in PPS. The overarching approach we term EPM. Within EPM are EPA, EQA, and then SPC (see Figure 12.5). These tools are excellent communications and problem-solving devices. They are essential for never-ending improvement and total customer support. As of this writing, for those DS employees who have been reorganized from the Air Force to the DLA organization, it is unlikely they will be given the support needed to continue to use these tools in team problem solving. However, those who remain with the Air Force are still being encouraged to do so. The destiny of TQM remains closely tied to the philosophy of an organization's leadership.

Figure 12.5
PPS Essential Process-Management Overview

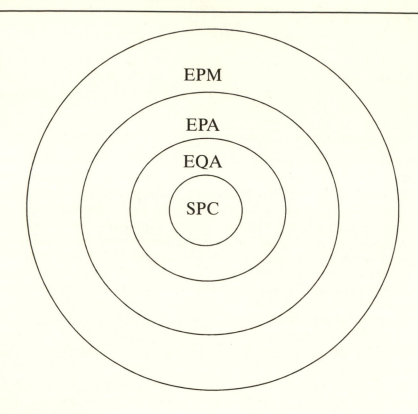

REFERENCES

DeMarco, T. (1978). *Structured Analysis and System Specification*. New York: Yourdon Press.

Deming, W. E. (1986). *Out of the Crisis*. Cambridge, MA: MIT-CAES.

Ishikawa, K. (1986). *Guide to Quality Control*. White Plains, NY: Quality Resources.

Keller, R. (1987). *Expert System Technology: Development and Application*. New York: Yourdon Press.

Imai, M. (1986). *Kaizen*. New York: Random House.

McMenamin, S. M., and Palmer, J. J. (1984). *Essential Analysis*. New York: Yourdon Press/Prentice Hall.

Mizuno, S. (1988). *Company-wide Quality Control*. Tokyo: Asian Productivity Organization.

Nelson, L. (1985). *MIT Video Course and Manual: Statistics in Quality Productivity and Problem Solving*. Cambridge, MA: MIT-CAES.

Yourdon, E. (1975). *Techniques of Program Structure and Design*. Englewood Cliffs, NJ: Prentice Hall.

Yourdon, E., and Constantine, L. (1976). *Structured Design*. New York: Yourdon Press.

_____ PART IV _____

Results, Revisions, Recommendations

A summary of the project as a quality-oriented effort is provided as are the results of the project to date. It is evident that the evaluation design of the project is less than adequate and recommendations are provided for improved evaluation management for TQM-oriented efforts that may be attempted in the future.

In the Appendix, Colonel David Naehring, Director of DS, describes the results of the project from the perspective of the executive-in-charge. From the civilian side, Colene Krum, a member of the original design team, reviews the progress made thus far by the project and addresses the prospects for the future of PPS. Both were deeply enmeshed in day-to-day management of the program. Jim Graham, Director of DOD Installations Assistance Office, a person familiar with TQM programs throughout the DOD, shares his observations about the unique characteristics of the project and his ability to share and transfer the program technology elsewhere. Finally, John Salas, President of Local Union 1857 of the AFGE comments on the project and the TQM approach from his perspective.

The host organization has undergone major reorganization due to changing national defense priorities and reduction in force. Anita Clevenger, the new manager of the project design team, who replaced Nelson after his retirement, discusses the project and its future in the Appendix, as well. Finally, recommendations for the manager seeking to undertake the transformation to quality in his or her own organization are provided by the authors.

Discussion and Final Assessment: The Overall Project at a Glance

This book introduced a new management paradigm that is emerging as a result of a changing global economy, which is customer-driven and competitive. As a consequence of such heightened competition, organizations have had to become more adaptive and internally more efficacious. We have termed the new model of management to be the "quality approach."

We presented an actual case example where some of the theory of the quality approach is being tested—Project Pacer Share (PPS). Its purpose is to test the practicality of the new approach in the workplace itself. Although a federal-government-sponsored effort, the implications of the approach include both business and government. The management approach in PPS, relying to a great extent on the philosophy of Total Quality Management (TQM), represents a substantive shift from the way others in government and business work. The quality approach has totally revised the concept of the organization as a pyramid-shaped system having substantial power located at the top of the organization and little power at the bottom. The new approach is customer-driven, having teams working together, using systematic approaches to problem solving, making continuous process improvements in order to excite long-term customer satisfaction. The leadership for such an effort is shared by organized labor and management—they are working together in partnership.

The Directorate of Distribution (DS), the host organization for the project, is deeply rooted in a system enmeshed in the traditional top–down, bureaucratic, management approach. It has made an attempt to transform itself to the new quality-driven approach. The driving force for the change in DS came from within rather than as a result of an external mandate or other type of environmental influence. Although the federal government had endorsed TQM-type efforts since the start of PPS, at the time of its inception, PPS was years ahead of government trends toward TQM.

The appendix contains a brief statement from the Director of DS, Col. David

Naehring. He joined the program shortly after the start of implementation. It was not his idea. He had no vested interest in it. His words reveal how he came to like it and lead it to new heights.

PPS is an official "experiment" cosponsored by the U.S. Air Force (USAF) and the U.S. Office of Personnel Management (OPM) and is officially authorized through the Civil Service Reform Act of 1978. As an experimental effort, the project is being assessed to determine whether or not it offers viable alternatives to the present Civil Service System (CSS). The OPM and the USAF are evaluating the impact of the new approach on productivity, quality of work life, and overall organizational effectiveness.

At the time of this writing, the project had just completed its third year of a five-year demonstration effort. It is possible that the project may be authorized to go beyond its five-year life. There are no definite commitments to continue it beyond five years. As an approach to improve quality, it has demonstrated itself to be a superior alternative to the old way of doing business. It is doubtful, though, that this outcome alone (e.g., quality improvement) will lead to changes in the CSS itself due to other political preferences.

The experimental nature of the project has been impeded by larger systemic changes that have taken place as a result of changed national policy toward defense spending, defense management, fiscal constraints forced on government as a result of the current condition of the national debt, and the like. These changing conditions at the national level have resulted in major reorganization within the AFLC and Department of Defense. Such reorganization has led to the breakup of DS, the host organization, at the end of the third year of the PPS demonstration, and the reduction of status of the organization from a directorate to a lesser level, a division. Some of the DS people are still working together as members of a larger organization, termed Technology and Industrial Support Directorate (TI). However, they will soon be split up, with about 800 employees have been transferred along with the processes they support to the Defense Logistics Agency (DLA).

In the fourth year of PPS experimentation, Nelson, the major designer of PPS, and McRorie and Naehring, the leadership force behind its implementation, are no longer at the helm. Naehring and Nelson retired, and McRorie reports to new leadership that now is responsible for the project. The new host organizations, TI and DLA, are less enthused about PPS. Thus it is unclear if PPS will have the same day-to-day hands-on management and provide the same assistance to the PPS design team that McRorie and Naehring were resolved to provide and did so, so remarkably well. Both Colene Krum and Dan Fuchs of the original PPS design team have moved over to TI and report to Anita Clevenger, the new PPS Project Management Officer. Anita is well schooled in the quality approach to management and is very capable. She will bring to the project a fresh perspective while having the benefit of Krum and Fuchs' exceptional talents and in-depth knowledge of the program. She will be challenged to be an advocate for PPS as others advocate for their own interests as the dust starts to settle after such an organizational and institutional upheaval.

After its review of PPS, the host organization at MCAFB has sought, unsuccessfully, to expand PPS throughout its entire organization—some 5,000 employees. The future role of the TPTB follow-on consultants in DS is unclear. They will need new sponsorship.

It is unlikely that DLA will opt to continue the PPS experiment with the same organizational development and EPM tools employed by DS. In fact, as of this writing, they appear to have opted to overtly withhold, rather than provide, support for them, for their management philosophy is not openly team-centered.

There is one added factor that will substantially impact the behavior of the host ALC, MCAFB. Despite its excellent performance in support of operation Desert Storm, it is widely rumored that one-third of all employees in the AFLC will be cut, through a major RIF, which is forthcoming. The Commanding General in charge of the AFLC, within which MCAFB is a part, has stated publicly that the future workload for the AFLC will only support three and one-half ALCs. As there are five ALCs at present, at least one ALC is likely to be eliminated. MCAFB at Sacramento, California, is politically the weakest center in the AFLC. Even the mayor of Sacramento has stated publicly that if Sacramento lost MCAFB, it would not hurt the community.

Such threats to the security of a dutiful and loyal work force at MCAFB are unique to the PPS setting. They will nullify much of the "controls" necessary for RAND or any other organization to measure and compare the performance of the MCAFB DS organization in its first three years with PPS against the other DS organizations within the AFLC without PPS. Any differences RAND may find between PPS results and other DS organizations may be more a result of the unique contextual changes at MCAFB than the project itself.

Thus, the PPS host agency, and the character of the demonstration itself, has been shaken from top to bottom and split apart. New leadership will create new policies and new styles of implementation (not necessarily good or bad—just different). Also, the receptivity of the interventions in the host AFLC is much more encouraging of the TQM approach to management and the interventions introduced by PPS than it was at the project's start.

Colene Krum, a project analyst with PPS from its inception, reflects on the project situation at the end of its third year, given the turmoil facing the DS employees. Her remarks are included in the Appendix entitled, "On Reflection."

PROJECT RESULTS: WHERE IS THE BEEF?

All social institutions or subsystems, whether medical, educational, religious, economic, or political, are required to provide "proof" of their legitimacy and effectiveness in order to justify society's continued support. Both the demand for and the type of acceptable "proof" will depend largely upon the nature of the relationship between the social institution and the public. In general, a balance will be struck between faith and fact, reflecting the degree of man's respect for authority and tradition within the particular system versus his skepticism and desire for tangible "proofs of work." (A. E. Suchman, 1967, p. 2)

As Suchman states, PPS, a federally sponsored demonstration project, is obligated to provide "proof" of its " . . . effectiveness in order to justify society's continued support." The RAND Corporation, an external consultation organization of considerable repute, was contracted to help provide scientific research to test for such evidence or "proof."

The employment of program evaluation into civil service reform is foundational to the Civil Service Reform Act itself, where its architects sought to link management, program evaluation, and personnel administration in ways to improve program management and performance (Wholey, 1984). Furthermore, an evaluation effort is expected to provide such proof that a program is (or is not) accomplishing its objectives in a timely manner, and to help decision makers steer the project toward desired outcomes.

Now at the end of its third year of demonstration, the RAND effort has not yet issued its assessment of the results of PPS in its second year. They are behind schedule. As the project is still in its formative stage, OPM needs the RAND findings to make informed decisions about the project's effectiveness—especially when it is being asked by the Air Force to expand the project.

The delay in the RAND study is not due to its lack of ability or will; it reflects the complexities of the PPS demonstration situation itself. Too many changes are occurring at too fast a pace to permit adequate controls for scientific measurement. This should not be surprising for the weaknesses in the evaluation of social experimentation have long been known to students of evaluation research (Campbell, 1957; Hyman, Wright, and Hopkins, 1962; Guttentag, 1972; Horst et al., 1974; and Scanlon, 1977).

Thus, the gaining of evidence to determine the worth of a demonstration like PPS may rely on expert judgment, political interest, and/or customer satisfaction rather than hard data. To date, the RAND Corporation has not been able to construct sufficient controls in its research design to conclusively demonstrate that changes noted in DS-wide performance have or have not been a result of PPS rather than some other intervening variable(s). After three and one-half years of RAND research, OPM has opted to end its contract with RAND and employ the services of the U.S. Navy to measure the effects of the project. This further weakens the measurability of the project from a control standpoint.

From an evaluative research perspective, the project is out of control. Sufficient controls do not exist to make valid comparisons regarding the overall functioning of DS with that of other DS organizations. Bottom-line-type differences found in the overall productivity of the host PPS organization cannot be conclusively tied to the PPS interventions, for they could have come from some other intervening factor that did not occur in the other DS comparison groups.

Measuring Project Components That Do Not Exist—Type III Errors

There is a difference between organizational rhetoric and organizational reality (Scanlon, 1977). Rhetoric is what the organization says it will do (or is doing). Reality is what the organization actually did (or is doing). Gain sharing never got to the total reality stage. Thus, any measure of it would be premature, because the intervention itself never fully existed. RAND has claimed it has not been able to find positive differences in productivity between PPS and the other four groups to which the project has been compared, a claim disputed by the ALC. RAND has, therefore, tentatively (in preliminary draft form) suggested that after two years, the gain-sharing intervention has not made a positive difference in organizational performance. Such findings may lead the decision maker to reject gain sharing as a positive element in the quality approach in government. However, the reason for the "no-difference" finding may not be due to the inappropriateness of gain sharing as much as it might be because gain sharing was never totally operational during the period of measurement.

Gain sharing was an intervention element that was to be tied to overall organizational performance, yet it never got implemented in a manner that was clearly understood by the employees themselves and the payouts were not readily tied to specific organizational or team-performance improvements.

This does not mean that the project's leadership didn't try to design it correctly and make it work. They were impeded by a reduction in the DS work load that had occurred as a result of cutbacks in defense spending and the warming of relations with the East Bloc nations of Europe. The gain-share formula tied the payout to the work volume. But the formula was not sufficiently developed to measure work unit performance with real-time feedback to those in the work units so performance could be constantly monitored by the employees themselves.

When the work load was reduced as a result of external forces beyond the control of DS, the gain share was negatively affected. Thus, any "outcome" or effect-type assessment of the impact of gain sharing would, in itself, be invalid. Such an assessment that attempts to tie the effects of gain share as a performance incentive within DS would be erroneous for it did not truly exist in the first place.

Although the rhetoric of PPS has been written in fairly precise terms in the *Federal Register* and elsewhere, the actual PPS program was different as a result of environmental and systemic factors that interfered with the conduct of the process itself.

Thus, the Air Force, OPM, or RAND cannot cite hard substantive evidence that a given number of dollars has been saved through PPS that would not have been saved otherwise—no one can. None can scientifically demonstrate through controlled experimentation that better service quality has occurred in DS when compared to other organizations as a result either. Contrarily, no one can demonstrate the project has resulted in excessive costs, decreased quality, or decreased productivity. We do not have conclusive evidence about the project's effects on the bottom line either way. The measurement criteria of the old paradigm are being applied to the new paradigm and this further complicates systems evaluation.

Evidence exists which strongly indicates the implementation of PPS has led to improved employee satisfaction with their leadership and improved team play. The data gathered by both RAND and MEDi, using separate measurements and population samples, point to significant improvements in quality-of-work-life measures. Such changes would be expected if one looked at the level of emphasis placed on interventions like TPTB; team follow-on training; "self-initiated followership," "customer-oriented leadership" training; customer-oriented behavior within the organization as well as external to it; JPGs; Quality Circles; team problem solving through EPM, EPA, and SPC; team facilitation training; and the TQM college. These interventions were clearly in place, were employed systematically, and positive behavior changes for quality were observed as a result of them.

EVALUATION BASED ON SUBJECTIVE OPINION AND POLITICAL PREFERENCE

Given the difficulty with the evaluation-research design for some of the reasons cited, the results of the project are not known. Scientifically derived "proof" has not been, nor will it be, gathered. Thus, the project's life will be decided upon by the rational persuasion of those for and those against it. This is not to be unexpected or even interpreted to be a negative aspect of project management. As Guttentag (1972) urged, evaluation research needs to pay more attention to contextual relevance, subjectivity, and political values to make it more useful to decision makers.

At this time, it appears some parts of the Air Force and organized labor are becoming increasingly in favor of the project, wanting to expand it, whereas OPM and other Air Force interests are more guarded, seeking more conclusive data to support the assumptions that the project is a viable alternative to the CSS as authorized in 1978 through the Civil Service Reform Act. Though the continuance of the experimentation with the CSS is in question, there is little question about PPS's contribution to quality. In 1990, OPM's Federal Quality Institute named MCAFB to be one of five recipients of the President's Quality Improvement Prototype Award—much as a result of the project's success.

PPS has not demonstrated scientifically through controlled experimentation that its six changes to the CSS should be implemented nationwide. However, when compared to the old system, it clearly is the choice of most of the managers and employees who have stayed the course and have lived with it for the past three years. As a TQM-type project, it has the popular and political support among those in DOD who place heavy emphasis on TQM throughout all levels.

This seems to fit the criteria proposed by Kuhn (Chapter 2) for the rejection of the old paradigm and the acceptance of the new paradigm (Kuhn, 1962).

It would be extremely rare to find a military commander who would be an advocate of the present CSS. They are especially excited by the prospects of pay banding, modification of job series like that in PPS, and the termination of supervisory level based on their employees' grade levels and spans of control ("grade creep"). These modifications are especially enticing to the military manager. The military leadership is generally in favor of the concept of gain sharing and the end of employee performance appraisal, but these two interventions are a bit more controversial than the others. By law, the military cannot participate in gain sharing. Yet, as working partners with civilians, the military makes a major difference in the success or failure of civilian teams accomplishing their own productivity improvements. If the military could participate with the civilians in gain sharing, then there would likely be more support for it as an intervention.

In the Appendix is a description of the project from Jim Graham, an official in the DOD whose job it is to spot examples of organizational excellence and share such throughout the DOD. His account attests to the high level of acceptability of PPS in the defense community.

After having spent three years with the implementation phase of the project, the authors are convinced that although not perfect when compared to the CSS currently in place throughout the nation, PPS offers greater prospect for improved government service (quality) and would be the "customers' choice" as a basis for improvement rather than the current CSS if the decision for its implementation would be left to those directly involved with it, those directly touched by it. The comments in the Appendix by John Salas, President of Local Union 1857 of the AFGE, attest to its viability.

From the eyes of the host agency in the Air Force, DS, where quality improvement was the goal and change in the CSS as *one* of many experimental interventions was the means to achieving it, the project was a stunning success. However, from the perspective of those who manage the CSS, it has failed to demonstrate through empirically supported measures that it is the more viable alternative to that presently approved by Congress and in place throughout the federal government today.

UNEXPECTED OUTCOMES

Cross Fertilization/Technology Transfer

Like Graham's statement in the Appendixes, since its inception, the project has received a lot of attention from hundreds of visitors from other government and private-sector agencies desiring to find ways to improve their own systems. Direct impact has been made in non-DOD agencies such as the Federal Aviation

Administration, General Services Administration, and the U.S. Postal Service, where various TQM tools and approaches used in PPS were directly implemented as well. Senior leadership of the Congressional watchdog organization, the General Accounting Office (GAO), made on-site visits and spoke highly of the initiative to other federal executives and leaders in public management.

Representatives of PPS were called on to make frequent presentations at OPM-sponsored executive seminar centers at Denver, Kings Point, and Oak Ridge to share the philosophy and intervention techniques, positives and negatives with managers and executives from all walks of federal life. They also prepared papers for presentations at professional conferences as well as publications in both refereed and nonrefereed professional journals. Nelson instituted an undergraduate degree program at the local American River College, which is now being extended into the California State University System. Presentations were made at the invitation of American organizations in Europe and for others abroad. TQM has also been introduced into the business school's graduate and undergraduate curriculum at Florida International University (University of Florida at Miami) by Gilbert. It is also being offered as a certificate program through the university's continuous education effort.

The TQM-type technologies introduced in PPS have been adopted by many government and business organizations throughout the country to improve quality. The U.S. Navy's Naval Supply Center, Pensacola has applied it throughout their work force. The Navy's Supervisor of Shipbuilding, Conversion and Repair, at San Diego not only has integrated the processes throughout its own organization, but has enabled its supplier, the private sector ship builders, to assume the quality approach within their own organizations. As a result, the National Steel and Shipbuilding Company has improved their work in getting ships out to sea for the Navy. At McClellan AFB, the quality processes introduced in PPS truly went "up the organization." They were introduced at the DS directorate level, then went upward to the ALC commander's top team, then upward to the AFLC headquarter where the Deputy Chief of Staff, Logistics, and its Cataloguing and Standardization Center at Battle Creek, Michigan, adapted them throughout their entire organizations.

New Approach to Labor–Management Relations

Among the exceptional outcomes of the project has been the collaborative partnership that emerged from organized labor, headed by AFGE President, John Salas (see his comments in the Appendix), and the DS leadership team. The decision-making model used went from one of collective bargaining/negotiation to true teamwork, where honest differences were raised; opposing points of view articulated and listened to; and win–win alternatives developed and implemented in the attempt to accommodate the interests of all.

At the initial phases of the project, when TPTB was just being introduced, it was clear that union and management were on different ends of the spectrum.

When together in the same room, both DS supervisors and union stewards would engage in subterfuge, rumoring negative things about the other. They were in a win–lose/lose–lose course. As discussed by Frank Mason (see the Appendix), they began to work together for the good of the organization and the people working there.

Clearly, the union has been better able to accomplish its goals as a result. It is doubtful that any other union in the federal government has been as involved in the decision-making process and in shaping organizational policy than has the AFGE at Sacramento—and management and the work force, in general, have clearly benefited from its involvement. Likewise, the union has actively been a champion of management policy with regard to PPS. And the union has clearly benefited.

A recent TPTB session provides an example of what is meant by unique union participation with the project. During the presentation of a team-building session, a few "difficult" employees started to rail against their supervisors—once a common occurrence. It was the union steward, Mike Hamblin, who brought the few disruptive employees in line. He let them know that their negative attitude was hurting the team. His positive leadership served as a role model for the rest of the members attending that workshop. As a result, they got involved and worked through some very important process problems that served to improve the overall operations of the group. Hamblin's approach has built greater respect from the employees and management for the vital role the union plays in DS. With gain sharing as an incentive, when the organization wins, everyone wins. Those employees who have become expert at "slow rolling" management and their teams and supervisors who have become expert at favoritism are being confronted by the PPS process. Such behavior is out of step with the quality movement going on there.

LESSONS LEARNED

Understanding Employee Anger and Frustration That Come with Change

When PPS began its implementation phase, there was tremendous anger that was expressed by employees and supervisors and managers toward whomever was the spokesperson for the project. The language used, tone of voice, and confrontational, aggressive, and challenging statements were shocking. It was hard to imagine employees talking that way to the leaders and to anyone else who was associated with their leaders's policies.

When implementing a new program like PPS, or any substantial change, employees need to have the opportunity to vent their frustration, and when doing so, they may not use the "King's" English or follow the course of tact and diplomacy guidance that "Miss Manners," Ann Landers, or Abigail Van Buren would suggest to us. When introducing substantial change in an organization, management has two basic tasks: "inform, inform, inform" and "listen, listen, listen."

Development of an Ability to Demonstrate Persistence

A team is not built in one session. Partnership between labor and management does not happen in one handshake. Customer-oriented leadership, self initiated followership, reliance on EPM, and a never-ending dedication to improvement for the customer do not happen quickly. Understanding and competence in EPM, SPC, and other TQM tools do not get internalized overnight. For these behaviors to be internalized and the quality approach to become an operational imperative, it takes persistence and time. "The need for patience is, perhaps, the biggest barrier [to TQM implementation] for Amercians. We like to see things happen now. We like to resolve problems now. Successful quality programs take time and tenacity," says Krone (1990).

The Need for High-Quality, Decision-Relevant Program Evaluation

This is an old theme that keeps cropping up in program management. However, where quality is concerned, it is essential. The evaluation approach employed in the TQM program must be directly tied to decision making and be directed at enabling the decision makers to steer the organization. "In TQM, if you get the process right, the product will be of high quality" (Ken Adams in Krone, 1990). The "best" evaluation for a TQM-type program is one that is EPM-oriented (e.g., internal systems improvement) as opposed to the "controlled experiment" type. Although it is necessary to measure the results (outcome) of a project, in TQM, outcomes will take time. Also, the evaluation needs to be timely so that the decision makers have the information when they need it.

The data collected by RAND were not timely for either OPM or PPS management. The information derived by them was not responsive to the shifting operational directions of PPS. OPM needed information to determine if the project was making a difference when the results of TQM are not going to occur for a period of time. This points to a serious and increasing problem identified by the U.S. Comptroller General regarding the capabilities of the Executive Branch to carry out effective program evaluation (Bowsher, 1990). Chelimsky (1990) reports that in the Executive Branch, there has been a greater reliance on external professionals to conduct program-evaluation research as a result of staff shortages. This has deterred the type of quick-turnaround studies that are essential to sound management practice.

In December 1990, we asked the PPS management for scientifically derived information about the project's effectiveness. They did not have such information, because the RAND (official external evaluator) evaluation had not yet been submitted to them, and that report would be for the second year of the project's life, whereas the project was moving into its fourth year.

In the future, it is recommended that the implementation of a TQM effort be seen as developmental, with the primary need for evaluation to be in helping those in project management to create viable TQM processes and demonstration alternatives. Before one can measure program effectiveness, the program needs to be in place and working, otherwise measures of program outcome would be erroneous, because the program, having consistently applied behaviors based on prescribed interventions, may never have existed in the first place.

The program needs to be modeled just like EPM would model any other process, where the processes are analyzed, and the plan, do, check, assess and support (PDCAS) theme put into operation at every level.

The key decisions needed to manage the program by all key parties concerned (in this case, OPM and DOD) need to be identified ahead of time so they can agree on the evaluation plan. Then the parties need to work together, as partners, to integrate evaluative information with decision making to help steer the project toward its goals. This has not happened in PPS.

Understanding the Need to Excite the Will to Quality Before the TQM Tools Are Applied

The normal way in which TQM is presented in organizations is to train the employees to understand that there will be a new way of working together based on the quality approach, and then the employees are trained in TQM methods like EPM, SPC, etc. This is not the best approach, although it is the most widely used approach.

We are aware of several federal organizations that have spent millions on training in TQM with little impact on the work teams themselves. The problem was they did not create the environment first in which TQM could function.

Team building and TQM problem-structured analysis techniques go hand in hand. Effective team building, where employees learn to value their role as suppliers to valued customers, will excite the will of employees to learn new techniques to improve their own teams' processes. Once that will to learn is internalized, employees will see the value in the problem-structuring and problem-solving tools discussed in Chapter 12, which are often associated with TQM. However, in organizational settings where team play is not a tradition, it needs to be first addressed and then reinforced through TQM training such as EPM, EQA, and SPC. All within the organization need to be held accountable for team play and quality service starting at the top.

If TQM training is provided on its own without the skilled introduction of team building, where employees are so delighted with the quality approach as a result of experience that they want to continue working for their customers, then the TQM tools will not be applied by them even though they understand them.

Strong Leadership Is Essential

When undertaking the change to the quality approach, strong leadership is key. As the organization is beginning from the bureaucratic, classic efficiency orientation, where the leader is at the top of the pyramid and is viewed to be the motivator, without absolute, unflinching, warlike commitment and zealous insistence from the person at the top, the energy for change will rapidly dissipate. In PPS, the leadership took steps to assure that all within the organization were held accountable for team play through the use of an outside consultant whose task it was to assure that the leaders themselves did, in fact, listen to their people.

Those in the middle levels of the organization are upwardly mobile. The quality approach is aimed at flattening the organization rather than keeping it as it is or making it more vertical. Thus, those in middle management who seek added "power" have the most to lose from the successful performance of the quality approach. Their employees are also functioning with traditional "fear." They will not become fearless unless the leaders insist on their widespread involvement in problem solving. The leader must take steps to assure everyone that expressing their differences with those in superior positions is important and will not lead to future retribution. If the leader is lackadaisical about this matter, fear will increase and employees will not be enabled to play the vital role they must play for quality to happen.

When making a cultural change, trust is a very fragile but essential factor. It must be continuously reinforced. The lesson here: act trustfully, ethically, integriously, again and again and again.

Constancy of Purpose Starts with the Tenure of Leadership

Bennis and Slater (1968) describe organizational and social life as having temporary players—everyone moving, a society of transient self-directed people with their briefcases as their offices, and with little permanence in any work group.

Such will not be desirable for the transition to quality, because leadership requires commitment and constancy of purpose. Organizations that foster rapid change in leadership will more likely inhibit quality rather than promote it. The military, for example, tends to move its leaders every two or three years. Such a policy makes sense from the developmental aspect of a leader getting broad exposure. However, when such leaders are expected to demonstrate their "leadership" with each assignment, such a policy fosters heroic behavior from the top rather than empowering behavior from the top. It places the true leadership obligations on the civilian leader, who is often a deputy to the military leader and experiences a role redefinition with each rotation of the military leader to whom he or she reports. Also, there is insufficient time for the military leader to develop a consistent culture before the changing of the guard. This policy of ever-changing leadership and temporariness is widely practiced in other large organizations as well and is creating like impediments to quality.

The Quality Approach Is Dualistic—Consistency and Never-Ending Improvement and Change

The quality approach requires a tremendous tolerance for technological change. Constant improvement means constant ambiguity. The stabilizing factors in such an environment are the people with whom one works and the dedication to customer support. Teams provide the socio-emotional support essential for individuals to both tolerate and encourage change in technology. Excessive change among the people working on the team can impede the team's adaptation to changing technology.

People Are, by Nature, Good

The entire theme of the quality approach is that when given the opportunity, when it is demonstrated that their performance truly matters, when they are respected as full partners (just like our Constitution demonstrates that to us with the guarantee of our rights), people will perform beyond expectation. That is an essential aspect of the quality model that is different from the classic, efficiency-oriented approach, which held that employees would need ''motivating,'' guidance, and close supervision because they were not trustworthy. In PPS, management demonstrated that to the union and the union demonstrated that to management. Employees demonstrated it to their supervisors and supervisors became partners with their people. Teams took more responsibility when given the invitation in TPTB than when directed to perform specific tasks via the old model. The quality model is an extension of the nation's first quality statement—the Bill of Rights. The two go hand in hand.

Partnerships Need to Be Developed between Government Agencies and Their Suppliers/Contractors

The relationship between the Pacer Share implementation team and the outside contractor, Gilbert, played an essential part in the overall success of the project. From the very first planning session, prior to the initial TPTB session, the PPS team and the contractor committed themselves to being a quality-driven team. The PPS design team was exceptionally supportive of the contractor's needs for information about the organization. The members of the team educated the contractor about the project situation. It continued to provide open, trusting, supportive information to the contractor throughout the program life. There was never a time when the contractor made a call or request to McRorie or the Pacer Share team managers and was denied. The contractor was treated as a valued member of the DS team.

Many times, government agencies do not understand or trust the contractor's situation and they mismanage the contractor as a resource. Government organizations would do well to contact the DS project implementation team to learn of the approach taken with the contractor. The DS organization was exceptional at overcoming the inherent distrust that is often the case between the consultants and government agencies. As a result, the DS organization was able to obtain exceptionally high commitment from the contractor and added services from the contractor (without cost) to help assure the project's success.

The Civil Service System Is in Need of Change

The project was initiated as a demonstration effort to learn about the effects of a new system incorporating six interventions to the CSS, as presented in Chapter 5. Due to methodological issues discussed before, the effects of the PPS interventions have not been determined, and may not be identifiable upon the end of the five-year period for which the project has been authorized.

However, after the first three years of implementation, if the employees, supervisors, and members of the senior DS management team were to have had the opportunity to vote for or against the overall civil service system as modified by the project today, we would predict they would choose the alternative offered them through PPS. The PPS interventions further enable employees and their work teams to provide better quality to the customer. They offer the employees more flexibility to adapt their tasks, technology, and organizational structure to accommodate to the ever-changing needs of the customer. If a purpose of the CSS was to be responsive to the needs and preferences of the work force, management, and labor, the PPS experience has demonstrated that the need for change in the system exists.

A PEEK TO THE FUTURE

In the Appendix are comments by Anita Clevenger, the new Project Management Officer (PMO) of the PPS design team. She replaced Del Nelson when he retired in 1990. She has a fresh perspective and the opportunity to enlarge the demonstration to other organizations within the AFLC, if not the federal government.

SUMMARY

Project Pacer Share is the most far-reaching experiment occurring throughout the DOD and the CSS. It is a substantive attempt at finding new, more effective alternatives to the present Civil Service System while finding ways to improve quality to the customer. At Project Pacer Share, managers and nonmanagers alike are learning to practice "followership" for their customers and one another. As a result, they are demonstrating a renewed respect for one another, their customers, and their suppliers. They are challenging a traditional way of doing business that is less focused on customer satisfaction and more focused on the more rigid rules of conduct that are tied to the authority one has with the position he or she occupies.

What is taking place in PPS is long overdue and is to be commended. It has confronted problems with the Civil Service System and attempted to provide a viable working alternative to it. It may not have come up with the best alternative, but it is demonstrating improvements to that system that merit serious assessment by both the legislative and executive branches of government.

In terms of culture, whether in the "old" CSS or the revised one under demonstration by PPS, the leaders have made the commitment to listen to their people as though they were their very own "customers." The work force is demonstrating greater ability to work in teams, using TQM tools to manage their processes by fact. They have renewed pride in what they do. They are becoming even strident in their commitment to their customers. For those in PPS, the customer is becoming job number one!

At the end of its third year of demonstration, DS had been absorbed into another organization, and PPS has new leadership with Naehring's and Nelson's retirement, and the leadership is equally as dedicated and eager to extend what has already been started. The TPTB will not be included as an intervention in the expanded host organizations. Thus, the method to excite the will to quality improvement will be different from that employed during the first three years of the project's life. Because the TPTB was a primary process intervention in PPS during the first three-year effort, the nature of teamwork and its quality focus will be altered.

As previously stated, the reorganization of DS wherein its functions have been broken out into other systems precludes the future analysis of the effect of PPS interventions on DS processes as compared to others beyond the first three years of project demonstration. Very simply, the DS organization no longer exists. However, analyses can continue to be made in terms of how people now define their work, how they work with others, how they lead, how they follow, and how decisions are made.

Although PPS may conclude in February 1993, it, as a TQM demonstration, has lent support to the observations of industrial prophets who are calling for a new paradigm in the way we do business in America. PPS has demonstrated that the quality approach is also right for government. Indeed, quality in government is blowing in the wind.

REFERENCES

Bennis, W. G., and Slater, P. E. (1968). *The Temporary Society*. New York: Harper and Row.
Bowsher, C. A. (1990). "Program Evaluation is Essential." *The Bureaucrat* 19 (Fall): 5–8.

Campbell, D. T. (1957). "Factors Relevant to the Validity of Experiments in Social Settings." *Psychological Bulletin* 54: 297–312.

Chelimsky, E. (1990). "Executive Branch Program Evaluation: An Upturn Soon?" *The Bureaucrat* 19 (Fall): 9–12.

Guttentag, M. (1972). "Subjectivity and Its Use in Evaluation Research." *Evaluation* I(2): 60–65.

Horst, P., Nay, J. N., Scanlon, J. W., and Wholey, J. S. (1974). "Program Management and the Federal Evaluator." *Public Administration Review* (July–August): 300–307.

Hyman, H. H., Wright, C. R., and Hopkins, T. K. (1962). *Applications of Methods of Evaluation.* Berkeley: University of California Press.

Krone, B. (1990). "Total Quality Management: An American Odyssey." *The Bureaucrat* (Fall): 35–38.

Kuhn, T. S. (1962). *The Structure of Scientific Resolutions.* Chicago: University of Chicago Press.

Scanlon, J. W. (1977). "Type III and Type IV Errors in Program Evaluation." In *Evaluation Management: A Sourcebook of Readings,* Gilbert, G. R., and Conklin, P. J., Eds. Charlottesville, VA: The Federal Executive Institute.

Suchman, A. E. (1967). *Evaluative Research.* New York: Russell Sage Foundation.

Wholey, J. S., (1984). "Management of Evaluation: Implementing an Effective Evaluation Program." In *Making and Managing Policy: Formulation, Analysis, Evaluation,* Gilbert, G. R., Ed. New York: Marcel Dekker.

APPENDIXES

Autonomous Work Teams

Sharon Carvalho, DS Employee and Member of Self-
Managed Work Team

Autonomous work groups have received a good deal of attention lately. As organizations move toward developing a participative style of management, autonomous groups seem a natural evolution. Although these work groups are gaining in
popularity in the private sector, the federal sector is often saddled in a maze of red
tape which can often confuse and frustrate even the most experienced insider.

In March of 1990 the Administrative Section in the Directorate of Distribution
at McClellan AFB in California was faced with the loss of its supervisor. In this
structured environment, the supervisor's role is quite clear—they make decisions,
they intervene, they act as a buffer, and they perform a myriad of administrative
tasks. With the support and encouragement from management, our group was
offered the opportunity to operate as an autonomous work group.

The group took on the collective responsibility for those jobs previously handled by the supervisor. The team consisted of ten members with a variety of
specialities, grades and levels of experience. It was the group who became
responsible for decisions, interventions, buffering, and the myriad of administrative tasks of the office.

On the outset, planning was an essential process. Although at times tedious,
the group's ultimate success can be attributed to the time taken to make decisions
early in the process. It was during the planning phase that the team empowered
itself to be the collective power structure. The team defined the roles and responsibilities of the members. Each team member had an equal voice and could
sign correspondence. The team leader was to act more as a focal point for the
group and lead team meetings.

During this planning phase, the group also defined office procedures for issues
such as work assignments, paperwork flow, leave accountability, and individual
taskings. It was decided that each procedure was open for reevaluation should
it be determined not to be working. A number of procedures was in fact revised
and work loads redistributed.

Group involvement and decision making were probably the most challenging, and at times difficult, aspects of the experience. Because of the diversity of tasks inherent to the administrative area, the group would have to address topics with which many were unfamiliar. The team process fostered greater interest and a sense of personal responsibility and involvement with one another's work. Team members checked each other's work for quality and subsequently learned more about one another's job. Great office interaction took place and the group became closer. Team members found they could more easily discuss problems with others in the group.

The team was established as a test for the organization. Management had been observing the office's interaction and level of work and gained union approval to test the self-managing team concept at McClellan.

There were no controls to evaluate the group's effectiveness other than the ability of the office to maintain the previously established level of quality, timeliness of work products, and continuance of job performance. Quality, timeliness and job performance improved under the self-managing concept.

Pacer Share—Where Do We Go from Here?

Anita Clevenger, Pacer Share Project Management Officer

The environment in which Pacer Share has operated has never been an isolated test-tube for evaluating the results of the project design. The project is in an operational setting, where workload fluctuates, organizational needs change, and people move. The amount of personnel and organizational changes involving the project has recently greatly increased. I became the new Project Management Officer (PMO) in September 1990, concurrent with a reorganization in which the Directorate of Distribution became a division of the Technology and Industrial Support Directorate (TI). My primary charter is to expand Pacer Share throughout TI and another directorate up to the 5,000 people limit for a demonstration project.

Several changes have taken place that create special challenges for continued project implementation. Funds for the continuance of TPTB presented by our external consultant will most likely not be available in the future as they were in the past. If we rely on in-house staff for team building it will be different than that which worked so effectively in PPS during the first three years of implementation. No doubt the momentum established with the In-house Team Building Follow-On Consultants will be affected as well. The introduction of another approach to team building will lead to variance in the team building efforts throughout the project.

All the members of the Pacer Share Steering Group, with the exception of John Salas, AFGE president, have changed either due to reorganization or personnel moves. In the midst of all this change, the Defense Logistics Agency has expressed their intent to allow the 800 to 1,000 people scheduled to move to DLA from the Air Force to continue with the project through its completion. And, last but not least, Del Nelson retired in November, 1990.

The net result of all this turmoil is that the project's continued success will truly prove the benefits of the interventions divorced from the original personalities and organizational environment. Can Pacer Share thrive when so many changes are occurring? It's too early to say.

The decision to expand the project was largely driven by fiscal and organizational needs. The AF is required to streamline its operations due to major budget reductions, and the project clearly offers opportunity to save payroll dollars. However, the ability to effect these savings with managers new to the project will not immediately be in place. The management effort required to support the project cannot be ignored. First, management needs to understand the project interventions; second, true labor–management partnership must be developed; third, a bonafide effort to exploit the freedoms available in the project design needs to be made. This will not happen overnight. Part of my job as the new PMO is to draw from distribution's experience to shorten the time needed to prepare the managers to operate under Pacer Share.

Although not always clearly stated, one of the basic tenets of TQM and team building is respect for people. Management has a mandate to allow individuals to contribute to the fullest extent possible. This is fundamentally different from the traditional culture: a system designed not for the few troublemakers or the few superstars, but one designed for the majority of the people, with the premise that their contributions are vital to the organization's success. A frequent criticism of Pacer Share is that it degrades the individual by emphasizing teams and seeking to build a cooperative rather than competitive environment. In fact, the success of a few individuals at the expense of many others is far more degrading to individuals than Pacer Share.

Because a culture change is needed to implement such an overwhelming change in the management, it's almost impossible to remain neutral about the project. Either one continues to resist change and oppose what is happening, or one accepts the change and develops the view of the world in which no other way of operating is acceptable.

This is the most exciting and difficult assignment I have ever had. However, Pacer Share is beyond the point of the PMO being in a position to singlehandedly affect its progress. It's impossible to foretell where the project will be at the end of the demonstration period, but my belief is that those who have accepted the project's view of the world will find it virtually impossible to turn back.

Job Proficiency Guides

Jim Flaggert, DS Director of Training

The cornerstone of the DS job skills training program is the Job Proficiency Guide (JPG). The JPG is an explicit document that lists the tasks an employee is expected to perform on the job. Also, for each task listed on the document, is a predetermined proficiency level which indicates the desired level of performance an employee must demonstrate before being certified as a journeyman technician.

Each skill area in the Directorate has its own JPG. For example, warehouse workers, packers, management analysts, and secretaries all have their own JPG. Currently there are sixty-seven different JPGs corresponding to the sixty-seven different skill areas within the organization.

The task analysis for civilian employees is done in the following manner. First, documents are gathered. These include the corresponding military specialty training standard, the civilian position description, the civilian classification standard, and applicable regulatory guidance pertinent to the job. From these documents a ''straw man'' JPG is put together. Next, the draft guide is sent out to subject matter experts in the organization for their review and comment. The subject matter expert's comments are incorporated into the guide and then the guide is sent to the civilian personnel office for their review. Once personnel approves the guide it is field tested on a group of users. Pending the result of this test the guide is either published or modified. During the process, differences are worked out between the participants.

Once a guide has been approved it is placed in an Individual Training and Certification folder. There is a folder for each employee and this folder is kept by the employee's supervisor. The employee has complete access to the folder at any time. Once the guide is received by the supervisor, the employee's mastery of the tasks is either certified as proficient or opened for training. Additional tasks not included in the guide can be entered on a continuation sheet provided or written directly into the guide. In some cases, some tasks are not required of an employee. These can be omitted from the employee's training plan.

Incentives are built into the JPGs to conduct training and certification with integrity and seriousness. Employees who are not proficient in the tasks covered by the job are considered trainees. They are so coded into the personnel data system. Being a trainee can limit promotion and lateral transfer opportunities, consequently trainees are interested in seeing that their training is given a high priority by management.

The possibility that employees could be certified prematurely is monitored. All employees must spend a minimum of 45 days as a trainee (most are trainees much longer). Supervisors are given an eight hour training course on how to properly manage the JPG program. The promotion system is designed so that an employee who does not know the job will not score very well.

Management of the program is accomplished by a central Employee Development and Training office in DS. This office was specifically created to develop the JPG concept and was given division level organizational status.

Specialists are assigned to the training office. They are functional experts, knowledgeable of the various occupations within the DS organization. They obtain or develop courses for employees who need instruction to meet certification requirements. Actual certification of task proficiency is the responsibility of the supervisor to which the employee is assigned, and not by the central training office. The central office does, however, audit certification records submitted by supervisors.

Prior to the JPG concept the directorate lacked a system to determine employee's current knowledge, skill, and proficiency levels. Like most other organizations in the old way of doing things, at best, the organization kept lists of courses their employees completed. But such training was not directly connected with the extent to which the employee's skill or proficiency level had increased as a result of the course, or if, indeed, the employee needed that course to do his or her specific job.

Training was managed more along the lines of "efficiencies" tied to how many employees received what training at what cost per person than how to enable every employee to be a "winner" on the job through developmental assistance and adult-like mutual effort between the employee and the supervisor.

In the old system, emphasis in employee development was on the final product coming off the line, not on development of employee skills. If an item was usually received, stored, found when needed, packed and shipped as required, then it was assumed the system was working well. This situation resulted in an inefficient use of resources. Slower workers produced slowly because enough fast workers were available to offset the delays caused by the slower workers. Workers who made mistakes were often moved to less critical areas.

Since emphasis was not placed on training, rework was common. For example, if a letter was improperly typed it was simply kicked back to be redone. If an item was "lost," search parties were sent out to find it. In many cases the causes of mishaps and the area of weakness in the system were not investigated or shared with others.

The implementation of the JPGs helped to turn these types of situations around. For the first time the job requirements of a specific skill area were clearly identified. What an employee had to know and how well the task had to be done was clearly stated. Management now had a document from which true work force certification could result.

By assigning each employee, supervisor, and manager their own guide, and then checking individual performance against the stated task and proficiency level for each task, employee skill deficiencies were identified and positive training programs (as opposed to denigrating actions) were developed to meet these identified deficiencies. In those cases where deficiencies were widespread, formal group sessions were scheduled. In those more individual situations one-on-one coaching was used. On-the-job training (OJT) was used whenever a thoroughly well trained journeyman was available to conduct the training. This created added pride and team work among the employees in the work group, as well.

The program does not discriminate between workers. By adopting the JPG concept the organization now can train its employees to do their jobs according to the guides. This commitment also means it is now necessary to follow up on nonperformance by employees since certification data is tracked by the training office. For the first time it is clearly known by management who is certified and who needs training. From this information, supervisors are held accountable for the training of their employees and organizational training plans can be developed. A supervisor who has uncertified employees will know exactly who they are and has a system to train them.

An additional benefit of using the JPG is their use as training tools for multiskilled employees. The central training office of DS has developed a training plan that combines specific jobs into more generalized positions. For example, in the past there have been secretaries, clerk typists and management assistants each occupying different positions. Today the directorate has combined these three positions into a single position by simply placing all three JPGs into the employees' individual training and certification folders and conducting the training necessary. This move toward generalists, rather than narrowly defined specialists, has had benefits for management and employees alike. For management, fewer resources are needed and skills imbalances are minimized. Benefits for employees include greater job variety and challenge as well as an increase in job security.

The JPG concept is now being expanded across the Air Force Logistics Command (AFLC). During the summer of 1990 a work force development committee convened at Wright Patterson AFB, Ohio, to look at the viability of training within AFLC. At a follow on meeting of key training officials held in October 1990 at San Antonio, Texas, the JPG concept was adopted as the model for the entire AFLC.

Efforts to Generate Support for Project Changes

Dan Fuchs, PPS Design Team

In the early design phase of the project, the design team attempted to enlist top managers and division chiefs in DS in the design effort. We needed their ideas and recognized that early participation would be of invaluable aid in gaining their support for the project at the time of implementation. If we could involve the division chiefs in this phase, they would develop some sense of ownership in the project and transfer this positive feeling to their subordinate managers and the work force.

This effort failed. The specific methodology we followed was to present the group several areas of design consideration (individual award systems, different types of productivity gain share systems), ask that they form into groups to brainstorm ideas on possible alternative systems, and meet a week later to present their status. The methodology followed, to a great degree, the methodology we used internally in the design team: perform a literature search to see what other federal agencies or companies in the private sector were doing; follow-up with phone calls to the agencies or companies that were actively pursuing some sort of program in that area; brainstorm alternative solutions; list the pros and cons of each solution, and either research a consensus (with supporting arguments on why we agreed on a particular solution) or submit position papers to the Deputy Director so he could make a decision on which alternative he preferred.

In the case of the division chiefs, there was no action on their part. After postponing several meetings because the groups had nothing to report, the effort died. From my viewpoint, there were two reasons for the failure of that effort: the "It's your job, not mine" and "The mouse that roared" ideas. The first reflects reaction to "special" task groups like our design team: There is some jealousy, if the group is perceived to be set up as an "elite" group with special status and an objective that is specifically defined. In such a case, those people outside the group may elect to withhold resources or cooperation and justify the lack of cooperation by saying that the entire task is solely within the realm of the task group. In other words, no one else has any ownership or responsibility to help find solutions. The second reflects the general feeling that we would not be able to change anything as ponderous as the Federal Civil Service System, so why should anyone else waste their time in what was perceived as a futile effort. If asked directly why they did not respond to the tasking, the official reason would be there were more pressing matters in the daily operations that required their time and attention. In fact, this was somewhat the position of DS and the ALC, in that the Personnel and Comptroller design groups were not formed until after OPM had officially approved the preliminary design. Only then would the ALC and DS management commit additional resources to further design development.

The failure to get active participation by senior managers tended to make the design effort and implementation more difficult. Employees are quick to pick up on their supervisor's attitude, even when the supervisor doesn't openly voice a position. Lack of positive action, or lukewarm backing is interpreted by subordinates as opposition. Change, especially a change as revolutionary as Pacer Share (PPS), is difficult at best. There is a tremendous amount of organizational resistance for this sort of change. People believe they know how the existing system works, and even though it may be deficient in some areas, they believe they know how to work within the system. The idea of abandoning the known system for some new system, with new rules, is threatening. In this instance, since supervisors weren't actively aiding in establishing the new design, the project became, in the eyes of the general work force, a product of the small design group. Neither the management nor the work force had any responsibility to help make it work, and the new system was seen as being imposed on the test group, the DS organization.

In an effort to counter the uneasiness of change, the design group limited its efforts to gaining employee input to small groups of employees who had expertise in specific areas that were needed. Only after the final design approval did we attempt, through educational means, to explain the program to the entire work force. From the beginning of the design phase, we wanted to keep the general work force as well informed of what we were considering as we possibly could. This involved meeting with QC or small groups of employees to brief them on how the design stood at that moment, and alternatives that were being considered. We were careful to tell them that the information we were discussing was ''true'' at that time, but since the design effort was still in progress, the final product would probably be somewhat different from what we know at the current time.

Some people could accept this as normal development of an idea and were comfortable; others, however, became somewhat negative when aspects of the final design were different in some detail from an earlier version they had been told about. In some way, they felt they had been purposely deceived in the earlier briefings. Some employees need concrete answers in absolute terms. Yet in the planning and policy formation stage of PPS, we could not give them such information. Such ambiguity for some caused them more harm than good; it disturbed them and caused distrust rather than the partnership we were trying to build.

As a result, we gradually began limiting our briefings and were careful about discussing anything other than the broad outlines of the design outside of the design group. We had decided that rather than fuel the confusion of concerning employees with the details of the project, we would wait until we had final design approval to discuss it in detail with the work force. However, we still continued to give periodic status reports to the senior management at directorate level staff meetings, to keep them informed of what we were planning, and the rationale for the specific interventions. The design group also used the extensive network of QC, active at that time, to informally provide some information to the work force. The particular setting of employees who had volunteered to participate in the QC effort and facilitators who could discuss the design in detail, was fairly effective in terms of gaining some acceptance of the design.

After we received final approval of the design (six months before the implementation date), the participation of the division chiefs became vital. Although we had the general framework of all the interventions, the design had to be fleshed out in terms of detail and policy for actually operating the directorate under the new rules. The design group had purposefully left the design broad, so the senior management could begin to ponder how to translate the opportunities into the management of the directorate.

The Deputy Director formed the division chiefs and the design group into an Implementation Team, which met every morning for four hours. The design group would present the philosophy underlying a particular intervention and an idea of what we saw as the benefit of the intervention compared to the old system. The division chiefs would then discuss how they could use the intervention to better manage the resources, the policy that would be necessary to carry out the duties, and specific rules of operation. Many of these details became the Demonstration Operating Instructions, replacing old operating instructions.

Finally, with the realization that the project would indeed be implemented in only six months, there was a sense of urgency to develop the details. Since they were now active participants in a daily effort that used a significant amount of their time, the senior management began realizing they were indeed the owners and operators of the project, whether they wanted to be or not. The extensive amount of time devoted to the implementation effort also sent a message to the work force that the managers were involved in the project, and it was going to be a fact of life.

The last major preimplementation effort was a series of briefings to all employees. The Deputy Director, with the appropriate managers and the design team representatives, would meet with several groups of employees each day (group size was kept small, approximately twenty people, to encourage open communication), to explain the details of the design, what we hoped to accomplish, and the benefits of the new system compared to the former system. Early in this effort, we determined that it was important that the division chief and the managers of the particular unit being addressed, be the chief "presenters," and also make a statement of support for the project. In this way, the people were being told by the managers they were most familiar with, what would take place. The format served to signify that the management had taken an active and responsible part of the design and served, to a small extent, to downplay the idea that it was a product of only a small group of people (the design team).

How Can a Unit Supervisor Support His or Her Team-Building Group?

Connie Fullmer, Unit Supervisor

One of the most important rules to remember is to never dominate the meetings or selection of projects! This is a time when the supervisor should pull back so the employees will feel total ownership of their team and its purpose. From the beginning the team needs to be and feel that they are empowered to tackle any problems they want and to make changes that they see necessary. Show your trust in their capabilities and decisions. Allow them to express their concerns and criticisms. If you get angry when they voice dissension, it will be the last time you will hear from any of them. No one is going to put their head on the chopping block when you are known for killing the messenger.

By pulling back I do not mean to suggest that the supervisor should be totally withdrawn. On the contrary, the supervisor is also a team member who's role is that of coach. When a team has reached a point in their discussion where they do not know what to do, this is an ideal time for the supervisor to lend guidance and help the team out. It is important, however, to let the team try to come to a solution themselves before interjecting, as this is also a learning experience on group interaction and problem solving. Along with the facilitator of the group, the supervisor should help to keep the team on track and customer oriented. One of the checkpoints in defining problems and testing proposals is to ask, "How will this benefit our customer?"

You can display your commitment to partnership with the team by taking on your fair share of assignments. Particularly when the team has met with a stumbling block or barrier that they are experiencing problems with. By taking on the responsibility to go and resolve the problem, you show your unwavering support of the team and your willingness to fight for their causes.

Give the employees the time and opportunity to attend SPC, EPM, ESA and Team Building classes that will enhance their team building techniques. As a coach, you have the responsibility to be trained in these skills also. This will enable you to help train and guide the team when they incorporate these new skills in their team building sessions. The team should meet at least once a week and more if the project they are working on requires it. The supervisor should ensure that time is allowed for these meetings. If there is a problem with a heavy workload or employees are off, the team will decide whether to postpone their meeting and schedule it for another time. This empowerment will also reinforce ownership of the team to all the members.

Observe group behavior and help the group recognize areas that could be improved, such as seeking the opinions of other team members by asking for feedback or by showing encouragement of another team member's ideas. One of the most common problems in group behavior is the team member who is withdrawn. How do you draw this member into the conversation? By asking this individual their opinion, you not only recognize them as a member of the team, but you are also telling them that their opinion is important and that you are interested in them. Many individuals who are introverted by nature may be waiting to be asked for their input and are not really withdrawn. Thus, you may be missing out on some very good ideas simply because you did not ask them.

This brings us to another point. A supervisor should always know the personality type of his or her employees. It will greatly enhance your ability to assess the situation, and you will know how to approach this employee in a manner best suited for them. If the member is withdrawn and not sure they want to be on the team, do not force the issue! You will have singled them out and now they are forced to take a stand for fear of losing face among fellow employees. The best way to draw this member in is by making team building FUN!

By making team building fun you improve employee relations, members' enthusiasm is elevated, and there is a feeling of unity and team spirit. But most of all, sooner or later the employee who is holding back will want to join in on all the fun! After all, who wouldn't want to come to work when they know that they have a say in everything, have the right to fix or change anything, and have fun while they're at it?

How EPA Works for Me

Connie Fullmer, DS Supervisor

I was one of the fortunate employees who was able to attend one of the first EPA classes presented here. I found the class to not only be educational but exciting, too. My interest was peaked from the very beginning and remained there throughout the course as well as everyone else's.

The class was divided into small groups of five and our final assignment was to flow chart an entire process we felt we could improve. Our group decided to look at the sick leave report that we were required to do on a monthly basis. After doing a rough draft of the flow chart, we could not believe all the hands that this report went through and the amount of paperwork, time, and manpower required to produce the report.

Out of the nine areas of waste that you look for, the sick leave report covered seven of those. They are:

1. Work-in-process. We found that there were three different units that were waiting for one unit to forward the report before they could consolidate it to enable them to forward it to another organization.

2. Equipment. The unnecessary use of copy machines in order to have a copy for yourself.

3. Expenses. The cost of paper, charts for briefings and the cost of labor.

4. Indirect Labor. Human resources used to report the sick leave could have been used for production and improvements to our processes.

5. Planning. Poor planning required the units to manually produce a report that is already accessible in the H073 computer system that keeps a daily accumulative account of leave taken. The Electronic Mail system could also have been utilized to report the reasons for the sick leave usage directly to the unit responsible for reporting to the commander.

6. Human Capabilities. Use of personnel for mundane duties leaves no room or time for the challenges and opportunities to create better ways to do the job. Personnel are, therefore, not utilized to their full potential.

7. Operations. The plan is not valid. It takes more time and money to report the sick
   leave usage than the sick leave costs the organization in the first place!

This is just one report from one organization on one base that is costing us
unnecessary money. Imagine what it is costing the government and taxpayers
to produce this report nationwide!

One of the more satisfying moments for me as a supervisor was to see the
excitement of the employees when we first started training them in EPA. For
the first time they could see where they could make a difference. In fact, many
could be seen working on the charts in their spare time. When they could actually
put the process down on paper, it became very clear to them the changes that
could and should be made. As we continued to flow chart a process, we soon
found out that not all of the employees were doing the same job the same way
thus incurring variance. For those employees who were new on the job, not only
did they receive training during EPA, but their "fresh eyes" helped us to see
the process in a whole new light.

I had one team that was combined of two different shifts. This was a newly
formed team who had just gone through the Team Building Seminar. When this
group first started out they were having trouble feeling like they were a team
and there was constant dissension. The Team Building Seminar helped these
employees to understand each other better and to work together as a family. On
the heels of Team Building came EPA and this provided them the opportunity
to work on a project together and cement their new relationships. This group
soon excelled in their quick grasp of EPA and surprised many of us by the
amount of work they accomplished in a very short time. Why? Because they
had fun at it! It was a time when they could not only get to know each other
better, but they had control over their jobs and what that job would consist of.

Another team I had wanted to pay particular attention to one area in their unit.
This job had always been a difficult one and they felt they could improve it. All
of the jobs in this office were different from one another and this made it difficult
for one person to cover another's desk. During their EPA, the others learned
this desk as well and could fill in at any time. The team soon developed a plan
to look at everyone's job not just to improve it but to learn each other's desk
for better coverage. This enabled the team to give full coverage to the office
which not only cut down on variance, but cut down on the manpower required
to fill in when some one is off.

I have a third team that is just getting started in EPA and it will be exciting
to watch the changes that come over it. Especially when its members see that
they can make their job easier by weeding out waste and unnecessary steps. I
feel that EPA is one of the most useful and beneficial skills I have learned. I
not only use it on the job but at home, too. The applications are limitless!

Observations of Project Pacer Share

Jim Graham, Director, Installations Assistance Office—
East Office of the Secretary of Defense

One of my primary functions is to identify examples of excellence and share them with others throughout DOD, so that quality improvement interventions can be transferred from one military installation to another.

Project Pacer Share came to my attention in the Spring of 1989. It was then that I made my first visit to McClellan AFB, Sacramento, California, and attended a Tactical Planning and Team Building workshop. I did not expect to find the level of employee involvement in decision making that I found on that visit. It was something I had never seen before in my entire career, both military and civilian, which spans almost thirty years.

Employees who often felt alienated from their organizations and supervisors were learning to work together as though they were partners. Management was extending itself to find a better way of working together to get a top quality job done for their customers throughout the DOD and the nation as a whole.

I have never seen employees, supervisors, and work groups so involved in problem solving processes and team work activities, treating one another as "customers." It was most impressive to see the willingness of management to truly listen to their people, to learn first hand what was in their way (including the managers themselves) in getting quality to the customer.

As a result of my visit to Project Pacer Share, I have had the opportunity to share my experiences with many others in both government and the private sector. The result of that project on the Defense community has been exceptional. Commanders (Army, Navy, Air Force, Marine, and Defense Agencies) are trying the team building approach fostered by Pacer Share. It's working!

Project Pacer Share is the most far reaching experiment I've seen occurring within DOD. It is a substantive attempt at finding new, more effective alternatives to the present Civil Service System and traditional approach to management. At Project Pacer Share, managers and nonmanagers alike are learning to practice "followership" for their customers and one another. As a result, they are demonstrating a renewed respect for one another, their customers, and their suppliers. It is my view that what is taking place in Project Pacer Share is long overdue and is to be commended. In that organization, leaders have made a commitment to listen to their people as though *they* are their most valuable "customers."

On Reflection

Colene Krum, PPS Design Team

The project started with three or four people who took a look at their organization and decided things needed to be better. They envisioned their organization as it might be. They defined the characteristics of the organization in which they would want to work. They specified the quality of customer service with which they would like to be identified. They researched the literature and state-of-the-art quality focused practices in both the private and public sectors in the United States and abroad. They dared to dream and then accept their own responsibilities to go beyond the dream itself, and attempt to make it their reality. They pinpointed the barriers that were in the way of attaining their goals for the organization.

It started out as their adventure, their intellectual game that soon became their work life. I was there from the beginning and, by all odds, what we accomplished went well beyond our own expectations.

Being a part of the design team, especially at the project's early gestation period, was a lonesome experience. We were asking our colleagues, some more senior than us, to share in our vision, take ownership of it, and radically change course. There were no maps, regulations, or guides to follow. To get to our destination, we had to find our own way. It was indeed a journey into the future, one that we would work on together as a team for nearly the next decade.

Although the personnel system in which our work life was structured did, indeed, support us, it was costly and limiting. It impeded our ability to accomplish our organizational goals and objectives while optimizing quality to the customer, being cost efficient, and fostering opportunities for continued personal growth, pride, loyalty, and team work among employees. We chose to improve it rather than just complain about it.

We stepped forward to make a difference. That step turned out to become a radical leap, at times almost a free fall, from our past way of doing things. What we perceived to be a fall into an abyss turned out to be a leap into a better world of work. It was fun!

None of us were experts in planned change, yet we had to move the idea for the creation of a quality oriented reorganization forward to those who were actually guardians of the very system that we were labelling as "the problem." We had to convince them that the system was in need of changing, even though they had learned to function in it better than most, as they had been promoted in it. Our challenge was to convince them that we had designed a better system than their own. It was like attempting to convince caterpillars to undergo their metamorphosis and dare to become butterflies without the caterpillar's being able to envision the transformation.

For some, helping them to recognize the need for change was easy, others took more convincing, while others would say, "It isn't broken, so don't start fixing things, because you'll tear apart a system that took years to perfect."

The project has just completed its third year of operation. We have been visited by interested members of literally hundreds of organizations whom we found to be much easier to convince that what we were doing was right than some of the very people in our organization who never wanted the change in the first place.

We have been among the very few who have had the opportunity to create an alternative and see it tried by others. We spent about five years developing the idea for PPS. It took many revisions and reformulations and rejections from others. Finally, we gained the "okay" to actually make a formal proposal to be considered by the highest levels of our own organization, OPM, organized labor, and Congress.

We were too busy to celebrate the project's approval, for we had too much to do and too little time to do it perfectly. We prepared briefings targeted for those in our own organization to learn about the project and its concepts. We prepared training modules to educate others about Deming's TQM and specific EPM tools that they could use. We watched from the sidelines while our outside consultant, Ron Gilbert, took our managers and their teams, week after week, year after year, away from their work places to introduce them to the new model of work where, as a team of partners, they could exercise total commitment to customer service. Through TPTB, we saw the emergence of *hope* from very talented members of the work force (both managers and nonmanagers, alike) who had nearly forfeited their will to be outstanding on the job by the negative attitudes that they had formed within themselves over time as a result of the old system. That hope soon turned to new initiatives and eagerness to learn and use the TQM tools that we had so eagerly wanted them to learn. Now they were doing it on their own.

As a result of TPTB, participants learned to live the rhetoric of TQM. We learned to actually respond as one another's suppliers and customers. We experienced empowerment rather than talked about it.

We saw teamwork turn into quality work—better services and better products being produced from the floor, the offices, and the organization. Hearing good news from our customers about our service began to occur daily. Before PPS, we heard good news from them mainly when they were getting ready to ask us for a favor.

At the end of the project's third year, when an AFLC-wide reorganization and national defense cutback threaten the very teams we had built and the existence of MCAFB itself, there remains PRIDE among the DS employees. That is the greatest reward members of the design team have received.

If we did nothing more, we created an environment that will be a bit less stifling for those who follow. We challenged the stifling effects of the system and, on many fronts, we were the victors.

From the start, we realized we had a once in a lifetime opportunity to create our own destiny. We approached it that way, and we, in DS, share pride in what we have done. And we are not through yet!

Recollections from an Original Design Team Member

Colene Krum, PPS Design Team

Dan Fuchs had completed his masters in systems management and was working in the systems design shop. I had just completed four years working with Procurement and Material Management redesigning jobs under the Orthodox Job Enrichment (OJE) program and had returned to the Management Resources Division in Distribution. Del Nelson was managing the Management Resources Division and heavily into the "Quality Circle" program. Both Mr. Nelson and I had attended the West Coast Productivity Conference held at the Sacramento ALC where we learned of the Demonstration Projects sponsored by the Office of Personnel Management (OPM). Mr. Nelson had previously formed an interdirectorate work group to design a change to the personnel system, but he could not get agreement, commitment, or unification of his ideas. The other directorate members withdrew from the work group, and Mr. Nelson then pursued the idea of applying for a demonstration project for DS alone. Mr. Jerry Tompkin, then DS's Deputy Director, was looking for a way to compensate employees adequately for the work they had done in their Quality Circles. He particularly was interested in whether productivity could be improved by correlating work achievement to team reward. Together Mr. Tompkin and Mr. Nelson established the project office which would develop the demonstration project.

Mr. Fuchs and I were selected to begin developing ideas that would reward productivity achievements. In the meantime, Mr. Nelson had been promoted to Chief of the Transportation Division of DS. So Dan Fuchs and I found ourselves (later to be joined by the union representative) in a small out of the way room and began extensive research into the productivity, quality, and gain sharing programs being conducted around the country. We also traveled to conferences, visited private companies, contacted heads of corporate structures, and spoke privately with research consultants about our ideas and sought their experience and counsel.

We were in contact with people on both coasts, the south, and as far north as Canada. D. L. "Dutch" Landon, Michigan Quality of Work Life Council; DANA-HYCO Corporation, Ashland Ohio; Bert L. Metzger, Profit Sharing Research Foundation, Evanston, Illinois; Mitchell Fein, Improshare; Hewlett-Packard; Chevrolet-Pontiac Canada Group; David T. Kearns, CEO Xerox Corporation; American Velvet; Motorola; and W. Edwards Deming are just a few of the people from whom we learned some of the pros and cons of incentive and productivity programs. Mr. William Batt, U.S. Department of Labor, quoted the following premise from Mr. George Schultz, Professor of Economics, MIT: "The average worker is able to make and, given the right circumstances, wants to make important contributions to the solutions of production problems. If you cannot accept this premise you need consider the quality of work life questions no further." This statement has been to a large extent what the Pacer Share project has been all about.

Neither Dan nor I had any knowledge of, nor had seen any of the work originally developed by the first team, so we started from scratch. With Dan's educational and systems background, and my manpower/management background coupled with my present experiences in teaching Orthodox Job Enrichment (OJE) techniques (building teams and enriching jobs), we began designing what would become Pacer Share.

Productivity gain sharing was the first change to be developed. One of the hardest sales was equal dollar shares. It was not difficult to sell equal shares to the work force nor the labor representative, but high level managers and employees were taken back by the idea that the work force should get the same productivity gain sharing as they received. The philosophy had to match the actions. We were saying to the work force that it was everyone's responsibility to improve productivity, provide quality service, and create a quality environment in which to work. We also said everyone is an equal participant, an equal share holder and equally accountable for where this directorate goes in the future. We created the Project name Pacer *Share* based on this philosophy. Each directorate employee has one share and is affected by the organization's successes and failures. It was therefore only ethical that if accountability, responsibility, and success belonged to the employee, then the employee should equally share in the benefits. The losses come in the form of RIFs, contracting out jobs, base closures, and promotion freezes.

My experiences in OJE gave me several insights into what keeps managers in the background of process improvement. For those who tried it and were successful, they suffered budget and personnel cuts, while their less successful counterparts reaped the savings. Some told me they could not afford to improve, save money, or admit there was something that could be improved because of the repercussions. Dan had also experienced some similar repercussions in the project he had participated in. Out of these experiences came the ideas for supervisory grading criteria, series consolidation, and productivity gain sharing. We had seen them as the roadblocks keeping both the manager and the worker safely in the status quo. After we took the first three concepts to OPM, we received permission to add other ideas if we desired. Mr. Nelson then added to the design his ideas for no appraisal, demonstration on call, and pay banding, an idea originally pursued by his inter directorate group.

The struggles are still vivid, and at times we wondered if we would be canceled before we ever began. If we had taken "no" for an answer, you would not be reading this today. As I remember, it was a time of "negative" influence that we just had to overcome. It went something like this. It can't be done, "they" won't let you, it's too ambitions, it will never work, the rules require . . . , it's illegal. How did we get from there to the success stories? We were told that series could not be consolidated; appraisals were required and necessary to control people; pay banding was already being tried and off limits to us; supervisory grading criteria without numbers and grade associations would be impossible; demonstration on call would discourage applicants; and productivity gain sharing would not be acceptable. The Deputy Director changed three times during this period. Each offered insights and leadership when it was most needed. We refused to take "no" as an answer. It was a difficult, at times trying struggle, but we met some creative and adventurous folks along the way who were willing to listen and risk their reputations on a vision of quality improvement so badly needed for both the work force and the Department of Defense. Without Congressional assistance, labor, and some very dedicated and sharp folks throughout the system, we could not claim the successes we have already achieved.

How did we get the support needed locally? It was a combination of early leadership from the then DS Deputy Director, Mr. Jerry Tompkins, who initially kicked off the effort to design the project in January 1983. The labor union got on board instantly, supported us, and have never left. AFGE agreed to represent labor on Pacer Share issues at an early February 1983 meeting. The RAND Corporation supported the project immediately as they saw that our ideas would benefit the entire federal government. OPM, San Francisco Office, guided us through some of the personnel roadblocks, then we met with the Washington, D.C. OPM group, which further provided the demonstration legal guidance and Federal Register help that we needed. We, in turn, taught them many aspects about productivity gain sharing projects, and helped them write the guide for doing demonstration projects. Although we were not their first project, we were, in fact, their first major project and learning arena.

We began designing the concept for change in January 1983, brought RAND in as the third party evaluator in August 1984, and attained concept approval from OPM the following August 1985. At that point, personnel and accounting were willing to join the project design staff to assist in designing the detailed changes to the personnel system and establishing productivity gain sharing formulas and measurement plans.

The rest is history still in the making. The journey through concept, to detailed design, and on into implementation is trying at best; if you aren't dedicated to the idea of making improvements that will help others, it is not a recommended journey. Those who are only interested in their own personal careers and successes need not apply.

The Team-Building Process: From the Perspective of the PPS Manager

Carl McRorie, DS Deputy Director

Prior to PPS, the DS organization was managed by individuals who headed their separate organizational domains, but were not working together as a team of managers who were mutually focused on getting quality to the customer through their own collaborative processes. Each manager was at the top of his or her "pyramid," but the vital collaboration needed among all the pyramids within DS was lacking. We needed to build a team; starting at the top.

To do this, we selected an outside third-party consultant rather than use one or more of our own in-house facilitators to conduct our first session. The selection of an outsider provided us instant expertise (education, experience, demonstrated results elsewhere) and added objectivity.

In our first session, TPTB demonstrated to me that through the two day team building process open dialogue could begin and individuals could come to see themselves and others with whom they worked as important and necessary members of a team. Perhaps, more clearly, the process demonstrates that each person truly is unique and has very valuable gifts that can be used and are of worth to themselves, the members of their teams, and the organization. Accordingly, the process can improve individual sense of self worth and enhance a sense of belonging—a sense of belonging that is so essential to improvement and involvement in daily work.

Given what I saw in our initial session with the DS management, I realized that TPTB could provide the starting point, the basic initial building block, for our entire effort(s) to improve the quality of work life and capability of our system. It demonstrated customer-oriented service and then provided the opportunity for the participants to believe it themselves.

As the manager of PPS, I had been struggling with a question for some time: "How does an organization (or manager) empower people?" Empowerment is a term used a lot, but in actuality has been more rhetoric than reality when it is espoused by managers of organizations. Fear runs rampant in organizations, and it causes people to withhold vital information and initiative to get the right things done the way they are supposed to be done.

During that first TPTB session, I saw many members of our management team take full ownership in, and exercise their own control over, the processes they managed. They were motivated as a team; more ''pumped up'' than I had ever seen them as a group. It wasn't just a motivational effort, however, for they also identified major problems in the way to doing better, more quality driven work for one another as well as DS's external customers. The results gained from the TPTB process brought me to conclude that, for the good of the organization and its customers, every employee in DS needed the same training in customer-oriented behavior, and the invitation to get involved in fearless team play—as though they were in business for themselves working to please their customers in all that they do.

Early on in the team building process, it seems that I almost had to insist that some of our supervisors and managers participate fully in the TPTB process. Some were highly resistant to their having to ''listen'' to their people—an actual component of the TPTB process. That was a role many supervisors felt uncomfortable in, as they had always seen the supervisor as the person doing the talking, not doing the listening.

We gained a lot of extraordinary substantive results and savings as a result of the TPTB process. However, when looking back, without management's unflinching insistence of keeping the process going, TPTB may have died soon after its first application with our top management team. As it journeyed further on throughout the organization and directly involved those closest to the work processes, the TPTB process resulted in substantial work improvement and team play throughout our organization and for its customers. It has literally saved DS hundreds of thousands of dollars through teams of employees working better together and involved in streamlining their operations, and developing new methods to perform the work itself.

In TQM, cultural change or work force involvement must be based on mutual trust, respect, and a feeling/belief of individual and collective value in the work force. TPTB gives those participating a glimpse of what it is like to work in an organizational setting where mutual respect, trust, and collective pride and self worth exist. Without TPTB and the insight it provides, the implementation of a meaningful TQM program would not be possible.

Every employee in our organization was introduced to the team building process. Partnerships were formed among members and their supervisors and their customers. The walls and parochial interests that impede collaboration were weakened (if not broken down).

Managing the team building process, seeing the extraordinary accomplishments and personal and team pride that emerged along the way have been a highlight in my career. Wherever our employees go as a result of reorganization, RIF, mission redirection, Center closing, or as a result of their own self-initiated career redirection, I am confident they will be more highly dedicated to quality and be builders of high performing teams. Team building is not a one-time thing. It is a process and, like everything else tied to quality, is never-ending.

The Labor–Management Evolution of Pacer Share

Frank Mason, DS Chief Management Negotiator and
Senior Manager

In June of 1988 I was assigned to the duty of Chief Management negotiator to go along with my new assignment as Chief of the Material Storage Division. The Division has 650 workers and at the time many union/management problems.

I can vividly recall the first negotiation session in June of 1988 as one of the most uneasy things that I had encountered. When we (the management team) walked into the meeting room, the union sat across from us with arms folded and the only person to speak was Mr. Salas, the president. The next six weeks were the typical proposal, counterproposal, caucus, etc., type meetings. I was at my wits end.

Prior to our next meeting I informed my team that if we truly want to make headway we (union/management) need to be open with one another and feel free to discuss our needs as problem solvers rather than self protection oriented win–lose negotiators. We then discussed this with the union president. He agreed that this was one of the first major turning points in our relationship.

(Note: During this period I was empowered by my director to be the negotiator. However, my director and the union president did not trust one another.)

With the commitment to be more open with one another, we decided to jointly attend a university sponsored seminar on cooperative labor–management relations. I convinced my director to go along with the team. The session proved very positive to all of us. This started the positive relationship between the director and union president and made my job easier.

The year 1989 was a period of rapid expansion of the building of trust between the union and management. A formal statement of partnership was drawn up and signed by the director and union president. At the time, I did not realize the significance of this. Only later through talking about it to various groups from other agencies and organizations of the federal government did I realize this was a first.

One of our most risky agreements took place in the spring of 1989. We had been talking about the importance of professional managers as well as union stewards. At the time, the union had twenty-three part-time stewards and management had a very elaborate time accounting system for them. We jointly agreed that the union needed full-time stewards. We agreed to give them two if they would do away with the part-timers. Management took a lot of criticism from the base labor relations and Headquarters for allowing this. However, as time has gone by, the whole base now has a full-time steward for each directorate and labor problems are being solved at the first level in most instances. As a matter of fact, this is now being done AFLC-wide.

Now for what I believe is the most significant thing we have done. As time went on it became apparent to me that to fully achieve labor–management cooperation and the quality oriented management concepts and ideals that go with PPS, we had to expand the negotiation process. I found myself making all of the decisions that affected four of the other divisions in DS. It was also true that most of my peers were getting uncomfortable with this.

The union president and I met off line in his office to discuss the strategy for forming a Labor–Management Council concept of negotiating. We both agreed, and the LMC was created. Membership is composed of all division chiefs, union stewards, cost accounting and is co-chaired by the union president and me. The co-chairs have the authority for agreements. Our final Charter was signed in January 1990.

In summary, I've learned that most of the fears that the union had about management centered around the issue that the union is the representative of the rank and file. One has to be very sensitive to this when dealing with work teams and many other issues centered around highly participative, team oriented, quality management. You must take care and ensure union participation on all issues concerning practice, procedure and working conditions. If you don't, people start asking, ''Why do I need the union?'' which undermines the viable role of the union itself. Thankfully, PPS enjoys a partnership with the union and all employees.

The Results of the Quality Approach: A View from the Director of DS

Colonel David Naehring

Entering the DS at McClellan AFB six months after the start of formal team building sessions, while the ink was still wet on our Total Quality Management plans, PPS provided a tremendous opportunity. I had missed the early union negotiations, resistance from supervisors to share power and control and the normal bureaucratic aversion to risk taking.

What I found during my first days at the helm was a two thousand person organization that had, by repetition over the years, developed a grasp of the essentials that needed to be done—they knew what had to be done each day to make the "big system" work. However, they had not yet developed an understanding of the interrelationship of our key production processes.

During an early meeting with our top managers from each functional area, I asked a simple question: "How many basic processes do we have in distribution?" The answers ranged from a "couple dozen" to "we never counted." As we've moved through the universal training of our people in team building it has been amazing to watch what happens when over 125 teams begin to focus on their basic processes, through the tools taught them in EPM, the interdependence among work areas, open communications and the honest expression of needs to improve customer performance. Over time, we have come to recognize that everyone in the work force touches several different processes and that we clearly have over a thousand different processes in motion every day.

There were rough times at the beginning, and we learned some lessons the hard way. When teams finished with the formal team building sessions, we expected that enthusiasm and motivation, so evident on the last workshop day, would sustain the team once they were back in the workplace. For a few teams there was spectacular early success and then a cooling off. Other teams just never got their collective act together, while the rest made a valiant but slow effort to keep things going but never really reached their potential. Working together, several teams diagnosed the problem, developed options and proposed that we start a cadre of "coordinators" (later known as in-house team building consultants) to facilitate team progress. These coordinators came directly from the work force and were trained in how to work with our team building philosophy. They began working with their new teams the day of "graduation" from team building class. Their solution worked. Today we have an outstanding cadre of in-house team building consultants who come from the ranks and have a strong commitment to delighting our customers.

While progress was being made in the organization—to switch from a traditional "supervisor knows best" philosophy to one of "let's tell the team the problem, as we see it, and get their ideas"—interesting stories with real heroes began to emerge. A supervisory team in our inventory ordering area saw what they initially perceived as a need for more computer terminals and clerks to better support local customers. When the team completed essential process management (EPM) analysis they found something other than what they expected to find.

Being a west coast depot, they knew that vendors on the east coast were hard for us to reach after 1:00 P.M. local time because it was already 4:00 P.M. on the east coast. They also knew that our local (west coast) customers had a need to reach us with their requirements until 6:00 P.M. The supervisory team came up with a simple but effective solution called "Expanded Customer Support Hours." The work force participated in developing a flexible work schedule that insured a portion of our people came to work at 6:00 A.M. while others set their start time to enable coverage until 6:00 P.M.

"Expanded Customer Support Hours" was a simple concept that serves as an excellent example of what can be done with team building. Had supervision taken unilateral action to declare that some people were to come to work at 6:00 A.M. while others were to come in later and stay until 6:00 P.M., we would have been tied up in union negotiations, possible unfair labor practice charges and a number of individual grievances—and perpetuated the perception that management was out to "get us" one more time. Working with the team and our union partner, we were able to quickly start the new hours, avoid the need for more computer terminals and people, reach suppliers during their operating hours and, most important, provide better support to our customers.

Another team, mostly blue collar workers in our shipping area, saw a need to improve the way consolidated shipments were handled. A consolidated shipment is an effort to reduce transportation costs by placing together, each day, all items being shipped to the same destination. The intent is to avoid single shipments and use one container as consolidated shipment. Sounds simple, but the process is fraught with opportunity for disaster. Any problem with a single item in the proposed shipment was reason to delay the entire consolidated shipment, and problems always occurred. The team did an essential process analysis, using the tools they learned in team building and their class on EPM. In a few weeks, the team was able to focus on why consolidated shipments were frequently late. They identified the subprocesses, including those that were broken and then developed and tried solutions that made sense to the team. The result was quick and effective. Customer support was improved. But almost as important was the knowledge of the process that evolved within the team as well as a confidence that they could diagnose a problem and then do something themselves—without supervision providing a text book answer to the situation. We believe this is ownership and employee empowerment at its best in DS.

Vision from the start of PPS and our quest for improved quality was based on a premise that within our work force we had over a thousand processes that worked daily in concert with one another. It was also our perception that not one of the processes was perfect.

Therefore, if we were serious about improving customer satisfaction and upgrading the quality of our product, an abundant opportunity existed. What was needed was a mechanism for attaining ownership for each process at every level of the organization and the tools and training for our people to be able to focus on making massive process improvement.

A dramatic shift in the role of the first and second level supervisor was also envisioned. There was one supervisor for every ten workers and we saw some opportunity to reduce this overhead and transition our supervisors from "people watchers" into coaches and facilitators for quality team performance. The problem surfaced very quickly. It was discovered that being a supervisor required knowledge of the supervisory process—how one reports performance to senior management, solves coordination problems, and maintains discipline in the work force. However, our supervisors did not really have in depth knowledge of the processes they supervised. Our supervisors had become generalists in our key production processes but specialists in the supervision process.

Our immediate objective became one of educating supervisors, from the top down, to become coaches—willing to make the transition from one who "commands" the troops and insures compliance to one who develops the team and coordinates activities toward meeting objectives. The supervisor needed to move into the new role as a resource provider and facilitator who was there to help the team to provide total customer satisfaction.

Some supervisors could not handle this new role and either chose to retire or asked to move out of supervision. Others went along with the new scheme on the premise that "this too shall pass" but had no real intention of ever changing their approach. We had to take action to move these folks into nonsupervisory jobs—it was not hard to find them. But most supervisors understood the changing environment and made a genuine effort to make the transition. They have become the heroes and heroines in our saga. With our new supervisor to worker ratio of 14:1 and a clear road map for moving this closer to 20:1 in the future, today DS is well on the way toward reducing overhead costs.

Essential Quality Analysis at Work

Willie Nesbit, PPS Project Analyst

I have had the opportunity to use EQA on several occasions. It is a way to look at the finer details of a process. It helps one understand both future and present processes that are going on. When I'm talking Essential Quality Analysis I'm talking P–D–C–A–S and the Standardized Fishbone tools. EQA is a structured way of enabling others to see your point of view in the language that they understand. We use plan, do, check, assess, and support very simply. We analyze a process and apply P–D–C–A–S in each section of that process and break it down even further through the application of the standardized fishbone (who, what, when, where, why, and how).

EQA has been used in a variety of processes in our organization by the workers themselves. It was used to show the "doubting Thomases," those individuals who were stuck in their old way of doing business, that other alternative actions were more viable. Its straightforward, rational application enabled such people to manage by fact while alleviating their fears and defensiveness.

What Team Building Did for Us

Joe Prater, DS Trucker

If someone would have told me that what I was going to attend that November in 1987 would change my life and for once I would be doing something I believe in so much, well I would have told them they were crazy. But not so, for so many years at McClellan I gave up and really had no goals on what the rest of my life would be. I was told for years the way to do my job—right, wrong, or indifferent. And like everyone else, I expected that from management and tried to make the best of it. At first I tried to change things, and management would either ignore me or just not pay any attention to me. We attended team building in November of 1987. I was against the concept at the start and did not want any part of it, just another program that would last a few months and be thrown out. Not the case, we were surprised to find an outsider (Dr. Ron Gilbert) there to teach the class and that in itself made a big difference to me because he could be objective and it was immediately obvious he was on everyone's team and would not be intimidated by those in management who were attending, too, and were expected to participate like the rest of us. Indeed, he could enforce the rules of fair play for all. He began by asking us what we expected out of the two days. He had us pick a number from one to seven, with "one," a waste of time and "seven," an extremely useful time.

I did not buy into it at first, but at the end of the second day I can truthfully say I found the experience to be a "seven." He gave us a challenge to make things better and to tell management how we think things can be improved so we could really deliver quality to our customers.

At team building our supervisors committed to us (and we to them) to work together to make DS a better place for everyone. Now two years later we have built a partnership with our managers. They listen to us and allow us to work out our problems as a team. There is a trust now, a bond, that I would have never believed could have existed before without team building. To make team building a success you must have trust and work in partnership; it takes a lot of hard work and understanding.

An example of what we were able to get done as a result of our team building is our shuttle service. We started a shuttle service with our tractor-trailer section. We started with just one unit and within two weeks we had to add another due to the demand for it. In its first year we realized a savings of over $346,000, and in 1990 our team has realized a savings of over $450,000 with the improvements that have been made and the changes to the way we do business.

If it was not for team building, none of the things that have made our job and work place so much better would have happened. We would still be in the same rut and unhappy in our jobs and still taking our jobs home to our family. Team building has given us the chance to be the very best we can be on our job and off.

One of the most important things that has come out of team building is the fact that we know who our internal customers are, and we have the tools such as EPM, ESA, and SPC [see Chapter 12] that helps us identify the customers. Before team building, we had no idea who our customers were; in fact, we really didn't care who our customers were, but now we do everything in our power to insure we are providing our customers with the best service possible. After identifying the customer, we have gone to them asking what we can do to make it better; we invite them to our team building meetings to discuss any problems we may be having or they have, and work out a win-win solution to make sure that what we do helps.

That's team building to me, people helping people to make it better. If team building were to end today and we were to go back to the old way of doing business before team building, I would be looking for another job tomorrow. I will never go back to the way it was, when management and the work force were separate, and we did what we were told by management rather than what we and our management know is right for the customer.

Before our team attended team building, we tried to make some changes in how we conducted our business. We went to our managers, and they told us to just do the job the way it was set up because it works. It didn't work. After our two days with Ron, we came back and presented a plan to our managers to start a shuttle service to our customers, a service that we wanted to try a year before but we were not allowed. The service consisted of a driver with a trailer that would pick up several places and deliver to our customers without dropping the trailer. We started with one test vehicle and within a three week period we had to commit another trailer, and two years later we have four flat bed trailers and one closed van. We increased our production by 56%. Team building works because the employees want it to work.

The Union's View of the Project

John Salas, President, AFGE Local Union 1857

This project made sense from its very inception. Having been a federal civil servant as well as a member of the military, I have been well schooled with regard to the problems and pitfalls of the federal personnel system. It is too rigid, too cumbersome, too inflexible, too entangled with rules that impede rather than facilitate creative and fair employment practices. Also, there were too many variances in the system wherein the treatment of employees was often a result of "creative" manipulation of rules rather than fair employment practices.

In a system of progressive grade levels, there were exceptions that made it possible for some people to be tied to the career ladder (e.g., going from a WG–5 to a WG–6, WG–7, etc.), while other employees could hopscotch from a WG–5 to a WG–8 and then be promoted to a WG–11. And all this could be done without substantive evidence that the employee who had been so quickly promoted was better than the employee whose career more closely followed the rule book. In fact, quite often the reverse was found to be true. The "fast burner" type employee was often less of a team player than the other employee who moved up the chain of command with his or her team.

Thus, from my perspective, the concept of pay banding in Project Pacer Share made a lot of sense, for it enabled all employees to enrich their work experiences and gain greater job skills, which are both beneficial to the organization and to the individual.

It took time for management and the union to create a working partnership in the project. At first we didn't trust each other—there wasn't much reason for such, as we had a history of adversarial relations. However, we did have one thing in common—we wanted to improve the quality of work for government employees. As Americans, we shared a common concern—we wanted to improve the work situations for employees so they could provide more quality work. As we (labor and management) began to work together in the early planning stages of the project, we began to realize we had a lot of common concerns. Neither the AFGE leadership nor the DS leadership viewed the federal personnel system to be an asset for quality. We agreed that the personnel system needs changing. Over time, we were able to pinpoint the flaws in the performance appraisal system and we agreed to eliminate it. We also agreed that the grade system was in the way to quality and we were very quickly able to agree on pay banding as a more viable alternative. Gainsharing made sense to us, but there were many bureaucratic obstacles to overcome before it would be considered to be a bona fide program component. As we moved forward in the program design phase, we found that we needed one another more than we thought. We, in the union, were able to muster vital political support in Washington that was essential to overcome the normal type of resistances that would come from higher levels of the OPM and DOD bureaucracies.

Upon approval of the project and its initial stages of implementation, the management of the project fell back to the old way of doing things whereby the union was a second-string player on the team. However, it didn't take the project long to realize that the only way the project could succeed was through a true partnership between the union and the organization.

We started out as partners in name only. However, over time, we became partners in action. Together, labor and management at MCAFB in Project Pacer Share joined forces to improve organizational planning, decision making, and employee relations and training to improve productivity and overall performance to the customer.

If America is to be able to regain its status as the hallmark of quality worldwide, labor and management will need to forge the type of partnership that we have begun at MCAFB through Project Pacer Share.

Guides to Supporting the Follow-On Coordinator

Lee Tefertiller, PPS Team Follow-On Coordinator

One of the most important roles in team building is that of the follow-on co-ordinator. Teams initially rely on this person for guidance in how to get their team set up and headed in the right direction. Therefore, support for this individual is of the utmost importance.

When we initially started the follow-on facilitation in PPS, we sat down with management and exchanged "needs" from each other. These needs were the result of how we felt the program should function. Having had no experience in the follow-on field, and no one's previous experience to call on, we were treading in unchartered waters.

Management's commitments to us were to "do whatever you need to do to make the teams successful and to back you 100 percent."
This support was provided in the form of:

1. Management legitimizing the facilitator's role in team building.
2. Assistance in development of role definition for supervisor, team leader, team members, and facilitator.
3. Assistance in development of team building guidelines.
4. Monthly communication meetings with team leaders.
5. Timely follow-up on action items from teams.
6. Time allowed for team members to do follow-up on action items.
7. Time allowed for training of the team leaders.
8. Time allowed for training in the necessary TQM tools to achieve process improvement.
9. Keeping aware of team progress and breaking down barriers for teams when needed.
10. Time allowed for planning sessions with facilitator, supervisor and team leader.

Without this type of support, the facilitator's role would be severely hampered, if not impossible. The commitment of management is vital to the successful implementation of team building in the work force.

A Team Leader's Challenge

David Thompson, DS Team Leader

I was selected by my team as team leader. I work with our supervisor, the recorder, the members of our team, and the team building consultants to help us address ways our team can provide better quality to our customers. We meet almost weekly as a team to hear from one another and our customers so that we can do our jobs better.

In the past, we only had staff meetings which were run by our supervisor. Those meetings were not as participative as our team meetings. In our team meetings we try to include everyone on the problem solving process.

Sometimes our meetings are spent on interpersonal issues. That is okay, as it helps us work through things that get in the way of our working together better. We used to spend more time on the personal issues rather than the work process issues. That is changing now. Our supervisor is becoming more like a partner to us than a "supervisor" working for management to control us and tell us what to do.

Being a leader is new to me. Like most other team leaders selected by their team members, I don't feel skilled in leadership and feel I need a lot of training so I can work better for my team and the customers we serve.

My team needs to realize that I am not a replacement for our supervisor. My role is very different from the supervisor's role. It is my greatest challenge to get the other team members to recognize that they are an equal partner with equal responsibilities to bear. This kind of participation is the ultimate support for the team leader and the continued team building process.

We do not receive extra pay or enjoy any special status as team leaders. We are usually elected by our peers because we are dedicated to make things better. However, we can never have too much encouragement and training for the work that we are supposed to do. Since we are not experienced in leadership of groups and group process, we need the help of our supervisors and team building consultants.

I am fortunate in that respect. I have a supervisor who is skilled in organizing and is secure enough to share his knowledge.

There have been many successful projects completed or put into place by teams within DS. Nothing succeeds like success, and we as a team need to see positive results from our efforts. Every time we accomplish one of our objectives, we are more motivated to try to improve again.

Recognition for our accomplishments is essential to our growth and should be given by our management in a timely manner—at the time we have done the job. In addition, when we get approval for one of our projects, the system needs to respond to it quickly rather than delay our progress by sitting on it. Delays in implementation of our projects have caused many team members to lose faith in the team process. My job is to be forceful and to help our projects get off the ground once we have approval to forge ahead.

Through our team building we are attempting to mobilize within a system that is geared to be ponderous. We cannot affect instant change on a system built on regulations that are intended to direct the movements of personnel and material through specific channels. We can affect a gradual change if we have the persistence to do so and management has the willingness to help us.

We need the courage to discipline ourselves. There are some among us who choose to resist any and all efforts proposed by the teams. When an individual is adamant in his refusal to cooperate, or is actually campaigning against team effort, action needs to be taken (and we need management and the union to help us here). There is no place on a quality team for disruptive people or people who have an attitude that they can't be fired and just cause dissension for dissension's sake. When we find people like this, we don't pass the buck to our supervisor to handle; the team itself helps deal with it.

We are working together better now than ever before. We want to become known as the people who are not satisfied with "only good enough for government work." When we work together we feel proud. Getting that extra satisfaction from our customer for a job well done is what motivates most of us on the team. That is what brings us pride.

The Project from the View of the Chief Union Steward

David Wheeler, Chief Union Stewart

A new relationship between labor and management has resulted since the Pacer Share Project. We have gone from a win–lose, collective-bargaining-type relationship to one that is more like a partnership. We work as a team with management to resolve conflicts now.

The Pacer Share Project has given the employees a greater voice in the way things get done. They are included more in the planning and decision-making processes than they used to be. It isn't only management anymore that says what is to be done, how, and by whom. The employees more actively share in the planning process now than before.

The union has a bigger voice now, too. We are much more involved in policy planning with management than before. We get involved before things are a problem—we are able to work with management to prevent problems now rather than having our major emphasis on correcting management's handling of employees. Prior to Pacer Share, we were in an adversarial relationship with management, having to defend the employee from unfair labor practices—often having to rely on confrontational tactics on behalf of the employees against management.

Today, we still get involved in the grievance procedure (although grievances have been cut drastically). But we work with management in such conflicts, using the conflict as an educational tool for all parties concerned to identify better problem-solving practices and employee–management performance procedures to assure fairness to all parties concerned.

The union is part of the larger DS team-building process now. We are partners in team building. Employees don't have to have a grievance in order to work with the union. We are viewed more as a positive resource by them than before when our role was more confrontational with management.

The union assists both management and the employees in policy planning and interpretation. We work much more closely with management and, as a result, we have gained a lot more trust and understanding of one another. At times, the union will speak on behalf of the management, because we now understand their perspective better. At other times, management will speak for us, the union, and it is okay, because we know that they understand and respect our role in the federal labor relations system and in the overall checks and balances which are vital to fair labor practices.

In my opinion, Project Pacer Share is a model of things to come in the future of labor–management relations in the federal government. OPM, the federal government's "personnel department," has speculated about management in the year 2000. They see management of the federal work force to be much more participative, wherein labor and management work together in more collaborative forms than now. They envision changes in pay grades and more employee empowerment. It sounds good, yet so distant from what is practiced in the federal government—except in Project Pacer Share.

There, in the Project, we have already forged the type of new patterns of labor–management relations that OPM describes for the future. We have demonstrated that we can work with management and the work force to produce more quality services while improving the quality of work life for America's greatest resource—its people. Working in Project Pacer Share has given us the opportunity to experiment with new labor–management roles, to get a sense of what the future might be like.

From the viewpoint of the chief union steward, the new working relationships we in the leadership of the union have forged with management offer extraordinary promise. We have developed a working model of things to come in the federal system.

Team Building Helped Us Get Campers to Protect Our Material

Donna Wolfe, DS Pickup and Delivery Driver

We truckers transported small packages in the back of pickup trucks. For many years we did this knowing that in bad weather, especially during heavy rains, the material we were transporting would get damaged. When material got damaged it made us truckers look bad—we were embarrassed to drop off material that was damaged, yet that was our job to get the material out as assigned. We used the plastic bags that we were told to use, but they were at times inadequate or out of supply when we needed them.

After our team building program in PPS, we realized we could have more to say about fixing this problem—one that may seem trivial, but meant a lot to us because when the material we were obliged to transport got wet, we were the ones who were blamed. We considered ourselves to be professional, and we didn't like having to be part of sloppy work. It was embarrassing.

The team of truckers pulled together to figure out what could be done about this problem. We gathered ideas about how we might cover the material or the pickup bed. We decided on getting some type of shell to cover the pickup bed that would both protect the goods and materials we had to haul and offered easy access, roominess for the cargo, easy maintenance, and durability. The team gathered information from local suppliers as to what was available, the cost, installation, time frame for completion, and feasibility.

We analyzed the information obtained and came up with our recommendation. It was not difficult to sell our supervisor on the idea for he was a member of the team like the rest of us. He was with us from the start, but did not play as active a part in the fact finding and analysis as some others of us who were more concerned about the problem.

Some other drivers in our unit did not participate in the fact finding, but were briefed on all phases of procuring the shells. Plus, they were asked to express their preferences with regard to the type of shell we would buy.

With our supervisor's support, we briefed upper management about our recommendation to procure camper shells to protect material during times of inclimate weather. We showed them examples of past damage because we were forced by schedule to transport material when it needed to be protected from the rain, but we had no way to do it and keep the tight schedule to get things moved out to the customer at the same time.

Our work with upper management in this project did more than get us the shells we needed (yes, we got approval to purchase four of them). By engaging in problem solving with them, it further helped us build a better partnership with them. When we had team building, we started the partnership with management that was needed for us to risk getting involved with them on this project.

Today, our truckers deliver a quality product to our customers with pride and knowledge that we add value to the overall mission at MCAFB and the defense of the United States.

Glossary of Acronyms

AFGE: American Federation of Government Employees is the labor union that represents most of the employees through collective bargaining in Project Pacer Share. It was a key architect and remains a central supporter for the project.

AFLC: [United States] Air Force Logistics Command is one of four major commands in the Air Force. It is headed by a four-star general and has five major centers throughout the United States Combined; it employs over 100,000. Its basic mission is to provide logistic support for the U.S. Air Force and other defense-related organizations, both domestic and international.

AI: Artificial intelligence is a computer program that emulates the decision processes of a human "expert"; it may or may not have the ability to learn and change based on experience.

ALC: Air Logistics Center is a major organization within the AFLC. It consists of five centers—Hill, Kelly, McClellan, Tinker, and Wright-Patterson Air Force Bases. PPS was initiated at the McClellan Air Force Base, one of five ALCs. Each ALC is headed by a two-star major general of the U.S. Air Force.

ANSI: The American National Standards Institute is the official government-sanctioned consortium of engineering professional societies that establishes national standards.

CEO: Pertains to the individual who is personally responsible for the overall conduct of an organization. Generally, this person is the president of the firm and is accountable to a board of directors or an electorate. The overall welfare of the firm or jurisdiction is the responsibility of the CEO.

CNET: A designation for the office of the Chief of Naval Education and Training command at Pensacola, Florida. This office is responsible for certain aspects of education and training throughout the U.S. Navy.

CSS: Civil Service System represents the many policies, procedures, rules, and actions taken on their behalf to manage people in the federal government. PPS was created and funded to improve its approach to managing federal employees for quality.

DABDA: The acronym that stands for the five phases of psychological change: Denial, Anger, Bargaining, Depression, Acceptance, based on the teachings of Dr. E. Kubler-Ross.

DD: The Data Dictionary is the collection of structurally defined terms that applies to a specific system/process in EPM.

DLA: [United States] Defense Logistics Agency is a major defense organization having the mission to provide logistical services and supplies to defense organizations throughout the world. As a result of defense cutbacks and reorganization of the AFLC, the DLA was identified as an organization in which some of the DS functions would be merged. The DLA merger became a concern for employees in the DS who had worked with one another for many years and now were going to be dismantled by some being transferred to DLA and others staying within the USAF.

DOC: Demonstration On Call employees are part-time or temporary employees who are part of the PPS work force but not subject to long-term protection (permanent status). They played a critical role in the TQM approach, for they were to be the first to be terminated in times of spending reductions and employee cutbacks.

DOD: [United States] Department of Defense is one of several cabinet-level departments that report to the President of the United States. PPS is sponsored by the DOD and is under demonstration under its auspices and that of the AFLC and McClellan Air Force Base, ALC.

DP: The Directorate of Personnel (DP) at MCAFB was actively involved in the design and implementation of PPS. Experts loaned to the project helped conceptualize the interventions and clear the way for the project to be implemented through their revision of the rules, procedures, and policies associated with the CSS that needed to be revised for PPS to become a reality.

DS: Directorate of Distribution is the organization in which Project Pacer Share was initially developed and implemented. It is one of five organizations so named within the U.S. Air Force Logistics Command. In this book, the DS pertains to the Directorate of Distribution at McClellan Air Force Base at Sacramento, California. Other DS organizations are at Hill Air Force Base, Ogden, Utah; Kelly Air Force Base, San Antonio, Texas; Robins Air Force Base, Warner-Robins, Georgia; Tinker Air Force Base, Oklahoma City, Oklahoma; and at Wright-Patterson Air Force Base, Dayton, Ohio. In late 1990, about the end of Project Pacer Share's third year of its five-year demonstration life, DS organizations at all five installations were disassembled as a result of a major Air Force reorganization. Today, DS is no longer the sponsor of Project Pacer Share.

DS (2): The Project Pacer Share design team headed by co-author Nelson reported directly to the DS director and deputy director. Through it, the design of the project was finalized and implementation of the effort was begun. Other key employees in the DS(2) design team include Dan Fuchs and Colene Krum.

EEO: Equal Employment Opportunity is a program aimed at providing affirmative action to assure members of minority groups (e.g., aged, Asians, Blacks, Hispanics, native American Indians, women) are protected against discrimination in the workplace.

EPA: Essential Process Analysis is a methodology used in EPM that enables employees to plan a process and analyze it to assure never-ending quality improvement. It includes specific symbols and a data dictionary that make possible the modeling of dynamic interactions within a work element or process using systems analysis concepts. It also specifically incorporates the "voice of the customer" into every process (see Chapter 12).

EPM: Essential Process Management is the overall name for the total quality systems/ process analysis, modeling, design, operation, and improvement effort using EPA, EQA, and SPC.

EQA: Essential Quality Analysis is the bottom-level process analysis and specification using a revised version of the Shewhart/Deming cycle to incorporate never-ending improvement in every process task, and using a revised, standardized Ishikawa/fishbone diagram to visually display the plan for every process.

ESD: Electrostatic discharge pertains to electrical transmission that may be generated from employees when handling material. Upon accidental discharge, it may destroy highly sensitive and expensive electronic gear.

FEA: Followership Effectiveness Assessment is a questionnaire instrument developed by MEDi that is used to assess individual and organizational followership effectiveness per definition of self-initiated followership presented in Chapter 11.

GAO: The U.S. General Accounting Office is the oversight arm of the U.S. Congress. It is a major institution through which Congress studies the effectiveness of the Executive Branch and its implementation of legislative policy.

GM: General Manager is an official designation of a specific group of grades and jobs in the U.S. Civil Service System; mandated by the 1978 U.S. Civil Service Reform Act, it includes managerial jobs that were formerly in the General Schedule (GS) grades 13 through 15.

JD: The academic abbreviation for the Doctorate of Jurisprudence (JD) degree, which is a general prerequisite for the practice of law.

JPG: Job Proficiency Guide is a process document developed for PPS employees to enable them to understand the work to be performed, assess their skills at performing the work required of them, and provide them training to gain the skills needed to do the job. It also facilitated greater partnership between employees and their supervisors.

LEA: Leadership Effectiveness Assessment is a questionnaire instrument developed by MEDi that is used to assess individual and organizational leadership effectiveness per definition of customer-oriented leadership presented in Chapter 10.

MA: The Directorate of Maintenance at MCAFB helped conceptualize PPS at its very earliest stages.

MBO: Management by objectives is a process of the mutual setting of goals, tracking performance, and evaluating results by supervisors and their subordinates. The term was first popularized by Peter F. Drucker. During the Nixon Administration, it was the management approach of preference in the federal government. Today, it is widely applied throughout business and government.

MBTI: Myers–Briggs Temperament Indicator is a measure of personality differences based on the work of Katherine Briggs and a series of questions developed by her daughter, Isabel (Briggs) Myers. It is founded in Jungian psychology and places emphasis on individual traits that, when combined, result in sixteen different temperament types.

MCAFB: McClellan Air Force Base is the host ALC of PPS (the project). It is located in Sacramento, California, and as of September 1990, it employed over 30,000 people— mostly civilian employees and USAF personnel. Its mission is to provide logistical support for Air Force and other DOD-related organizations. By the end of 1990, it was strongly rumored that it had been targeted for closure should the AFLC have to undergo a cutback in funding. It is the smallest of the five ALCs in the AFLC.

MEDi: Management Education and Development, Inc., is a management-consulting organization employed by PPS to introduce Tactical Planning and Team Building, leadership, followership, and Myers–Briggs temperament assessments into the DS organization.

MTM: Sometimes seen as M-T-M, Method-Time-Motion, this is the industrial-engineering technique for measuring the precise time a task or series of tasks takes to perform so a "standard" can be set to measure the efficiency of a given process or organization. Frequently used in the DOD for forecasting personnel requirements.

NOSC: The DOD acronym for the U.S Navy's Naval Ocean Systems Command, headquartered in San Diego, and co-host for the first U.S. Civil Service demonstration project (with the China Lake Naval Weapons Systems Development Laboratory).

OD: Organizational development is an applied behavioral science process for increasing an organization's effectiveness. It is focused on the facilitation of change through specific, planned activities. It usually includes the involvement of an outside change agent and the application of action research wherein data are systematically gathered and used to help identify the specific changes needed and to assess the effects of the interventions employed.

OJT: On-the-Job Training is an approach to employee development that systematically exposes employees to actual job experiences where they can learn how to perform the work expected of them. OJT is usually provided others through co-workers, fellow team members, or their supervisors at the actual job site than by "professional" trainers or educators in settings away from the job site, such as classrooms or workshop settings.

OMB: The U.S. Office of Management and Budget is the management arm of the U.S. Office of the President. It is responsible for the preparation and implementation of the annual budget of the United States. It also guides other agencies within the executive branch with regard to overarching management philosophies, policies, and approaches.

OPM: [United States] Office of Personnel Management is one of two sponsoring agencies of Project Pacer Share. Congress, in the 1978 U.S. Civil Service Reform Act, charged OPM with oversight/sponsorship of all demonstration projects. It is the federal government's "personnel department." Without its sponsorship, many of the innovations initiated by the project would not have been possible. OPM continuously monitors and evaluates the project to assure the project does what it is supposed to do according to law. It also is involved in the measurement of the project's results or in the oversight of an independent, third-party measurer (such as RAND).

P–D–C–A: Plan, Do, Check, and Assess are steps taken to analyze a process flow. They represent an interactive process for never-ending improvement in TQM.

P–D–C–A–S: This is a revision of P–D–C–A. It is more systems-oriented with the last step being used to "support" the system. Originated by DS and PPS, it is part of the overall SCED process.

PFD: Process Flow Diagram is a state-of-the-art flow chart that replaces conventional ANSI (and other) flow charts. It allows a "top–down" analysis of an entire organization, showing total interdependency of all the processes.

PGS: Productivity gain sharing is a means, somewhat like profit sharing in the private sector, by which an organization and the people in it share the dollar benefits of increased productivity.

PMO: Project Management Officer is responsible for the implementation of PPS. The term is used to designate the organization (and leader) in charge of a given program of a project. It is a legal organizational authorization of responsibility.

PPS: Project Pacer Share refers to the Pacer Share Demonstration Project; all major projects in the DOD are assigned "nicknames." In the project nickname, the word Pacer identifies it as a project of the Air Force Logistics Command (now being merged with the Air Force Systems Command). The word Share, chosen by the project team, signifies the intent of the project to model a system in which accountability, responsibility, authority, and benefits are shared by all members of the organizational team, management, nonmanagement, and labor.

QC: Quality Circles is a term identified with Japanese management. It is a form of group decision making through a team of employees in an intact work unit. With their supervisor (often as facilitator of the team), the employees apply TQM tools such as those described in Chapter 12 to improve work processes. QC was started in DS in 1983 and continues today as one of several mechanisms to empower employees and improve work processes.

RAND: A corporation employed by OPM to conduct the external evaluation of PPS. It is located in Santa Monica, California, and provides both ongoing and final outcome assessments of the project.

RIF: Reduction-In-Force is a personnel action that is in response to funding cutbacks. It identifies a given number of employees who are to be terminated from a federal agency. The DOC employees were employed in PPS, so that in times of a RIF, they would be laid off so the more permanent employees would be protected.

SCED: Standardized Cause and Effect Diagram is a unique integration of the fishbone and Deming Cycle techniques applied in essential process management. It was developed by the PPS analysts and employed throughout the DS organization for continuous improvements. (See Chapter 12.)

SPC: Statistical Process Control is an analytic approach used to identify exceptional variation in an organizational process. It relies heavily on statistical frequencies, probabilities, and prediction. It is a subcomponent of EPM.

TI: Technology and Industrial Support Directorate is a new organization that has been established as a result of reorganization throughout the AFLC. It is the new host organization for PPS, replacing the DS, which was eliminated as an organization in the fall of 1990.

TPTB: Tactical Planning and Team Building is an intervention designed and introduced by co-author Gilbert (see Chapters 8 and 9). Every employee in PPS was provided training in TPTB. It was the central training and development intervention activity employed in PPS in its first three-year phase. Through it employees were introduced to the quality approach, leadership, and followership essential to creating quality for the customer.

TQM: Total Quality Management is a term that represents and entire school of management thinking. It is centered on an integrated approach for improving processes through specific methods and approaches. PPS was specifically designed and authorized to test its applicability to the federal workplace—especially in the AFLC. There are several approaches to the quality model (TQM). PPS is based, in large part, on the approach of W. Edwards Deming.

USAF: The U.S. Air Force is one of three major branches of the armed forces. It is part of the U.S. Department of Defense and is accountable to the Executive Branch. The Project Pacer Share effort was designed and implemented under the sponsorship of the USAF.

Bibliography

Albrecht, K. *At America's Service*. San Diego, CA: University Associates, 1989.

Albrecht, K., and R. Zemke. *Service America!* New York: Dow-Jones Irwin, 1985.

Bass, B. M. *Leadership and Performance Beyond Expectations*. New York: The Free Press, 1985.

Bates, M., and D. W. Keirsey. *Please Understand Me*. Del Mar, CA: Prometheus Nemesis, 1978.

Bennis, W. *Why leaders Can't Lead*. San Francisco: Jossey-Bass, 1989.

Bennis, W., and B. Nanus. *Leaders: The Strategies for Taking Charge*. New York: Harper and Row, 1985.

Bennis, W. G., and P. E. Slater. *The Temporary Society*. New York: Harper and Row, 1968.

Blanchard, K., and S. Johnson. *The One Minute Manager*. New York: Morrow, 1981.

Bowsher, C. A. "Program Evaluation is Essential." *The Bureaucrat,* Fall 1990.

Bradford, D. L., and A. R. Cohen. *Managing for Excellence: The Guide to Developing High Performance in Contemporary Organizations*. New York: John Wiley, 1984.

Campbell, D. T. "Factors Relevant to the Validity of Experiments in Social Settings." *Psychological Bulletin* 54, 1957.

Campbell, J., with B. Moyers. *The Power of Myth*. New York: Doubleday, 1988.

Carlzon, J. *Moments of Truth*. New York: Ballinger, 1987.

Chelimsky, E. "Executive Branch Program Evaluation: An Upturn Soon?" *The Bureaucrat,* Fall 1990.

Chin, R., and K. D. Benne. "General Strategies for Effecting Changes in Human Systems," in Bennis, W., K. D. Benne, and R. Chin. *The Planning of Change,* 2nd ed. New York: Holt, Rinehart and Winston, 1969.

DeMarco, T. *Structured Analysis and System Specification*. New York: Yourdon Press, 1978.

Deming, W. E. *Out of the Crisis*. Boston: MIT-CAES, 1986.

Fayol, H. *General and Industrial Administration*. New York: Pitman, 1949.

Fiedler, F. E. *A Theory of Leadership Effectiveness*. New York: McGraw-Hill, 1967.

Garvin, D. "Quality on the Line," *Harvard Business Review* 61 (September–October), 1983.

Gilbert, G. R. "Effective Leaders Must Be Good Followers Too." *Government Executive,* June 1990.

Gilbert, G. R. *Followership Effectiveness Assessment.* Boca Raton, FL: Management Education and Development, Inc., 1987.

Gilbert, G. R. "How to Be a Customer-Oriented Supervisor," *Government Executive,* February 1990.

Gilbert, G. R. "Jump-Start Your Team for Quality," *Government Executive,* November 1990.

Gilbert, G. R. *Leadership Effectiveness Assessment.* Boca Raton, FL: Management Education and Development, Inc., 1987.

Gilbert, G. R. *Leadership Effectiveness Within the Directorate of Distribution at MCAFB.* Boca Raton, FL: Management Education and Development, Inc., May 1988.

Gilbert, G. R. "Making Government a 'Quality' Place to Work," *Government Executive,* November 1989.

Gilbert, G. R. *Managing for Quality in the Directorate of Distribution, McClellan Air Force Base: A Review of Quality Practices and Followership Performance in the Directorate.* Boca Raton, FL: Management Education and Development, Inc., May 1989.

Gilbert, G. R. *The TQS Factor and You: Learn to Lead Yourself, Manage Your Boss, Delight Your Customer.* Boca Raton, FL: Business Performance Publications, 1991.

Gilbert, G. R., R. W. Collins, and R. Brenner. "Age and Leadership Effectiveness: From the Perception of the Follower," *Human Resource Management Journal,* August 1991.

Gilbert, G. R., and A. C. Hyde. "Followership and the Federal Worker." *Public Administration Review* (November/December), 1988.

Gilbert, G. R., C. Krum, and A. E. Nelson. *The Pacer Share Project: A Federal Demonstration Perspective on Pay, Gainsharing, and Quality.* Portland, OR: Western Social Science Association, April 1990.

Gilbert, G. R., and C. W. Whiteside. "Performance Appraisal and Followership: An Analysis of the Officer on the Boss/Subordinate Team," *Journal of Police Science and Administration* 16: 1, 1988.

Guttentag, M. "Subjectivity and Its Use in Evaluation Research," *Evaluation* I, 1972.

Hersey, P., and K. Blanchard. *Management of Organizational Behavior,* 4th ed. Englewood Cliffs, NJ: Prentice-Hall, 1982.

Horst, P., J. N. Nay, J. W. Scanlon, and J. S. Wholey. "Program Management and the Federal Evaluator," *Public Administration Review* (July/August), 1974.

Hyman, H. H., C. R. Wright, and T. K. Hopkins. *Applications of Methods of Evaluation.* Berkeley: University of California Press, 1962.

Imai, M. *Kaizen.* New York: Random House, 1986.

Ishikawa, K. *Guide to Quality Control.* New York: Quality Resources, 1986.

Jung, C. G. *Psychological Types.* New York: Harcourt & Brace, 1923.

Keller, R. *Expert System Technology: Development and Application.* New York: Yourdon Press, 1987.

Knowles, M. S. *The Modern Practice of Adult Education.* New York: Association Press, 1973.

Kroeger, O., and J. M. Thueson. *Type Talk.* New York: Delacorte Press, 1988.

Krone, B. "Total Quality Management: An American Odyssey," *The Bureaucrat,* Fall 1990.

Kubler-Ross, E. *On Death and Dying.* New York: Macmillan, 1969.

Kuhn, T. S. *The Structure of Scientific Revolutions*. Chicago: University of Chicago Press, 1962.

McCallum, J. S. "The Japanese Industrial Miracle: It is Not Hard to Explain," *Business Quarterly* 51 (Summer), 1986.

McCauley, M. H. *Jung's Theory of Psychological Types and the Myers-Briggs Type Indicator*. Gainesville, FL: Center for Application of Psychological Type, 1981.

McMenamin, S. M., and J. J. Palmer. *Essential Analysis*. Englewood Cliffs, NJ: Yourdon Press/Prentice Hall, 1984.

Meindl, J. R., et al. "The Romance of Leadership." *Administrative Science Quarterly* 30, March 1985.

Mizuno, S. *Company-wide Quality Control*. Tokyo: Asian Productivity Organization, 1988.

Myers, I. B. *Gifts Differing*. Palo Alto, CA: Consulting Psychologists Press, 1980.

Nelson, A. E. "Performance Appraisals, Fact or Fancy," paper presented at a Deming Four-Day Seminar in Washington, D.C., 1988.

Nelson, L. *MIT Video Course and Manual: Statistics in Quality Productivity and Problem Solving*. Boston: MIT-CAES, 1985.

Pearce, J. L., W. E. Stevenson, and J. L. Perry. "Managerial Performance Based on Organizational Performance: A Time Series Analysis of the Effects of Merit Pay," *Academy of Management Journal* 28, 2, June 1985.

Pearce, J. L., W. E. Stevenson, and J. L. Perry. "The Productivity Paradox," *Business Week,* June 1988.

RAND Corporation. "Pacer Share Demonstration Project: Preliminary Second Year Results," June 1990.

Reich, R. B. "Entrepreneurship Reconsidered: The Team As Hero." *Harvard Business Review, May–June 1987.*

Scanlon, J. W. "Type III and Type IV Errors in Program Evaluation," in Gilbert, G. R., and P. J. Conklin, *Evaluation Management: A Sourcebook of Readings*. Charlottesville: The Federal Executive Institute, 1977.

Scholtes, P. Unpublished article for Joiner and Associates, Madison, Wisconsin, 1988.

Semler, R. "Managing Without Managers," *Harvard Business Review,* September/October 1989.

Shingo, S. *Zero Quality Control*. New York: Productivity Press, 1989.

Smith, P. B., and M. F. Peterson. *Leadership, Organization, and Culture: An Event Management Model*. London: Sage, 1988.

Suchman, A. E. *Evaluative Research*. New York: Russell Sage Foundation, 1967.

Suchman, A. E. Unpublished paper on the elements of profound knowledge, 1990.

Vroom, V. H., and A. G. Jago. "Decision Making as a Social Process: Normative and Descriptive Models of Leader Behavior," *Decision Sciences* 5, 1974.

Walton, M. *The Deming Management Method*. New York: Dodd, Mead, 1986.

Wholey, J. S. "Management of Evaluation: Implementing an Effective Evaluation Program," in Gilbert, G. R. (ed), *Making and Managing Policy: Formulation, Analysis, Evaluation*. New York: Marcel Dekker, 1984.

Yourdon, E. *Techniques of Program Structure and Design*. Englewood Cliffs, NJ: Prentice-Hall, 1975.

Yourdon, E., and L. Constantine. *Structured Design*. New York: Yourdon Press, 1976.

Index

About the Authors

G. RONALD GILBERT, team builder consultant for Project Pacer Share, is Associate Professor of Management at Florida International University at North Miami, and President of Management, Education, and Development, Inc. of Boca Raton.

ARDEL E. NELSON was formerly Project Manager of Project Pacer Share at McClellan Air Force Base in Sacramento, California. He is currently Chair of the Management Department at American River College at Sacramento and Principal at Nelson and Nelson Management Consultants.